MOBFILES

MOBFILES
MOBSTERS, MOLLS AND MURDER

GEORGE ANASTASIA

Camino Books, Inc.
Philadelphia

Manufactured in the United States of America

1 2 3 4 5   11 10 09 08

Library of Congress Cataloging-in-Publication Data

Anastasia, George.
  Mobfiles : mobsters, molls, and murder / George Anastasia.
      p. cm.
  ISBN 978-1-933822-14-3 (alk. paper)
  1. Mafia—Pennsylvania—Philadelphia Metropolitan Area—Case studies. 2. Organized crime—Pennsylvania—Philadelphia—History. I. Title.

  HV6452.P4A63 2008
  364.1'060974811—dc22   2008020310

Cover and interior design: Jerilyn Bockorick

Photo on page 2 by Brad Nau

"Mafia Prince" is excerpted from George Anastasia, *Blood and Honor* (Philadelphia: Camino Books, Inc., 2004).

"Wife and Mother" is excerpted from George Anastasia, *Mobfather* (Philadelphia: Camino Books, Inc., 2006).

This book is available at a special discount on bulk purchases for promotional, business, and educational use. For information write to:

Camino Books, Inc.
P.O. Box 59026
Philadelphia, PA 19102

www.caminobooks.com

For Angelina

CONTENTS

PROLOGUE

In 1976 my newspaper, the *Philadelphia Inquirer*, sent me to Atlantic City to cover the start of the casino gambling era. In addition to writing stories about the "unique form of urban renewal" that was going to spark an economic renaissance, I was told to track the presence of the mob.

Part of the big debate during the run-up to the referendum in which voters approved the legalization was the question of whether casinos would bring organized crime to the city. Of course the answer was that the mob already *was* in the city, but the issue became a hot topic and remained so after the dice started rolling.

In those days, I wrote about the mob in conjunction with other stories about how the city was being revitalized. Then in 1980 Angelo Bruno, the longtime Mafia boss of Philadelphia and South Jersey, was assassinated.

Bruno was gunned down as he sat in a car smoking a cigarette in front of his row house near 10th Street and Snyder Avenue in South Philly. It was a Friday night. I remember it well because my brother-in-law was getting married the next day and I was at a rehearsal dinner when the hit went down. Consequently, I didn't cover the Bruno murder. But I guess it would be fair to say I've been writing about the aftermath for the past 28 years.

The slaying of Don Angelo was the seminal event in the demise of the Philadelphia crime family. Everything that came after—the chaos, the petty jealousies and the wanton violence—stems from that night. Bruno had been boss for 21 years. He ran a quiet, highly efficient organization.

He was from the old school. Don't call attention to yourself. Make money, not headlines. And he made a ton of it. Bruno was a millionaire a couple of times over when he got popped. A lot of the guys in his crime family, however, weren't as well off. And that may have contributed to the disgruntlement that led to his killing. It certainly was a factor in what followed.

Greed and treachery replaced whatever honor and loyalty had existed.

I began writing more and more about the organization. And by the 1990s, I had made it my beat.

I think it's fair to say that during that period the Philadelphia branch of La Cosa Nostra had become the most dysfunctional mob family in America. There have been six mob bosses during the period I have been writing about the organization: Bruno, Phil Testa, Nicky Scarfo, John Stanfa, Ralph Natale and Joey Merlino.

Bruno and Testa were killed. Scarfo, Stanfa, Merlino and Natale are doing time, although Natale is in a protected witness wing of a federal prison.

After he was indicted and looking at a potential life sentence for drug dealing, he cut a deal with the feds, becoming the first sitting American Mafia boss to turn publicly on his organization.

In fact, over the past 20 years, the Philadelphia family has had more cooperators per capita than any other crime family in the country. Omerta is like the city's famous Liberty Bell. Cracked and inoperable.

The sometimes sensational testimony of those turncoats and the hours and hours of secretly recorded conversations from FBI wiretaps and from wiseguys wearing body wires have laid the organization bare. Honor and loyalty? Forgetaboutit. Secrecy is also a thing of the past.

Couple those factors with more sophisticated law enforcement techniques and the devastating application of the Racketeering Influenced and Corrupt Organizations (RICO) Act and you have a formula for investigative success.

In case after case, the Philadelphia family has taken a hit.

I've been around to write about most of it. What follows are some of the highlights—stories that over the past 28 years have appeared in the *Inquirer*. During that time I've been fortunate to work for many good editors. From the top, people like the legendary Eugene Roberts, Max King and Bob Rosenthal. They set the tone that made the paper what it was—at one point one of the finest in the country. Now Bill Marimow is in charge and I think that's our best shot at getting back to where we once were.

It would be impossible to name all the other line and word editors who have had a hand in shaping the stories that appear here, so I ask forgiveness in advance for those I may have overlooked. Over the years these have included Lois Wark, Butch Ward, Bob Samsot, Dan Biddle, Fran Dauth, Dave Tucker, Dave Taylor, Avery Rome, Michael Mills and Francisco Delgado. To them and to all the other copy editors and line editors who made what follows better when it appeared in print than when it first appeared on their computer screens, I say thank you.

MOBFILES

Joey Merlino and his motorcycle

MOBSTERS

In the early 1990s, the *Inquirer* had a two-year correspondents program for aspiring young journalists. These were primarily kids just out of college who wanted to be reporters. They would come to work in the paper's suburban bureaus, get some experience, work for about half the salary of regular reporters, and then, after two years, move on to what was hopefully a better job at a decent paper as a full-time staff writer.

One of the correspondents working out of the Cherry Hill, New Jersey, office where I am based was a young woman who had grown up in South Philadelphia. She was, in fact, from the same neighborhood as Skinny Joey Merlino and a dozen other young wiseguys who were then making names for themselves in the underworld.

One of them, a guy named George Borgesi, would complain to her about the stories I was writing, claiming I always took the government's side and that I believed everything the cops told me. I told her to have him give me a call.

He did.

Our first conversation didn't go very well. He wanted to vent. But he kept calling and over time we developed a relationship. I started to quote him as "an underworld source" and several times I wrote stories that juxtaposed the police version of events with his. He loved it. It was like a politician who realizes that with access to the media he can put his spin on the news. I thought it was great having another take on events and, more important, having access to someone who I could call to verify information.

One of the journalistic dangers of reporting on organized crime is that you seldom hear from the other side if you screw up. Make a mistake in a story about an elected official and he or she will be on the phone the next morning demanding a clarification. Screw up a story about some wiseguy and you don't hear a word. He might think you're a jerk who doesn't know what he's talking about, but it's not in his interest to set you straight. At least that's the way it used to be.

That changed in the 1990s. Part of it had to do with the John Gotti syndrome, the concept of gangster as celebrity. What's the point of being a wiseguy if nobody knows who you are? It's a philosophy that flies in the face of the idea of omerta and the secret society, but I think helps explain how and why the mob started to come apart.

But it was more than that in Philadelphia. The new mobsters were not really Mafiosi in the true sense of the word. They were corner boys. Born and raised in South Philadelphia, second- or third-generation Italian-Americans, their loyalty wasn't to some Old World concept of men of honor. Their loyalty was to one another and to the corner where they grew up and came of age. And on the corner you don't want anyone else to have the last word. That, I think, was the key reason guys like Borgesi and Merlino were accessible. Not just to me, but to certain television reporters as well. Dave Schratwieser and photographer Brad Nau had at least as much access to Merlino as I did at this time.

In fact, they recorded one of the greatest one-liners in South Philadelphia mob history. It was Merlino at his best. There was a report floating around that Nicky Scarfo, from prison, had put a $500,000 contract on Merlino's head.

Schrat and Brad, naturally, sought Joey out for comment.

When asked what he thought about the hit contract, Merlino gave one of those classic half smiles of his, shrugged and then said, "Give me the half million and I'll shoot myself."

During their rise to power and while they were targets of an intense FBI investigation, Merlino and Borgesi were always available. I had their cell phone numbers. On several occasions we had lunch. Typically during one of these sessions Borgesi would badger, complain and worry. But Merlino was something else.

Smooth is the word that comes to mind. Very personable. Always asked about my family. Loved to talk sports and politics. Studied the papers and could tick off details about how and where the FBI had screwed up, be it Ruby Ridge or the Whitey Bulger investigation. He never, however, gave up much that would figure into a news report.

Smooth. Like a politician.

Merlino, I think, understood better than Borgesi what was going on. I was using them as sources. A reporter, after all, is only as good as the information he has access to. And they, in turn, were using me to open another line of intelligence. What was I hearing? Who was under investigation? When were indictments coming down?

My rule was never to give up anything that wasn't going to be reported in the paper anyway. Their rule, it was clear, was never to talk about anything that could be incriminating. That's the way the game was played. I was fine with it.

At around this same time I got a phone call from another wiseguy.

I had written several stories about mob boss John Stanfa and the co-terie of mobsters who were emerging as his go-to guys. One of them was Ron Previte. Previte was especially interesting because he was a former Philadelphia cop. Now, according to investigators, he was a major rack-eteer.

Previte called to say that he thought I had an undue interest in his life and he would like to meet me. It was a calculated challenge. If you write about these guys, you can't back down when they confront you. I said I'd be happy to meet with him as long as it was in a public place. He suggested the Silver Coin Diner in Hammonton, New Jersey, which was his base of operation.

A few days later we had lunch. This was in the spring of 1993. We've been talking ever since. Previte is probably the most erudite mobster I've ever met. He is also one of the shrewdest. Six years later I would learn that he was an informant and that, for two years beginning in 1997, he wore a body wire and recorded conversations for the FBI.

Throughout that investigation he would meet me for lunch or dinner or we would talk on the phone. Like Merlino and Borgesi, I figured he was a source and he was using me the same way I was using him.

He, of course, had bigger things in mind, telling me repeatedly that some day I'd write a book about him. I'd asked how that would be possible without his going to jail since, among other things, he had openly discussed the various underworld gambits—from loan-sharking and gambling to prostitution and extortion—that he had been involved in for years. He'd just smile and say we'd work it out.

I did write the book. It's called *The Last Gangster*. It's the story of the investigation that brought down Merlino, mob boss Ralph Natale, Borgesi and a host of others.

Once the book came out Borgesi, who by then was in prison, stopped talking to me. He said I made Previte out to be a hero when he was nothing more than a rat.

In fact, Previte was what he had always been—an underworld mercenary whose first allegiance was to himself.

What follows is a series of stories, some of which appeared in the now-defunct *Inquirer* Sunday magazine, while others appeared in the daily paper. They profile some of the mob figures I have written about over the past two decades.

Merlino and Previte were two of the most fascinating.

Merlino's Way

Joey Merlino has been in jail for 18 months awaiting trial on racketeering charges that include allegations of murder, conspiracy, drug trafficking and extortion. If convicted, the 38-year-old reputed mob boss could spend the rest of his life in jail.

This summer, he was confined to his 10-by-12-foot cell for 23 hours a day because prison officials claimed he was a security risk. The four months of administrative detention also meant no personal phone calls, no visits, no television and no books. Only after his lawyer threatened a civil rights suit was Merlino able to join the prison's general population.

Today he and six codefendants live at the new federal detention center at 7th and Arch Streets, where they spend much of their time scrutinizing the evidence in the 37-count indictment against them, a document that runs 97 pages and includes a description of all manner of murder and mayhem. Consequently, it has not been the best of times for the dark-eyed Mafia prince whose brooding good looks and well-documented swagger have made him Philadelphia's one and only celebrity gangster.

The evidence in the case is voluminous. There are transcripts and tapes from thousands of hours of conversations secretly recorded by the FBI during an investigation that stretches back to 1993. And there are six former wiseguys, including the onetime boss of the Philadelphia mob, ready to testify. Yet Merlino, who has listened to more tapes and read more transcripts than most of the lawyers in the high-profile case, says he's not worried. He says, in fact, that he and his codefendants will be "totally vindicated."

Last month, when one of those codefendants was speaking to a reporter on a prison phone, Merlino happened by. Never shy, he took the opportunity to offer a quick critique of the government's case. Calling out in the background because it was not his phone time, Merlino said the authorities had built a case with no foundation.

"We got them right where we want them," he declared.

It was quintessential Merlino. Bold, brash and full of the bravado that has defined his life as a wiseguy.

There has never been a mobster, reputed or otherwise, in Philadelphia like Joseph Salvatore "Skinny Joey" Merlino. He is the John Gotti of Passyunk Avenue. The Al Capone of 9th Street. And while his current living conditions have put a decided crimp in his style, when it comes to living large in the world of wiseguys and wannabes, nobody does it better than Skinny Joey.

They knew him at the Palm, the swank Center City restaurant that caters to the city's movers and shakers. He and two or three associates would dine there at least once a week, usually drawing more stares and attention than the caricatures and portraits of local celebrities that decorate the walls in the dining area.

He'd order the crabs—soft-shell in summer, stone in winter—or a pork chop. He drank ginger ale with dinner, usually passed on dessert and would finish with coffee and Sambuca. Then maybe a beer at the bar before heading over to the Continental, the chic martini lounge at 2nd and Market. A few drinks with friends, the entourage growing as the night progressed, and then it was off to Delaware Avenue, where things would really get interesting.

Merlino and about a half-dozen other macho young wiseguys would pull up to the Eighth Floor in a Mercedes, a Cadillac, maybe a customized four-wheel-drive Jeep or Land Rover. Dressed in the latest from Armani or Versace, their hair coiffed, their nails buffed and manicured, they would glide toward the entrance. Lines would part. Cover charges would be waived. They'd be escorted to the best table or given the best seats at the bar, attended to by a bevy of waiters and waitresses who laughed and smiled and tripped over one another to provide the best service.

All the while, of course, there were stares and nods and whispers.

"It's Joey."

"Skinny Joey."

"Merlino."

His swagger, his cockeyed grin, his South Philadelphia who-gives-a-damn-let's-party attitude are a magnet for women looking to be bad and for guys who think they are. As a result, Merlino has given the Philadelphia mob an identity. He's brought a face and a personality to a local institution that, like so much else in this city, has operated in the shadow of its bigger and better-known New York counterpart.

He is a mob boss for the new millennium, a rock and roll gangster whose egocentric sense of entitlement is an underworld reflection of the me-first style of the 30-somethings who are making their mark on Wall Street and Madison Avenue and in Silicon Valley.

Arrogant or confident? Self-involved or self-assured? Whatever your take, Merlino is somebody who merely by being himself has managed to push people's buttons. To many, he is the dark side of the generation gap, the mob's version of the spoiled son who takes the privileges that others have earned and assumes they are his birthright. And while there may be enough evidence to justify the charges against him, there is also a sense that, unlike any of the other racketeering cases that have decimated the Philadelphia mob over the past 20 years, this one is personal.

To federal officials, Merlino epitomizes the braggadocio and violence of an organized crime family that has been careening out of control for two decades. He is a thug, an arrogant, self-centered lowlife whom the media have turned into a star, a vicious criminal who deserves to be in prison for the rest of his life.

There are three murders and two attempted murders in the case pending against him. Prosecutors allege that Merlino ordered the violence. There are a half-dozen other gangland hits, including two of the more notorious in Philadelphia history, that authorities believe Merlino planned and/or carried out. The blood, the bullets and the grieving families of those who died paint a somber backdrop to the life and times of Skinny Joey, federal investigators say. Yet there is something about Merlino that softens the public's perception—a certain style, a panache that allows him to be seen not as a roguish outlaw, but as a free spirit challenging authority.

Older mob bosses used to operate in the shadows. Some even denied their own identity. Angelo Bruno told people that he was a salesman for a vending machine company. Carlo Gambino was in the olive oil business. It was a facade, a front. And on a certain level, it diminished them.

Merlino is what he is. And he doesn't seem to care what anyone thinks about it. Before his arrest, he was a regular part of the city's social and celebrity landscape. His name turned up in the gossip columns, he held court at the coffee shop he opened on Passyunk Avenue, he served as the well-dressed but modest host of an annual holiday dinner for the homeless. He sat in box seats at Phillies and Flyers games, where he would often sign as many autographs as the players.

"Joey is a guy who dances to his own beat," said Frank Friel, a former Philadelphia police captain and organized crime expert in an interview two years ago. "He epitomizes the new La Cosa Nostra. He enjoys the trappings.

"Joey is gonna do what Joey wants to do, until and unless someone stamps him out."

For most of the 1990s, Merlino dodged the bullets and bombs of rival wiseguys while dancing two steps ahead of a federal investigation bearing down on him. Two of the city's previous three mob bosses wanted him dead. So did a major drug kingpin. The bosses, Nicky Scarfo and John Stanfa, are now in jail, probably for the rest of their lives. The kingpin, Louie Turra, committed suicide in prison two years ago.

The third boss, Ralph Natale, is far from a Merlino supporter, but instead of firing bullets, he plans to do his sniping from a witness stand. The first sitting mob boss ever to become a government witness, Natale is Merlino's chief accuser in the pending racketeering case.

That, in itself, says a lot about Merlino, whom the FBI alleges once served as Natale's underboss. In no other city have federal authorities been willing to make a deal with the boss to get the number-two man. Imagine federal prosecutors giving John Gotti a get-out-of-jail-free card in order to convict Salvatore "Sammy the Bull" Gravano.

But Skinny Joey is different.

Federal authorities will not comment on the pending case or any of the targets named in the indictment. But four years ago, veteran FBI Agent James Maher, who heads the bureau's organized crime office in Philadelphia, had this to say about Merlino:

"Maybe he thinks he's Al Capone or John Gotti. Capone used to feed the homeless in Chicago. Gotti used to have those big Fourth of July celebrations in New York. Look where they ended up. Capone died of syphilis, and Gotti's going to die in jail."

"They got a case, bring it on," Merlino said in an interview around that same time. "If not, leave me alone."

Merlino has never been afraid to use the media to make a point. In fact, he frequently talked with reporters about the allegations that swirled around him, about the FBI agents who dogged him, and about the threats and murder attempts that became so much a part of his life.

When a television reporter informed him two years ago that authorities believed jailed mobsters had put out a $500,000 contract on his life, Merlino responded in typical fashion. His dark eyes flashed just a hint of sarcasm. Then, in the machine-gun staccato cadence that is his normal conversational style, he quipped, "Gimme the $500,000 and I'll shoot myself."

He has been described as a mob boss, as the leader of a young, renegade branch of the local crime family, as a rising star in the underworld. He may, in fact, be all those things. But underneath, Joey Merlino is a guy from the corner, quick with a quip, often self-deprecating, always looking to make a score.

"You got anybody we can rob?" Merlino asked an associate in one of the hundreds of secretly recorded conversations that are now part of the federal case against him. That one question may say it all.

During his rise to the top, Merlino surrounded himself with like-minded associates whose loyalty was not to an organization but to one another. Members of Merlino's group, many of whom are now codefendants, grew up with him, went to the same South Philadelphia Catholic grammar school (Epiphany of Our Lord), hung out on the same street corner—12th and Wolf—and by and large wound up doing the same things at age 35 that they were doing at 15. This, more often than not, included following Joey's lead.

A few years ago, a young woman who had grown up with Merlino and his associates returned to the neighborhood for a visit. She went "clubbing" with the guys one Saturday night and was astounded by the preferential treatment her old friends received. They hit five or six establishments along Delaware Avenue that night before ending up at an after-hours club. The scene, she said, was always the same.

"We were waved right through the lines," she recalled. The best tables had been reserved in advance or were quickly made available. "It was like they knew we were coming."

The drinks flowed steadily. And though the clubs were crowded, no one was allowed to approach the table unless Merlino or someone close to him nodded OK. That, of course, didn't stop dozens of young women from tossing napkins with their names and phone numbers at the young wiseguys, particularly at Skinny Joey. Some even flashed their breasts.

9

"I was amazed," the young woman said.

But she was also struck by something else. "Other than the fact that they all had wads of money in their pockets, these guys acted no differently than when we were growing up. They were still the guys from the corner."

"You know there's this image of Joseph that's not reality. It's just not the way he is. He doesn't like to call attention to himself. He doesn't think of himself as a celebrity."

Deborah Wells Merlino—tall, thin and with the striking features of a fashion model—is sitting at a dining room table with her mother-in-law, Rita Merlino, trying to explain just who this man—her husband and the father of their young daughters, Nicolette and Sophia—really is.

It is a long, rambling and cordial conversation, with both women trading quips, asides and anecdotes while deftly dodging questions and issues they prefer not to discuss. One frequently will answer a question posed to the other. Both refer to "Joseph," never "Joe" or "Joey."

Rita Merlino has served coffee and offers a slice from a huge, sticky cinnamon bun with nuts that she has brought back from a local bakery. Her dining room and adjacent living room are done in soft beige and light-brown tones. The two-story brick rowhouse is in the 1900 block of Hartranft Street, a quiet, upper-middle-class neighborhood.

Rita Merlino, a short, 60-something mother and grandmother, is wearing a sweatshirt and sweatpants. She is a boisterous product of South Philadelphia and proud of it.

"You won't get this in Jersey," she says as she cuts a slice of the cinnamon bun, puts it on a plate and slides it across the table to her guest who, she knows, left Philadelphia for the New Jersey suburbs decades ago.

Deborah Merlino, in her early 30s and wearing a stylish blouse and dark slacks, smiles at her mother-in-law. The younger Mrs. Merlino, who traces her origins to Korea and New York City, is soft and reserved with a Downtown Manhattan air of steely self-confidence. The contrast in their styles is as obvious as their devotion to "Joseph."

Deborah says she met her husband while working as a hostess at the Saloon, a posh South Philadelphia restaurant. He asked about her and arranged, through friends, to go out with a group of people they both knew. The thing she remembers most about their early dates was that he was totally without pretense. And that he made her smile.

"People ask me, 'Do you know who you married?'" she says. "I married a guy who made me laugh like no one else I'd ever gone out with. I married a guy who made me feel like it was all right to be myself."

The only son and middle child, Joey Merlino was "quiet and shy" as a boy, his mother says. "But with a hard head. He could be stubborn. You don't know." She points to a portrait hanging over the couch in the living room. It is Joey and his sister Maria, at ages four and five. "Look, look at that. See those eyes. He was always like that." The eyes are as dark as midnight, serious and somber.

Deborah pulls out a picture of Nicolette, a beautiful young girl who, her mother says, wants to know when her daddy is coming home. She has her father's eyes.

"People think all these things about us," Deborah Merlino says. "But that's not the way it is."

For example, she continues, her husband has always liked nice clothes. So to imply that his wardrobe is some kind of "Godfather chic" is totally inaccurate.

"He was always interested in fashion," she says.

"Even as a boy growing up, he always dressed nice. So did his father," adds Joey's mother.

Once, Deborah says, she and her husband were having dinner at La Veranda, the stylish Italian restaurant on the Delaware River. This was shortly after *Philadelphia* magazine named Merlino one of the city's best dressed.

"We were sitting at a table for two, and there's a group of people at the next table. I can hear them talking about us, and I see them craning their necks. They want to see what Joseph is wearing and what kind of shoes he's got on. I wanted to scream. He just laughed and told me not to worry about it."

Another misconception, they say, is that his acts of kindness and generosity are attempts to court the media.

"We grew up poor," Rita Merlino begins. "We've always been generous. My husband and my father-in-law were the same way. Ask anybody, they'll tell you."

"Joseph is just like that," Deborah adds. "He enjoys people." And people seem to enjoy him.

Two summers ago, a friend recalls, Merlino was out riding his motorcycle, a cherry-red Harley-Davidson. He was tooling down South Street, his thick black hair blowing in the warm Sunday afternoon breeze. As usual, he was not wearing a helmet. Moments later he was stopped by a police officer. A small crowd gathered as the officer began to write a citation for the safety violation. Merlino mimed a you-got-me shrug. The crowd loved it.

"All of a sudden, they start chanting," says the friend. "Jo-ey. Jo-ey. Jo-ey."

Merlino smiled. Now it was the beat cop's turn to shrug. He handed Merlino the citation, but let him drive off. The motorcycle roared down South Street, drowning out the chants.

"Jo-ey. Jo-ey. Jo-ey." It is all part of the street legend.

Back in 1992, for example, as he was establishing himself as a singular force in the underworld, Merlino and several of his associates used to frequent a local South Philadelphia beauty salon where, each week, they would get manicures.

11

Around Christmastime, Merlino persuaded the shop owner to host a holiday party. This was several years before he launched his own, larger celebration on Passyunk Avenue. An associate in the catering business put out a spread. Pasta, veal piccante, clams casino. All kinds of salads, vegetables and desserts. And all day long, customers and neighborhood residents were invited to partake of the food and good cheer. Late in the afternoon, several young African-American girls, 10- and 11-year-olds, happened past. The beauty parlor owner invited them in and soon was piling food onto plates for them. Merlino smiled.

"What are you doing?" he asked the hostess. "That's not how it's done."

"But it's Christmas," she said.

"I know," said Merlino. "And this is how it's done."

With that, he pulled out a wad of cash and, as each little girl left the beauty salon with a plate of food, he handed her a $20 bill.

"Buy something nice for your mother for Christmas," said the young wiseguy with a smile. The girls' faces lit up. The source of the cash, of course, is another matter.

The IRS has been tracking Merlino's income for years, trying to determine where he gets his cash and whether he has paid Uncle Sam what is owed. Over the past decade, Merlino has listed several sources of income: the coffee shop, which was open for about two years in the mid-1990s, a job in a steak shop, and a job in a construction company office. But none seems to justify the lifestyle he's been able to lead.

Before Merlino was jailed, he and his wife lived in a $285,000 condominium in an upper-middle-class neighborhood just west of Broad Street near the stadium complex. Deborah and the girls are still there. They would summer in a rental at the Jersey Shore. They drove late-model, expensive cars. Mercedeses. Jeeps. Cadillacs.

In one recorded conversation during the current investigation, Merlino complained about the IRS dogging him, even going to Boyd's, the men's store where he sometimes bought his clothes.

"They're trying to get me on a tax case now," he said. "Subpoenaed everybody." They even subpoenaed his wife's work records, he said.

For most of the marriage, Deborah Merlino has worked at a series of well-paying office jobs. Federal authorities believe they may be fronts, ways for people to funnel money to her husband. In the taped conversation, Merlino said he may have been remiss in paying some taxes, but that his wife always paid what she owed.

"I made $200,000," Merlino said. "And my wife made, she paid, you know, paid hers. She made . . . $300,000 in two years."

Deborah Merlino says they used her earnings to cover household expenses. Most of her husband's other income, she explains, came from gambling.

"He's a gambler. It's a vice, but he loves to gamble. And he's very good at it." There is, of course, another side to that story.

Merlino got the nickname "Skinny Joey" for obvious reasons, and because his cousin, also named Joseph, was chubby. The two families lived in the same South Philadelphia neighborhood, near 10th and Jackson. The cousin, who was known as "Fat Joey," eventually moved to the Jersey Shore.

Skinny Joey stayed in South Philly. He attended Bishop Neumann High School but was bounced out during his senior year for "disciplinary reasons," says his mother. "After," she quips, "they collected the tuition payment." By then Joey had already started working as an apprentice jockey, mucking the stalls and giving the horses their morning workouts. Eventually, he got to ride in races at nearly a dozen area tracks, including Philadelphia Park and Atlantic City.

"He was good," says Rita Merlino, proudly recalling a race he won at Pimlico. But he was growing. At five-feet-five and 130 pounds, he was still known as "Skinny," but was already too big to jockey. There were, however, other "opportunities" on the horizon.

Merlino had just turned 18 in March 1980 when Angelo Bruno, Philadelphia's longtime mob boss, was killed. Bruno had been the don for 21 years. He ruled with an iron fist covered with a velvet glove. When Nicodemo "Little Nicky" Scarfo succeeded Bruno, he didn't see the need for the glove. The Philadelphia mob has been on a bloody downward spiral ever since.

Salvatore "Chucky" Merlino, Joey's father, was one of Scarfo's best friends. Soon Joey was the son of the underboss. He hung with the sons, brothers and nephews of the "made" members of the Scarfo organization and became part of what federal investigators referred to as the "Jayvee Mafia," as in Junior Varsity. They would run errands, serve as gofers and hang on the corner outside the mob clubhouse, at Camac and Moore Streets, just off Passyunk Avenue.

"This kid grew up with Cosa Nostra," said Nick Caramandi, a Scarfo crime family soldier who later became a government informant. "He knew all the moves just because he was always around it. He knew it better than some guys 20 years older than him."

He knew about all the trappings, of course. The sacred "making," or initiation ceremony, where a mobster swears to live and die for "the family." And the time-honored code of silence, omerta, which for generations kept La Cosa Nostra isolated and protected from law enforcement. But for Merlino, the business of the mob was always personal. Sometimes, in fact, it seemed like a South Philadelphia soap opera, a never-ending story of love, betrayal, honor and treachery with interchangeable characters whose relationships overlapped in a maze of pathos and violence.

The wedding was set for the last Saturday in April 1984. The gowns had been purchased. The invitations were ready to go in the mail. There would be 700 guests, all the top wiseguys from the city and emissaries from several of the big New York families. In Philadelphia, it was billed as the

Mafia wedding of the decade, perhaps the century. Maria Merlino, Joey's older sister, a beautiful, dark-haired Mafia princess, was to marry Salvatore Testa, the young, charismatic son of the late mob leader Philip "Chicken Man" Testa. The elder Testa had been Angelo Bruno's underboss and was Scarfo's mentor and ally before he was brutally killed in a 1981 bomb blast that ripped the front porch off his South Philadelphia home.

The proposed Testa-Merlino wedding, the joining of underworld royalty, was almost medieval. It would bring two prominent families together in an alliance that would solidify the future of the organization. But Salvatore Testa, a fearless young wiseguy who himself survived a series of murder attempts, had the poor judgment to break off the engagement just weeks before the nuptials were to take place.

"They were gonna have a big affair, I think at the Bellevue," recalled Caramandi. "They were even talking about trying to get Stevie Wonder or somebody like that to perform. I think they could have done that. They had a lot of connections."

Salvatore Merlino, Caramandi said, was livid when the younger Testa balked at marrying his daughter. And Scarfo, growing in paranoia and distrust, used the "insult" to the Merlino family as a pretext to turn on the young mobster, whom he saw as an eventual rival. In September, nearly six months after the canceled wedding date, Salvatore Testa was shot and killed, his body unceremoniously dumped along the side of a rural road in South Jersey.

"It's easy to be generous with other people's money," says an investigator who has tracked Merlino for years and who admits he is put off by the Robin Hood image that some attach to him. For years, federal authorities contend, Merlino has lived high on money that he didn't earn, that in many cases he simply stole.

His first serious jail time came after his conviction for a 1987 armored truck heist in which $357,150 was stolen. Merlino was in his mid-20s at the time. His father had just been convicted and sentenced to 45 years for racketeering along with Scarfo and a dozen other wiseguys. Joey himself had just come out of prison and was still on parole for stabbing a patron in a bar fight in Atlantic City.

The armored truck robbery was an inside job. One of the guards on the truck arranged to dump sacks of cash at a prearranged location. Merlino and an associate then grabbed the loot. After that, the plan started to fall apart. The guard, who was expecting a piece of the take, never saw any money. There were some heated arguments. Threats were made. Shots were fired and eventually the guard ended up talking to federal authorities. Before it was over, Merlino's associate also turned government witness. Both men testified at the 1990 trial that led to Merlino's conviction. Merlino was sentenced to four years in prison and did a little more than two before being released on parole in 1992. The money has never been recovered.

"Joey is for Joey," said a source familiar with the incident. "Always was, always will be. These kids around him don't get it. Maybe now, while they're sitting in jail, they will."

The sentence Merlino got for the truck heist, say the federal prosecutors who handled the case, was the price Merlino was willing to pay for the cash. The gossip in the underworld is that Joey's father, sitting in a federal prison in Atlanta, is still angry that his son blew all the money in less than two years.

"Joey is the kind of guy, if he's got $5,000 in his pocket, he's gonna spend it," says another associate, "because tomorrow he's gonna go out and get $5,000 more."

"These guys all ought to wear stocking masks because they're nothing more than common thieves," former mobster Ron Previte said several months before his role as an FBI informant became public.

Previte claims that during the 1997 football season, Merlino bet heavily with a sports bookmaking operation that Previte was running. Merlino lost a total of $212,000 and reneged on the debt. It was, say others, part of a familiar pattern. Merlino loves to gamble. In most cases, he would collect when he won and would refuse to pay when he lost.

On the corner, they call this "guzzling" somebody. It's a scam usually aimed at a bookmaker who doesn't have the right affiliation, an outlaw operating outside the bounds of the underworld. But you don't guzzle members of your own organization. You don't scam bookmakers who have been in business for years, who have established a track record and who do the right thing with the right people.

Gambling is the foundation of the entire underworld economy. The rules are clear and self-evident. If you lose, you pay.

Merlino seemed to think it was his privilege to walk away from his debts even as he accumulated wads of cash from various underworld players. His house was listed in someone else's name. The cars he drove were leased by associates. (Previte, for example, was paying the monthly lease on one four-wheel-drive vehicle, with money supplied by the FBI.) There is even talk that a Boston-based mobster bought membership in the Merlino organization by agreeing to "lend" Merlino $100,000. The unspoken understanding, of course, was that the loan would never come due. Others who had lent Merlino money knew the drill. In fact, Merlino used to joke about it.

"Crime don't pay," he'd say. Then he'd flash one of his crooked smiles, and his eyes would dance in happy defiance. The message was clear: In Philadelphia, Merlino was crime. And he didn't pay.

On October 31, 1989, Nicky Scarfo Jr. was having dinner with an associate at Dante & Luigi's Restaurant in South Philadelphia. Soon after the salads were served, a man wearing a Halloween mask and carrying what customers thought was a trick-or-treat bag walked up to Scarfo's table, pulled out a semiautomatic MAC-10 machine pistol, and opened fire. Scarfo was hit eight times in the arms and body, but miraculously survived. Joey Merlino has been the suspect in the shooting for the past 11 years.

Informants have identified him as the masked gunman. Nicky Jr., in a telephone call secretly taped by the New Jersey State Police, told his jailed father that Merlino was the hit man.

"He's a snake, this kid," the elder Scarfo replied. But authorities have never come up with enough evidence to make a case.

For a time, the Halloween hit—carried out in a crowded restaurant in front of dozens of innocent patrons—was considered one of the most notorious acts of violence in the storied history of Philadelphia's underworld. Now, it takes a back seat to the August 31, 1993, attempt on the life of mob boss John Stanfa, whose car was strafed with machine gun fire from an unmarked van as the two vehicles sped on the Schuylkill Expressway in the midst of weekday-morning rush-hour traffic.

Stanfa's son, Joseph, took a bullet in the face during the ambush, which came in the midst of the war between mob factions headed by Stanfa and Merlino. Authorities have long suspected that Merlino had ordered the Schuylkill hit as retaliation for an attempt on his life several weeks earlier and for the murder of his longtime friend Michael Ciancaglini.

Ciancaglini, like Merlino the son of a jailed mobster, was one of Merlino's best friends. The two young wiseguys had grown up together and, after Merlino was paroled in the armored truck case, they staked a claim to the underworld legacy of their fathers. (Joseph Ciancaglini Sr., like Salvatore Merlino, was convicted in the 1988 Scarfo racketeering case and is doing 45 years in jail.)

Their clash with the older, Sicilian-born Stanfa was both generational and cultural. He referred to them derisively as the "little Americans" and told associates they were not smart enough or tough enough to be real Mafiosi. They called him "the greaser."

On August 5, 1993, as Merlino and Ciancaglini walked toward a clubhouse they had opened near 6th and Catharine Streets, two Stanfa gunmen drove by in a car and opened fire. Merlino took a bullet in the buttocks and fell to the pavement. Ciancaglini threw up his arm to protect his head. A bullet struck him in the chest. He died on the sidewalk.

"We both went down together," Merlino said in a phone conversation the FBI taped the day after the shooting. "I knew I wasn't hurt that bad. . . . It looked like maybe he just got shot in the arm or something. . . . I turned around. He was, like, 'I'm dyin'.' All blood was coming out of his mouth."

Nicky Jr. had been shot eight times and survived. Mike Ciancaglini got hit once and died.

"It was just bad luck," Merlino said in the same conversation, adding that he wished he could have changed places with Ciancaglini. Merlino was single at the time. Ciancaglini was married with three young children.

"They're all fighting and over what?" an anguished Maria Merlino, Joey's sister, asked in another phone conversation taped at the time. "Jail time or coffins." Her brother, however, didn't see it that way.

"They can't kill me," he said. "[I got] the devil in me."

Three weeks later, bullets were flying on the expressway. Like the Scarfo hit, no one has ever been charged in that shooting.

When he is brought to trial sometime next year, Joseph Salvatore Merlino will be the fourth reputed Philadelphia mob boss to face serious criminal charges in the past 14 years. Two, Scarfo and Stanfa, were convicted and likely will spend the rest of their lives behind bars. The third, Ralph Natale, in an unprecedented development, is a cooperating witness, joining a long list of lower-ranking mob turncoats who make up what is derisively referred to as the South Philadelphia boys choir.

Natale was facing a potential life sentence for dealing methamphetamine when he decided in August 1999 to start singing. It is all part of the decline and fall of the organization that once dominated the local underworld. To compare the Philadelphia mob as it existed under the late Angelo Bruno to the world of the wiseguys of the new millennium is like "comparing a filet mignon to a Big Mac," said former federal prosecutor Louis Pichini.

"And that might be an insult to the Big Mac," added the prosecutor, who brought down the Scarfo organization.

"Bruno was like the CEO of a Fortune 500 company," Pichini said. "These guys are in Chapter 11 bankruptcy. The old mob had substance. It had power. It was a revenue-producing organization. This mob has none of that."

It is, Pichini says, little more than a street gang. "We give them names and ranks and list them on charts, but they're no different than some mopes from North Philly."

"There's no sense of loyalty or honor anymore," said Michael Lorenzo, a former Philadelphia Police Department organized crime investigator. "This is the 'Me Generation.' All they care about is themselves."

Joey had the buyers all lined up. The sales were guaranteed, he said. All he needed was the merchandise. "I'll sell them on the street myself," he said. "I can sell them in two days."

The date was June 10, 1999, and Merlino was deep in conversation with Ronnie Previte, the wiseguy who was wearing a wire. Previte had been setting up cocaine deals in Boston that would soon lead to the drug trafficking charges for which Merlino would be arrested, but this conversation was not about blow. It was about Rolex watches.

The mob boss of Philadelphia wanted to get his hands on hot watches. He had 10 buyers lined up. Rolex watches, especially the two-tone kind, he said, were "better than . . . money."

Earlier, Merlino and Previte had discussed stolen bicycles, ceiling fans and baby formula. Somewhere, Angelo Bruno was rolling over in his grave.

Bruno had invested in real estate, had hidden interests in legitimate companies, bought Resorts International casino stock when it was selling for $2 a share and cashed in after it split three-for-one and rose to $150. He was a millionaire when he died, a mob boss who knew intuitively that to survive you had to make money, not headlines.

Joey Merlino's life, on the other hand, is incandescent, a high-wire act played out in headlines, chic clubs, box seats and the glow of television cameras. There are no shadows. It may not be the smartest way to run a mob family, but for a guy from the corner it doesn't get any better than that.

Fortune Favors the Bold

JUNE 30, 1999

He cut a wide swath through the Philadelphia-South Jersey under-world for most of the 1990s. He was a player, a major mob money-maker, an intimidator and occasional head buster. But for a good part of that time, Ron Previte, 55, was also a confidential law enforcement source, first for New Jersey authorities and more recently for the FBI, ac-cording to several New Jersey law enforcement sources who asked not to be identified.

For the last two years, Previte has been working with federal authori-ties, recording hundreds of conversations while moving through a series of deals involving drugs, extortion, gambling and hijacking. The arrest of re-puted mob boss Joseph "Skinny Joey" Merlino and 10 others on Monday capped that undercover work and shined a spotlight on the underworld's newest informant. Even without that attention, the six-foot, 280-pound Pre-vite was hard to miss.

Previte, who once boasted in an interview that he "learned more about being a crook" during the 10 years he spent in the Philadelphia Police De-partment than at any other time in his life, is the FBI's latest weapon in its battle with the local branch of La Cosa Nostra, a battle that has resulted in the jailing of dozens of top mob figures in the last 10 years.

Operating with the same guile, wit and stone-cold bravado that he dis-played in the underworld, Previte may have put the final nail in the coffin, several law enforcement authorities believe. If it wasn't Merlino picked up on tape allegedly approving a cocaine sale, then it was former mob boss Ralph Natale bragging about his power.

"There's only one boss in Philadelphia. . . . That's Ralph Natale, and that's where the [expletive] it's at," Natale allegedly said during a meeting with Previte and others in March 1998. The taped comments were included in the criminal complaint made public Monday when Natale, in jail on a parole violation, was charged with setting up a series of methamphetamine deals. Bail hearings for most of those arrested Monday, including Merlino, are set for tomorrow, when even more details about the investigation could be disclosed.

"Fortune favors the bold," Previte said over lunch one day nearly four years ago, unknowingly quoting one of the tenets of a philosopher he had never read but whom he understood intuitively. Previte was an underworld Machiavelli, and his decision to turn on his former associates is a classic gambit right out of *The Prince*.

According to a source close to the investigation, Previte decided that the Mafia—at least what passes for the Mafia in the Philadelphia and South

Jersey area—was a losing business proposition. While he had generated tens of thousands of dollars for Natale and Merlino, he didn't respect them. He thought they were shortsighted and greedy.

"Nobody wants to work anymore," Previte has told those in whom he is now confiding. "All they want to do is rob people."

The comment is ironic. Several years ago, Previte said: "I enjoy what I'm doing. I enjoy robbing people. I'm not a nice person." But that was in a different context. Previte said he "worked" at his profession. He was a master at setting up deals, establishing legitimate and quasi-legitimate business operations that, in conjunction with his illegal activities, created a constant flow of cash.

"This is not a sideline to him," one longtime Hammonton associate said of Previte more than five years ago. "This is his life."

Previte, in a series of interviews over the years, offered a self-portrait. Operating out of Hammonton, where he has lived for 20 years, Previte built a base of operations in the underworld even before he was formally tied to the mob. After leaving the Philadelphia police force in the late 1970s—he resigned under pressure and with a reputation for brutality—he went to work as a security officer for the Tropicana casino in Atlantic City.

He later joked that he left the Tropicana "in handcuffs" in 1985, claiming that during his years there he scammed more than a million dollars from the casino through a series of ripoffs ranging from stealing supplies to robbing hotel guests. Previte managed to avoid being charged with any crime despite the allegations by casino officials. He left the Tropicana "under a cloud" and with the understanding that he would not work in the casino industry again.

But by the mid-1980s he had already established himself as a full-service underworld entrepreneur, dabbling in almost any illegal enterprise in which there was a profit—drugs, prostitution, gambling, loansharking, extortion.

By 1994, Previte had aligned himself with Mafia boss John Stanfa. Through Stanfa, he was formally initiated into the mob. He survived the bloody underworld war that pitted Stanfa against Merlino and then managed to reposition himself with Natale and Merlino after Stanfa and nearly 20 associates were convicted in 1995.

While there was some speculation that Previte had avoided arrest because he was an informant, it did not stop him from moving up the ladder in the Natale-Merlino organization. He was listed as a "capo"—a captain or street boss—in a 1998 organizational chart put together by federal and New Jersey law enforcement authorities. By that point, he had already been wearing a wire for the feds for more than a year.

Previte recorded conversations with most of the major players in the organization, including Natale and Merlino. He insinuated himself into the middle of a series of drug deals that he recorded and that, on occasion, the FBI was also able to videotape.

Taken into protective custody last week, he is now preparing for the next phase of the operation. He will be one of the government's key witnesses if and when the cases growing out of the undercover operation go to trial. At some point, it is expected that Previte will face criminal charges for his activities. Often, cooperating witnesses are charged with lesser crimes or receive lighter sentences.

The Devil to Pay

APRIL 8, 2001

He says he did it for his family, not the family. He says he gave most of his adult life—including the nearly 16 years he spent in prison for drug trafficking and arson—to the Mafia and decided he couldn't give any more.

"If there is any life left for me, any time, I'll give it to [my] family. No more La Cosa Nostra."

This was mob boss Ralph Natale back in November, explaining to a federal jury in a Camden corruption case why he decided to become a cooperating witness following his 1999 arrest on drug-dealing charges.

No one bothered to ask the 69-year-old underworld kingpin if the prospect of spending the rest of his life in jail might also have been a factor in his decision to cooperate. No one asked if he was thinking about his family—his wife of more than 40 years and his five grown children—when he came out of jail in 1994 and went right back to a life in organized crime, dealing in meth and murder and taking charge of one of the most violent and dysfunctional mob families in America.

The smart money says those questions and others intended to challenge Natale's character, motives and credibility will be asked in as many ways and as many times as possible by defense attorneys as Natale testifies in the racketeering-murder case of reputed mob leader Joseph "Skinny Joey" Merlino and six codefendants. The trial is under way in a ninth-floor courtroom of the federal courthouse at 6th and Market Streets. Natale is the chief government witness.

As such, Natale, the smooth-talking mob boss, is the newest poster boy in the government's war on organized crime. The first sitting American Mafia boss to agree to testify for the prosecution, he is a major trophy for law enforcement, particularly the Philadelphia office of the FBI. But he is also, in the eyes of a growing number of critics of the Justice Department, a glaring example of a prosecutorial system gone awry, part of a disturbing win-at-any-cost trend in which convictions are more important than overall justice and in which a guilty verdict, no matter the cost, is all that counts.

Going easy on a low-level wiseguy to get testimony against the bigger fish in an organization is a time-honored tactic of law enforcement. But, critics ask, isn't there a threshold that should not be crossed when making a deal with the devil? Are there wiseguys to whom no deal should be offered?

Natale has admitted that he was a mob boss, that he headed a South Jersey methamphetamine distribution ring, and that, during an underworld

22

career that stretches back to the 1960s, he was involved in eight gangland murders and four attempted murders.

He faces a potential life sentence. But it is no secret that, because he has agreed to testify, he hopes to walk out of prison. And that, says Frank Friel, an organized crime expert and former top law enforcement investigator, is the moral quandary that the prosecution faces whenever it considers making a deal with a cooperator.

"What's the larger good?" asks Friel, a former captain with the Philadelphia Police Department who worked on the highly successful federal-city organized crime task force in the 1980s. "What's the value to society when the government throws back the covers and gets into bed with . . . Natale?

"The theory has always been that if you cut off the head of the snake, the snake dies. But do you make a deal with the head?"

Alan Hart, a former IRS agent and private investigator who now heads the criminal justice department at Burlington County College, has similar qualms. "The job of the government is to get justice, to get to the truth," he says, "not to get a conviction at any cost."

Of course, government prosecutors have stock responses that they put before the jury every time a mobster-turned-informant is attacked by the defense. "Swans don't swim in sewers," they say. "We can't get a priest or a rabbi or the leader of the Chamber of Commerce to come in here and tell you about the defendants because the defendants didn't associate with those kinds of people."

"It's a value judgment," says Robert Carroll, a former prosecutor who headed the New Jersey Division of Criminal Justice.

Carroll, who successfully used the testimony of confessed mob leaders Alfonse D'Arco and Philip Leonetti to win convictions in a high-profile Toms River organized crime case several years ago, says the ultimate target is not the individual, but the enterprise. "Whether you're going up the chain or down the chain [in terms of an informant's position in the crime family], the question is where can you do the most damage to the organization."

"The only thing that matters is whether the witness is telling the truth," adds Frank DeSimone, who has seen the issue from three sides: as part of the prosecution offering a deal to get at another defendant, as a criminal defense lawyer engineering a deal to get his client a reduced sentence, and as the lawyer of someone convicted based on an informant's testimony.

DeSimone was representing Leonetti when the former underboss of the Philadelphia-South Jersey mob became one of the most important government witnesses in the country. Sentenced to 45 years in prison in 1988 on murder-racketeering charges, Leonetti had his jail time reduced to five years, five months and five days as a result of his cooperation and testimony.

Society, DeSimone said, is constantly wrestling with issues of right and wrong, constantly trying to "balance morality." Jurors, he said, bring that with them to the courtroom.

"It's not about the deal these guys get," DeSimone said. "The question is, 'Is he telling the truth?' All the other stuff is . . . irrelevant."

In the last 20 years, federal authorities throughout the country have racked up a series of staggering convictions that have decimated mob families from New York to Los Angeles. High-tech surveillance has resulted in audio and video tapes that have allowed juries to see and hear the mob in action.

The multipronged Racketeering Influenced and Corrupt Organizations (RICO) Act has provided a legal framework for attacking a criminal enterprise, rather than individual criminals. And informant testimony has shattered the once sacred code of silence—omerta—around which the Mafia structured itself. The results have been scores of convictions. But at what price to society?

Increasingly, critics contend, the government has crossed the line in seeking cooperators and in making them offers they can't refuse. Consider the underworld trinity of Salvatore "Sammy the Bull" Gravano in Manhattan, Gregory Scarpa in Brooklyn, and James "Whitey" Bulger in Boston. They are prime exhibits for critics who contend that, when it comes to mob cases, overzealous FBI agents and federal prosecutors too often equate winning with justice.

Gravano, perhaps the best known, testified against mob boss John Gotti. The Bull, who was Gotti's onetime friend and underboss, admitted his involvement in 19 mob murders. He described himself as Gotti's enforcer.

"When he barked, I bit," he told a federal jury during a 1992 racketeering trial not unlike the one now under way in Philadelphia.

Gotti was convicted and sentenced to life in prison. Gravano, because of his cooperation, got five years. He was released, and got a book and movie deal and a new identity. He popped up later in Phoenix, boasting about how he wasn't afraid of the mob, about how he wasn't going to hide, about how he had started his own construction business and was going to live his life to the fullest.

Last year, Gravano was arrested and charged with heading a multimillion-dollar narcotics ring that was selling the drug ecstasy to teenagers and young adults in the Phoenix club scene. Gravano's wife and their adult son, daughter and son-in-law were also charged. What happens if Gravano is convicted? Does he still have a federal get-out-of-jail card to play?

How much was convicting John Gotti worth? For years that question has plagued the families of Gravano's 19 murder victims. Now it can also be asked by the families of anyone whose life was ruined by the drugs Gravano was peddling after the FBI helped him start a new life.

Gregory Scarpa is dead. He died of AIDS, the result of a tainted blood transfusion while he was in the hospital being treated for bleeding ulcers. But in the early 1990s, Scarpa was a major player in the Colombo crime family in Brooklyn, one of the leaders in a factional, internecine power struggle that left a dozen mobsters dead.

Defense attorneys now contend—and courtroom testimony has provided corroboration—that while Scarpa was out and about committing murder and mayhem, he was a so-called top-echelon informant for the FBI. That's the highest rank the bureau can attach to a cooperator. More troubling, documents indicate, an FBI agent may have been feeding Scarpa information about members of the rival faction of the Colombo crime family during the bloody war. Some defense attorneys have said in appeals proceedings that Scarpa used that information to track down and kill his rivals.

While no charges have resulted from the allegations, the handling of Gregory Scarpa was clearly not the FBI's finest hour. Several convictions have been overturned because Scarpa's role as an informant was never disclosed. One FBI agent assigned to the case, Christopher Favo, testified that he was concerned that the bureau had been compromised by Scarpa, that instead of Scarpa's being used by the bureau, Scarpa was using the FBI.

"It was like a line had been blurred . . . over who we were and what this was," Favo said.

While many of the circumstances surrounding Scarpa's deal with the FBI remain in the shadows, there are floodlights beaming in all directions in the case of James "Whitey" Bulger and his FBI handlers. A legendary crime figure from South Boston, Bulger is now on the FBI's 10 Most Wanted list. Two books have already been written about the case. There is talk of a movie.

It is, by any measure, a saga, a sad and sorry tale of those sworn to uphold the law stooping to the level of those they were investigating. Bulger and his underworld partner in crime, Stephen "The Rifleman" Flemmi, were FBI "top-echelon" informants for nearly 20 years, helping the feds build a series of cases against members of the Boston-based Patriarca crime family. The convictions, an ongoing investigation now shows, not only removed wiseguys from the streets, but also paved the way for Bulger and Flemmi to expand their own criminal enterprises, which ranged from drug-dealing and extortion to gunrunning and murder.

One FBI agent has been indicted and another has turned government witness as federal prosecutors try to sort out two decades of internal corruption. Among the allegations are that Bulger and Flemmi, with tips provided by the FBI, killed individuals who had tried to inform on them. Bodies have been dug up, special grand juries have been convened, and dozens of mobsters have asked that their convictions be overturned because evidence against them was tainted.

Bulger disappeared shortly before he and Flemmi were indicted in 1995. Investigators believe Bulger, whose brother was once the president of the Massachusetts Senate, was tipped off several days in advance that an indictment was coming.

Many of the seamier details in the Bulger-Flemmi FBI fiasco have been outlined in a 600-page report issued by U.S. District Judge Mark L. Wolf in 1999. The report was based on 80 days of hearings and testimony from 46 witnesses.

Testimony included Flemmi's allegation that he and Bulger were once told by one of their FBI handlers, "You can do anything you want as long as you don't clip anyone." Clip is underworld shorthand for murder. Yet Wolf noted in his report that the FBI maintained its relationship with Bulger and Flemmi even after the two surfaced as suspects in a series of gangland killings.

Wolf also noted that, in clear violation of FBI regulations, two agents accepted gifts and money from the two wiseguys and dined with them socially. Wolf found that both Bulger and Flemmi used their relationships with the FBI to advance their own criminal operation.

The report also included an anecdote that captured the attitude Bulger brought to his role as an undercover operative for the FBI. In 1985, Bulger learned that the Drug Enforcement Administration had planted bugs—listening devices—in his car. He subsequently found and removed the devices, which were worth between $15,000 and $20,000. When DEA agents, who were monitoring the bugging, heard what was going on, they rushed in to recover the equipment. At that point, Bulger expressed surprise that he was being bugged and allegedly said to them, "We're all good guys here. You're the good good guys and we're the bad good guys."

Ralph Natale claims he's 66. Other documents, including FBI reports, list him as 69. It's a minor point, but it speaks to the vanity of a man who clearly enjoyed the trappings of wiseguy life. In his testimony last year during the corruption trial of former Camden Mayor Milton Milan, Natale came across as someone who liked being center stage. He referred repeatedly to his reputation and his prestige and how he was the only person the major New York crime families would entrust with rebuilding the beleaguered Philadelphia mob in the early 1990s.

Dressed in a neatly tailored business suit, his goatee sharply trimmed, his bald head shaved clean, Natale was relaxed and at ease as he told the jury about his life in La Cosa Nostra. His mob pedigree, he explained, dated back to the 1960s. He came up as an associate of then-mob boss Angelo Bruno.

Some wiseguys now claim Natale was nothing more than a gofer for Bruno, but that's all part of the petty bickering that has been going on behind the scenes since Natale flipped. Those in Merlino's camp describe Natale as a "liar" who is making up stories to fit the government's version of the case. He was the boss in name only, they contend. "A legend in his own mind," they say.

Natale, in turn, has repeatedly bad-mouthed his former confederates. Not long after he got out of prison, he referred to them as "fine young men" and told a television reporter they were the kind of people with whom he would be honored to "share a foxhole." Now, as revealed in tapes of his prison phone calls, one's a "punk," another's a "drunk." One is a "homo" who "beats his wife" and another is strung out on cocaine.

Natale told the jury in Camden that he eventually took over the South Jersey Bartenders Union for Bruno, who secretly controlled it. And, he added with no small amount of pride, he became an enforcer for the boss, carrying out two murders to ensure the mob's continued control of the union.

In a line that sounded a lot like the well-publicized "when-he-barked-I-bit" phrase that Gravano used at the 1992 Gotti trial, Natale arrogantly described his relationship with Bruno this way: "I was his dog. When he had a problem and it was serious, he would set me free."

Natale's criminal career was short-circuited in 1979 when he was convicted of drug trafficking and arson. The arson was in connection with an insurance fraud scheme. He spent the next 15 years in federal prison, where, he now contends, he made the kind of underworld connections that paved his way to the top of the Philadelphia-South Jersey mob after he was released in 1994. In fact, he contends, he was the "unofficial" boss while serving time. This was the case, he said, even though he had not yet been formally initiated into La Cosa Nostra.

When he was finally released, Natale went about his business like someone trying to make up for lost time. Most afternoons he would hold court in the Currier & Ives Room, the third-floor bar and restaurant at Garden State Racetrack. There he would meet with associates to discuss business, share drinks, and place bets on races all over the country. He loved it. He called the bar his "office."

Evenings were reserved for dinner meetings, again with friends and associates. He would sit at the head of the table in a fine restaurant regaling his young mob associates with stories about the old days when he was a "hitter" for Bruno, bragging that if things got tough he could still "put on my work boots."

Tanned and fit—he jogged nearly every day around the Cooper River in Pennsauken, where he lived in a penthouse apartment—Natale would puff out his chest and hold his cleanly shaved head high whenever he walked into a room with his 30-year-old South Philadelphia girlfriend on his arm. The woman had once been a good friend of Natale's youngest daughter. She was also well known to Merlino and his associates, a fact that caused at least some of the friction that developed between Natale and the Merlino faction. On more than one occasion, Natale berated a young wiseguy for failing to show the proper "respect" to his lady. Those who had been chastised thought Natale was being ridiculous.

"She was a girl from Broad and Snyder, and he wanted us to treat her like Princess Di," one Merlino associate said in an interview.

Natale's run at the top of the mob was short-lived. He was jailed on parole violation charges in 1998, and a year later, in June 1999, was indicted for running a methamphetamine ring. A conviction would have resulted in a long jail term. He was facing the very real prospect of dying in prison. At the end of August, after putting out feelers for several weeks, he made his deal with the government.

Now he has pleaded guilty not only to the drug dealing, but also to murder and attempted-murder charges and to heading a mob family. On paper, at least, he is looking at a life sentence. The reality, say those who have followed this kind of case in the past, is a probable five- to 10-year sentence imposed after the conclusion of the Merlino trial. At that point, sometime this summer, Natale will already have been in jail for three years. If he is given credit for that time, a five-year sentence would mean almost immediate release.

Not a bad deal. But what could be worth letting an eight-time murderer off so easily? Prosecutors and FBI agents say it's because Natale is able to link Merlino and several of his top associates to three unsolved murders and two attempted murders.

That Natale, as mob boss, authorized those hits appears to be of little concern to those who have brought the case. Merlino, the swaggering, in-your-face South Philadelphia celebrity gangster, has clearly become the federal government's top priority. Yet it was Natale who was the primary target of the initial investigation.

Beginning in 1994, authorities allege, Natale and Merlino took over the mob that had been headed by their underworld rival, jailed mob boss John Stanfa. It was that year, Natale says, that he was formally initiated into the mob by Merlino. And, by the fall of 1995, when Stanfa went to trial on RICO-murder charges (he was convicted and sentenced to five life sentences), the FBI was already bugging Natale's phone, his apartment and his favorite meeting place at Garden State Park.

Hundreds of hours of secretly recorded conversations, with Natale discussing all kinds of mob business, were picked up on those bugs. In several conversations, Natale also complained about informants, berating them as weak and unable to stand up "like a man."

Two years later, in 1997, Ron Previte, a top Natale associate who had been secretly cooperating with law enforcement for more than 10 years, agreed to wear a body wire. Previte recorded hundreds of additional conversations for the FBI.

The Previte tapes, which included wiseguys discussing everything from drug deals and extortions to construction contracts and the effectiveness of Viagra, became the basis for the arrests and indictments of Natale and Merlino on separate drug charges in 1999.

Information on Previte's tapes was used to expand the drug case against Merlino to include charges of gambling, extortion and receiving stolen property. Already, prosecutors had a sweeping racketeering indictment against the younger mob boss. But Natale offered more. In cutting his deal with the government, he promised to deliver information about several mob hits, including the 1995 slaying of Billy Veasey, a South Philadelphia shooting that had long stuck in the craw of the FBI.

Veasey was gunned down a block from his South Philadelphia home on the morning of October 5, 1995, just as his brother John was about to take the stand as a government witness in the racketeering trial of John Stanfa and seven others.

John Veasey was an admitted hit man for the mob who turned on Stanfa. Among other things, he had confessed to the 1993 drive-by shooting in which Merlino was wounded and Merlino's best friend, Michael Ciancaglini, was killed. The killing of Billy Veasey was immediately read as an attempt to silence John Veasey.

Although other motives were mentioned during the five years the FBI investigated the shooting, the murder probe was given high priority because many agents considered it an affront. This, after all, was the brother of a protected government witness. The killing occurred in broad daylight as Billy Veasey, a sometime bookmaker and construction company operator, was leaving for work.

The message the murder sent throughout the underworld was that the feds could not protect everyone; that if you were considering cooperating, you or someone close to you might pay the ultimate price. That is still part of the current theory behind the shooting. The other is that revenge, not intimidation, was the reason Billy Veasey was whacked.

"It was a brother for a brother," Natale is said to have told authorities. He alleged that Merlino and two of his codefendants, George Borgesi and Michael's brother John Ciancaglini, admitted to him that they were involved in the shooting.

"It was an honor to do this for Michael," Natale has quoted John Ciancaglini as saying.

Borgesi, Ciancaglini and Merlino have all been charged with the Veasey killing as part of the overall racketeering indictment. Natale, as boss, has told investigators that he authorized the hit. He also said he approved the murders of Joe Sodano and Anthony Turra, two other killings that are part of the current case.

The Turra murder charge, like the Veasey killing, is built almost entirely around Natale's testimony. It will be his word—and his credibility—that will make or break those parts of the 36-count racketeering case.

The Sodano hit raises different questions about the way the government has framed its case. Sodano, a Newark mobster, was killed in 1996 for failing to show the proper "respect" to Natale and Merlino, according to the charges. The murder, prosecutors say, was ordered by Natale and Merlino. Peter "Pete the Crumb" Caprio, a North Jersey mob capo, or captain, got the assignment.

Caprio then enlisted hit man Philip "Philly Faye" Casale to do the actual shooting. Casale is, among other things, a convicted child molester.

Caprio and Casale, like Natale, are now cooperating with authorities. Thus, in its quest to convict Merlino of the Sodano murder, the government has cut deals with three other mobsters, including the two who carried out the hit. It is that kind of math that drives defense attorneys screaming into the night.

"I don't think you should ever cut a deal with a murderer," says Edward Crisonino, whose clients have included Stanfa and several prominent North Jersey wiseguys. "That's where I'd draw the line. . . . But the whole federal system is based on getting people to rat. They don't care what the person's done. . . . They seem to think what they're doing is justice, that the deals are worth what they're getting."

The difficulty, Crisonino and other defense lawyers say, is getting the jury to look at the broader picture, to look beyond the specifics and see a pattern that defense lawyers believe is an abuse of the justice system.

"It's a total perversion of the system," says Joseph Oteri, a prominent criminal defense attorney in Boston who has spent years defending alleged wiseguys and suspected drug dealers in cases built around informant testimony.

"Prosecutors and FBI agents are interested in building their career statistics. It's about how many notches they can get on their guns," says Oteri, who also defended Thomas Capano in the Anne Marie Fahey murder case.

"The prosecutors all think they're the ones wearing the white hats and everybody else is a [jerk]. . . . But it's a breakdown of the system. It's not supposed to work like this. And that's what people should care about."

Frank Friel, the former Philadelphia police captain and recognized organized crime expert, thinks the larger good was overlooked. Prosecutors already had a substantial case against Merlino before "flipping" Natale. But someone, Friel believes, fell in love with the idea of "getting a reigning mob boss" to cooperate. As a result, Friel and others believe, Natale's actual value as a witness may have been overshadowed by his pedigree.

"What is the cost in terms of dollars and cents?" he asks. "And in terms of risks and rewards? When you have an organization that is as dismembered as the [Philadelphia mob], is it in society's best interest to make a deal with the target of the investigation? At what point do you say, 'Enough is enough'?"

The Hit Man

He talked of the murder plots and the mob hits that have rocked the Philadelphia underworld. He called himself a triggerman, the shooter in two notorious slayings, and said he had his body tattooed to commemorate the events. He told a grisly tale of deliberately setting his already badly burned hand on fire to create an alibi in the aftermath of one of those shootings, and he described beatings, extortions and plans to blow up rivals with a bomb that he and his associates called "the egg." And on the one occasion when he recalled his mother, who has been dead for several years, he paused, and, in full view of the jurors, blessed himself.

So went the debut of confessed Mafia hit man John Veasey yesterday as a witness in the racketeering trial of mob boss John Stanfa and seven associates in U.S. District Court.

Five days after his brother was gunned down in South Philadelphia, the dark-haired and broad-shouldered former mobster swaggered into court and swore to tell the truth. He wore a blue business suit, white shirt, red tie and a self-assured smile, and he eyed Stanfa and the other defendants repeatedly, occasionally shaking his head in what appeared to be mock disgust or sympathy. On at least one occasion, he appeared to be pulling the trigger finger of an imaginary gun aimed at the defense table.

Veasey is the first of five former Stanfa associates scheduled to testify for the prosecution. The government's case is built around their stories and a series of more than 100 secretly recorded conversations, most of them made by the FBI during a two-year investigation.

Last Thursday morning, just hours before Veasey was supposed to take the stand, his brother Billy was shot and killed in a gangland ambush not unlike the ones that John Veasey described from the witness stand yesterday.

The murder of Billy Veasey, believed to be a mob warning to John Veasey and other current or potential government informants, has not been mentioned in court. The shooting is the focus of an intensive police and FBI investigation.

John Veasey's appearance as a witness was delayed until yesterday because of the murder, but several sources who know the tough-talking former hit man said the killing had hardened his resolve to help the government make its case against Stanfa and the others.

Veasey's testimony, which is expected to resume today, was a gritty tale of underworld chaos, most of it stemming from the bloody war that raged in 1993 and pitted those loyal to Stanfa against a rival mob faction reputedly headed by Joseph "Skinny Joey" Merlino. The marching orders of the organization at the time, Veasey said, were "to kill anybody aligned with Merlino." Shotguns, machine guns, rifles with telescopic night sights, and the "egg," an eight-inch pipe filled with gunpowder, were all part of the arsenal in the war, he said.

Under questioning from Assistant U.S. Attorney Robert Courtney, one of four federal prosecutors presenting the government's case, Veasey, 29, described elaborately planned murders that were never carried out and mob hits that occurred on the spur of the moment. He admitted his own involvement in the August 5, 1993, shootings of Merlino and Michael Ciancaglini that left Merlino wounded and Ciancaglini dead, and in the September 17, 1993, murder of Merlino associate Frank Baldino in the parking lot of the Melrose Diner.

Those shootings, and many of the other crimes Veasey talked about, were detailed in a 13-count racketeering indictment returned against Stanfa and his codefendants last year. Veasey's testimony, delivered in South Philadelphia tough-guy jargon, put a more graphic spin on the government's legalese. He described several key events.

THE STALKING OF JOEY MERLINO

Veasey said he was recruited by Stanfa's reputed acting underboss and codefendant, Frank Martines, to help murder Merlino in July 1993. At the time, he said, he was working for a construction company owned by Stanfa's brother-in-law. On several occasions, he said, he went with Salvatore Brunetti and Philip Colletti to an area around 2nd and Market Streets where Merlino was living in an apartment.

Colletti, like Veasey, is a government witness and is expected to testify in the case. Brunetti is one of eight other defendants scheduled to be tried sometime next year on the same racketeering charges.

The plots included using a rifle with a telescope and firing on Merlino from a car parked on a highway ramp near the apartment; bursting into Merlino's third-floor apartment with guns blazing; and planting the "egg" under his car.

Veasey said that when he asked the other two if a bomb might kill other people, he was told: "As long as it ain't a girlfriend or somebody like that, it don't matter."

Anybody considered "with" Merlino, he said, was fair game. None of the plots was ever carried out.

THE MERLINO AND CIANCAGLINI HITS

Veasey said he and Colletti happened to be watching a clubhouse at 6th and Catharine Streets on August 5, 1993, when they spotted the two targets. "Let's get 'em," he recalled Colletti saying.

They drove by in a car as Merlino and Ciancaglini were walking and opened fire as they passed. Veasey said he was shooting a 9-mm from the back seat and Colletti was firing a .45 from the driver's window.

"I seen Mikey Chang [Ciancaglini] hit the ground, get up and fall down again," Veasey said. "I saw Joey Merlino spinning around."

Ciancaglini died of a gunshot wound to the chest. Merlino was wounded in the buttocks.

THE FIRE

Veasey said that Colletti used a car leased in his own name to carry out the hits and that they decided to burn the vehicle. He said they were at Colletti's parents' home, near 18th Street and Passyunk Avenue, at the time.

"I didn't have no money on me," Veasey said. "I got a milk carton, gallon container, out of the refrigerator, emptied it, borrowed a dollar and walked over to a gas station and bought a gallon of gas."

He, Colletti and Colletti's wife, Brenda, drove to a deserted area near 19th and Johnston Streets, Veasey said. While Colletti cleaned out the car, Veasey said he poured gasoline all over the interior and around the outside.

"I saw some change in the car," Veasey said. "I went to get it just as he [Colletti] threw in the match. My left hand caught on fire."

Veasey said he and Colletti struggled to douse the fire that spread to his shirt and pants as the car went up in flames. He came away from the incident with a badly burned left hand—"the skin was coming off"—but he could not go to the hospital because of the fear that an injury report might link him to the murder car.

Later that night, Veasey said, he returned to his own home near 8th and Washington Streets. He said he made a point of stopping to talk and have a cigarette with neighbors who, he said, thought he was coming home from work.

"I kept my left hand in my pocket," he said.

Once in his own house, Veasey said, he went into his yard, where he had a barbecue grill, and poured lighter fluid on his burned and blistered hand. Then he set it on fire.

"I screamed and told the neighbors I had burned it trying to light the grill," he said.

THE MELROSE MURDER

Veasey said he, Frank Martines and Giuseppe Gallara, also awaiting trial next year, were driving past the parking lot of the Melrose on the night of September 17, 1993, when they spotted a Cadillac owned by Merlino associate Frank Baldino.

"The opportunity presented itself, and we took it," Veasey said.

He said they waited in a car until Baldino left the diner, then Veasey and Gallara ran up and opened fire. Then, he said, they kept running around the block where Martines was supposed to meet them in the getaway car.

"Martines was going down 15th Street [as planned]," Veasey said. "But he wouldn't let us in the car. He thought he was being followed or something . . . . We just shot a guy. We had the guns in our hands, and he wouldn't let us in the car. I'm hollering, 'Open the door, Frank. Open the door.'"

Eventually, he said, he and Gallara got into Martines' car. They later switched to a car driven by Thomas Rebbie, another Stanfa associate now cooperating with the government. Veasey said they drove in Rebbie's car to "the Lakes" in South Philadelphia, where Rebbie threw the two guns.

THE "MAKING" CEREMONY

Because of his role as a hit man, Veasey said, he was formally initiated—or "made"—into the Stanfa crime family. The ceremony occurred in a room at the Penn Towers Hotel in University City. It involved the pricking of his trigger finger with a pin, dabbing the blood with toilet paper, and then burning the paper in his cupped hands while he swore allegiance to the organization. Veasey appeared less than overwhelmed by what other mobsters have described as solemn and often seminal occasions.

"I already burned my hand once for this family," he remarked when the paper was lighted. He also said he could not partake in the wine and drinking celebration that followed "because I had to report to my parole officer that night."

SHAKEDOWNS

Veasey said he was also part of a crew that extorted money from bookmakers, gamblers and loan sharks for the Stanfa crime family. The payments sought ranged from hundreds to thousands of dollars weekly. The targets were guys with names like Georgie Stumps, Tony Video and Billy Bones. Those who balked paid a different price, Veasey said matter-of-factly.

One bookmaker who refused to come up with $5,000 was pulled over on the street by Veasey and John "John Gongs" Cassasanto, another defendant awaiting trial next year.

"I punched him in the mouth a couple of times," Veasey said. "I took his car keys and threw them down the sewer. Gongs got a knife and cut all his tires and cut up his car seats. . . . It was a brand-new Cadillac. I told him, 'That's $5,000 worth of damage.'"

The owner of a newsstand who was booking numbers was also targeted. "I told him a newsstand is only made of wood," Veasey said.

But Veasey said he drew the line when Sergio Battaglia, a Stanfa codefendant, threatened another target's sickly mother.

"I told him to leave him alone," Veasey said. "I felt sorry for the guy," he added. "That wasn't right. I lost my mother."

Then he blessed himself.

THE TATTOOS

Veasey said he had tattoos drawn on his body to commemorate special events, like the mob hits he took part in and his initiation into the organization.

Jurors were shown a photo of one, a tattoo of a .45-caliber revolver that is on Veasey's upper back behind his left shoulder. There are two bullets next to the gun, symbols, he said, of his involvement in the murders of Ciancaglini and Baldino. Over top of the gun are written the words "Someone Talked" and under the gun the words "The Enforcer."

Veasey also showed the jurors his right ankle and the tattoo there of Chinese symbols that he said stood for "faithful" and "loyal," apparent references at the time to his loyalty to Stanfa. While that tattoo is still in place, Veasey's appearance on the stand has made a mockery of its symbolism.

A Wiseguy Looks Back

NOVEMBER 20, 1994

Growing up in Newark in the 1960s, all he ever wanted to be was a wiseguy, says mob informant George Fresolone. In his Eastside High School yearbook, under his graduation picture, his goal was "bookmaker." Thirty years later, having climbed up and down the mob ladder, he is considered one of the most notorious Mafia turncoats in the country.

No regrets.

That's the message from somewhere in Middle America, where Fresolone is building a new life.

"If somebody came to me and said they could erase all that has happened and I could go back to being a wiseguy, I wouldn't do it," the former bookmaker, loan shark and leg buster said in a lengthy telephone interview last week.

"This is the life I want to lead now. It's a life I wouldn't give up . . . . I don't regret what I did one bit."

Struggling to get a new business started, hoping that a book he has coauthored "takes off," and worrying about mortgage payments and monthly bills, Fresolone says he is a happy and content "working stiff." It is a new experience for the burly 41-year-old who celebrated a birthday on Friday with his wife and three children.

For 20 years, he was more likely to mark those kinds of special occasions with his other "family," hanging out with wiseguys at clubhouses in the Down Neck section of Newark, where he grew up, or at an Atlantic City casino, or a posh New York restaurant.

The turnabout began in 1988, when Fresolone, who says the mob's time-honored values of loyalty and honor had been replaced by greed and treachery, agreed to become a "confidential source" for the New Jersey State Police. A year later, he took it a step further, wearing a body wire and a transmitter and recording hundreds of conversations in a massive undercover investigation dubbed "Operation Broadsword."

The high point—for investigators, at least—came on July 29, 1990, when Fresolone wore a transmitter and body wire to his own mob initiation ceremony and recorded the secret Mafia rite of passage for the state police. No one had ever done that before.

Thirty-eight mob members and associates from six crime families that operate in New Jersey were indicted as a result of the year-long Broadsword investigation. Most pleaded guilty and are now in jail.

Earlier this month, Fresolone capped his work for the state when he took the witness stand for the first time, testifying in Camden County Superior Court against Anthony "Tony Buck" Piccolo in the one racketeering case that went to trial.

Piccolo, after a two-week trial, was found guilty Wednesday of conspiracy to commit racketeering and being a leader of organized crime. The 72-year-old mob leader faces up to 20 years in prison when sentenced on January 13.

"All I ever wanted to be was a wiseguy," Fresolone said. "That was all I knew. It's the way I was brought up."

Fresolone's father, who died when he was a child, had been a numbers writer for a small branch of the Angelo Bruno crime family that operated in Newark. When he graduated from high school, Fresolone went to work for Pasquale "Patty Specs" Martirano, the Bruno crime family soldier for whom his father once worked.

"Patty was like a father to me," Fresolone said. "He taught me everything about this business. But it was different then."

Like other Philadelphia crime family members who have become government witnesses, Fresolone traces the demise of the organization to the gangland murder of Angelo Bruno in March 1980. The shotgun assassination of the longtime crime boss set in motion a series of other underworld shootings—in all, 28 mob members and associates were killed—and ushered in the bloody reign of mob boss Nicodemo "Little Nicky" Scarfo.

"When I first started out, this was a thing of honor," Fresolone said. "But after Ange [Bruno] got killed, you saw a lot of unnecessary killings for no reason. Everybody was out for themselves. There was no loyalty anymore."

That, Fresolone acknowledged, is not to say that murder wasn't a part of mob life during the Bruno years. But it was different.

"If somebody hadda go, they didn't just kill him on the street and leave the body," he said. "They used to do it right. Wrap him up. Put him in the trunk of a car. And go bury him in the woods somewheres.

"After a couple of weeks, people don't see the guy, they start to ask, 'Where's Joe? Where's Joe?' You'd say, 'I don't know. Maybe he ran off with a broad.' See, they mighta thought he was dead, but they didn't know."

Scarfo, with a penchant for violence and a fascination with headlines, changed all that.

"Maybe because he was so little, he wanted to show how big he was," Fresolone said of the five-foot-three former mob boss. "He wanted to leave bodies on the street. All that does is attract the attention of the FBI, the police and the media. And that was the destruction of the Scarfo family."

Fresolone, who served a two-year prison term in 1984 on gambling charges, said he agreed to cooperate with the state police in 1988 after being charged along with Martirano and three others in a racketeering case. He did it, he said, both to protect Patty Specs—who had fled the country and was dying of cancer—and to get out from under a potentially heavy prison sentence.

"I did what I had to do to help myself," he told the jury. He later explained that if he cooperated, the state agreed not to pursue Martirano in hiding. It was at the time, he said, when the organization was in turmoil, when several top members had begun cooperating, and when most of the leadership, including Scarfo, was in prison.

Since he flipped and became a government informant, Fresolone has learned a lot about both law enforcement and the media. After being relocated and given a new identity, he worked with state police detectives and state prosecutors analyzing evidence and interpreting the tapes that were at the heart of the Broadsword indictments.

The best test of how devastating those tapes were, detectives and prosecutors say, is that most of the defendants opted not to stand trial but to plead guilty instead. Those nailed by Fresolone included John Riggi, the boss of the New Jersey Decavalcante crime family; Joseph "Scoops" Licata, a capo, or captain, in the Scarfo crime family; and Nicky Scarfo Jr., whom Fresolone was assigned to guard after the younger Scarfo was shot and wounded in a 1989 gangland ambush in a South Philadelphia restaurant.

Nicky Jr. went into hiding in North Jersey shortly after Fresolone began working undercover for the state police. Among the tapes played at the Piccolo trial earlier this month were three phone calls from Nicky Sr. in prison in which he discussed mob business with his son, including a plot to kill rival Joseph "Skinny Joey" Merlino, who was suspected of being behind the botched restaurant hit.

Now, with the Piccolo trial behind him and his obligations as a witness-informant apparently over, Fresolone is hoping to bring that story to a broader audience. Last week, as the jury deliberated Piccolo's fate and ultimately brought back a guilty verdict, Fresolone was on the phone touting *Blood Oath*, which he co-authored with Washington-based journalist Robert Wagman.

"I did 33 radio shows in two days," he said wearily as he ticked off some of the cities in which his voice was heard. "New York. Philadelphia. Kansas City. St. Louis. Cleveland. Detroit. Chicago. San Diego. Washington. Charlotte. Des Moines. Providence. Denver. Pittsburgh. Akron. Miami."

The live interviews, arranged as part of a publicity blitz, included several call-in shows. Questions, he said, ranged from the mob's involvement in legitimate businesses to his fear of possible retribution. (The mob will go wherever there is a chance to make money, he said in response to the former. He will always look over his shoulder, but he is reasonably comfortable with his security and new identity, he said of the latter.)

"People seem to be fascinated with wiseguys," he said. "They see the way it's portrayed in the movies and on TV. And in certain instances, that's the way it was. You see these guys with nice clothes, big cars, diamonds on their fingers, beautiful girls around them. Money in their pocket."

For a brief moment, Fresolone almost sounded nostalgic. Then he was back talking about his new business venture and his new life. The company he owns is in a service industry. He solicits clients. For security reasons, he did not want to get more specific.

"I do the work myself," he said. "I go to work every day. Someday I'd like to get to the point where I can just run the business and have other people work for me."

His wife is happy. His children—two sons, ages 15 and 13, and a daughter, 11—are in good schools. He gets to watch them grow up. He goes to their baseball and basketball games. Takes them to karate lessons. Helps with their homework.

It is all new. And he is enjoying every minute of it.

"I don't miss organized crime one bit," he said. "I wouldn't think about going back. . . . When you're in that, what is there to look forward to? You know it's almost inevitable what's gonna happen. Look at the guys I was around. You wind up in jail. . . . or you wind up dead in the trunk of some car."

No regrets, he said.

Crazy Like a Fox

JUNE 9, 1997

Vincent Gigante, the last big-name Mafia boss in America, is mentally incompetent. Demented. Schizophrenic. The Last Don? Forgetaboutit.

Gigante, 69, is the Lost Don, his life a neurological fog of agitation, paranoia and confusion. Or so say his lawyers and doctors.

He is, they argued last week, incapable of caring for himself. More important, they contend, he is unable to participate in his defense in a criminal case in which he is charged with running the most powerful organized crime family in the country.

Although dressed up in fancier medical and legal terms, those were the arguments offered in a federal courtroom in Brooklyn, as defense attorneys launched yet another attempt to keep Gigante from standing trial on federal racketeering charges that date back to 1990.

The trial is scheduled to begin June 23. The case includes seven murders and three attempted murders, all allegedly carried out on Gigante's orders as a leader of the Genovese crime family. Among the hits were six gangland slayings that changed the face of the Philadelphia mob in the early 1980s.

Prosecutors contend that Gigante, who did not attend last week's hearing, has been feigning mental illness for years to avoid prosecution. His act, they say, has included a penchant for walking around his Greenwich Village neighborhood in a bathrobe and mumbling to himself. More recently, they said, he has claimed to hear voices and to communicate with God.

"God is my lawyer. . . . He takes care of me" is what one medical expert, testifying for the defense, said Gigante told him during an interview last month.

The expert, neuropsychologist Wilfred van Gorp of the Cornell University Medical College, said tests that he and a colleague administered indicate Gigante has an IQ of 68, a score that would place him in the bottom 2.2 percent of the population. But prosecutors, referring to an earlier court ruling that labeled Gigante a "shrewd, able and powerful man," contended that the hallucinating and the low test scores are just part of Gigante's act.

"He's crazy, all right," said one federal investigator. "Crazy like a fox."

U.S. District Judge Jack Weinstein appeared to agree. On Tuesday, he dismissed a defense motion to bar the start of the trial on grounds that Gigante was suffering from dementia brought on either by vascular problems related to a heart condition or by the early onset of Alzheimer's disease. Weinstein said that new evidence offered by van Gorp and another

40

medical expert was simply not persuasive and that Gigante and his lawyers should prepare for trial.

Gigante, who was under court-ordered guard in a New York City hospital for the past month, was released on $1 million bail on Thursday. He returned to the Upper East Side townhouse of his girlfriend, Olympia Esposito, with whom he has been living off and on for 20 years. Gigante has three children with Esposito, according to law enforcement authorities. He also has three grown children with his wife, who lives in North Jersey and is also named Olympia.

While Gigante's mental condition remains the topic of debate—the New York tabloids now refer to him as "The Oddfather"—there is no doubt he has serious medical problems. Gigante has had heart surgery three times, the most recent earlier this year. He is also heavily medicated.

Testimony at last week's hearing indicated that the man who federal authorities contend is the most powerful mob boss in America is a walking medicine cabinet, taking daily, prescribed doses of Thorazine, Percocet, Pamelor, digitalis, Valium and various sleeping pills. Among other things, government prosecutors contended that the combination of drugs could have contributed to the fuzzy mental state of the alleged mob boss and skewed the results of the mental tests administered by the defense medical experts.

None of this, of course, has anything to do with the actual charges in the racketeering case—crimes of murder, murder conspiracy, bribery and extortion that have gotten lost in discussions of "positron emission tomography tests" and "dementia syndrome."

Gigante was first indicted in 1990 in a bribery and conspiracy case involving bid rigging and construction contracts in New York City. Several other defendants were tried and convicted, but Gigante was severed from the case because of his mental and medical problems. Three years later the indictment was expanded to include a series of murders and murder conspiracies, including a plot to kill rival mob boss John Gotti. All of those were linked to the government's contention that Gigante was a powerful and shadowy figure who ran the Genovese organization, arguably the largest and most feared mob family in America.

"It's an enormously disciplined family and always has been," said Dick Ross, a retired FBI agent who investigated mobsters for nearly 30 years. "Gigante looks and talks like a thug, but he's a very bright guy."

He is also the only major mob leader in the city—and one of the few in the country—to escape the onslaught of investigation, prosecution and conviction that in the last 10 years has rocked the American Mafia to its foundations.

"The guy acts like a fruitcake 23 hours a day," says one law enforcement investigator who has tracked Gigante for years, "but he finds one hour someplace each day to run the biggest Mafia family in the United States.

"Is he crazy? He's the only one not in jail. Maybe he's a genius."

A legendary underworld figure, Vincent "The Chin" Gigante first attracted attention when he was fingered as the shooter in an attempted rubout of New York mob leader Frank Costello in 1957. (He was acquitted after a witness, a hotel doorman, changed his testimony.)

Authorities say he was a major player under Philip "Cockeyed Phil" Lombardo, Frank "Funzi" Tieri and Anthony "Fat Tony" Salerno, all former Genovese crime family bosses. Gigante, in fact, may have outranked Tieri and Salerno, even though they were assumed to be family bosses.

"They always tried to hide who really was in charge, who had the real spheres of power," said Ross.

Gigante was identified as the boss of the family after Salerno was sentenced to life in prison in New York's famous "Mafia Commission" trial in 1986.

Gigante is said to have little direct contact with members of his organization, issuing orders through a few confidants. Investigators say associates have been ordered not to refer to him by name. Many have taken to simply rubbing their hand or fingers over their chin as a way to signal who they are talking about, according to investigators.

Gigante's behavior has been well documented over the years. On one occasion, detectives who went to his home to serve a subpoena found Gigante standing fully clothed in a running shower. It was about that time, in the mid- to late 1980s, that he was often seen walking around Sullivan Street, near his mob clubhouse, in a bathrobe and slippers.

"He puts on a show if someone is watching," said Ross.

But while he bumbled and mumbled his way around Greenwich Village, law enforcement sources say, the Genovese family remained one of the best organized and most disciplined crime groups in America. All that is of particular interest to local investigators, given the current state of the Philadelphia mob.

Things began to deteriorate in Philadelphia with the March 21, 1980, assassination of mob boss Angelo Bruno. Most law enforcement authorities now believe that it was Bruno's consigliere, Antonio "Tony Bananas" Caponigro, who was behind that hit. According to law enforcement and underworld sources, Funzi Tieri and other leaders of the Genovese family led Caponigro to believe that a move against Bruno would not cause problems with the Mafia Commission, the since-fragmented underworld high court controlled by the five New York crime families.

After Bruno's death, Caponigro went to a meeting in New York expecting to be anointed the new boss of Philadelphia, according to the sources. Instead, he and his top associate and brother-in-law, Freddy Salerno, were brutally killed. Within months, two other Philadelphia mob figures suspected in the Bruno killing, Frank Sindone and John Simone, also turned up dead.

Gigante, say federal authorities, was behind those killings. They are four of the crimes listed in the racketeering case pending against him, together with the murders of two other Philadelphia mobsters, Frank Narducci Sr. and Rocco Marinucci, and a charge that Gigante plotted to kill the flamboyant John Gotti, the reputed Gambino crime family boss. That intrigue and history provide a backdrop for recent developments in the Philadelphia underworld.

Federal and local law enforcement authorities say that the Genovese family has backed reputed boss Ralph Natale and his alleged underboss, Joseph "Skinny Joey" Merlino, for the last three years as they move to reorganize the fragmented Philadelphia crime family. Most of their major moves, investigators say, have been cleared or approved by Gigante, a man who, the pending indictment indicates, helped create the turmoil that has raged in the Philadelphia underworld for 17 years.

The Underboss

SEPTEMBER 22, 1997

The question, Frank Martines says, is simply this: If he is serving four life terms for ordering a series of murders during Philadelphia's bloody 1993 mob war, then shouldn't the hit men who pulled the triggers also get life?

"What kind of system do we have?" Martines asks. "Where's the justice when you can kill somebody and then, because you talk, they put you back on the street?"

The question, posed by Martines during a lengthy interview last week in the visiting room of the federal penitentiary in Florence, Colorado, hangs over a series of court proceedings that begin today in U.S. District Court in Philadelphia.

Over the next 10 days, a federal judge will sentence six mobsters who cooperated with the government in the 1994 racketeering case that brought down Martines, mob boss John Stanfa and more than a dozen other Stanfa associates. The cooperators include admitted hit men John Veasey, Philip Colletti and Rosario Bellocchi.

All three have pleaded guilty to racketeering-murder charges and face potential life sentences as a result. All three, however, are expected to receive substantial reductions in those sentences because of their cooperation. As part of their plea bargains, federal prosecutors have filed the necessary motions to permit Judge Ronald Buckwalter to deviate from the sentencing guidelines. What that will mean in terms of prison time, however, is uncertain.

Robert Courtney 3rd, one of the prosecutors in the Stanfa case and chief of the organized crime unit in the U.S. Attorney's Office, said last week that he could not comment on any sentence until it was imposed. But in general, he said, the ability to prosecute conspiracies involving organized crime, drug trafficking and terrorism "often depends on the cooperation of insiders." And it is the policy of the Justice Department, he added, to recognize that obtaining that cooperation "is in the public interest."

It is a familiar story in organized crime cases here and across the country—cases that have ended with the convictions of scores of top Mafia figures. In every case, admitted mobsters have cooperated with authorities, pleaded guilty to a series of heinous criminal acts, testified, and in return, received the equivalent of a "get out of jail free" card.

Anyone who travels in law enforcement or underworld circles can tick off the names of a dozen or more informants who are now living with new identities in other parts of the country while their former partners in crime sit in prison cells. In Philadelphia those who walked would include Nicholas Caramandi, Thomas DelGiorno and Philip Leonetti, the former mob underboss who admitted to his involvement in 10 gangland slayings, but who served a little more than five years in prison after he agreed to cooperate.

Then, of course, there is Salvatore "Sammy the Bull" Gravano, the government poster boy for mob informants. Gravano was the star witness in the 1992 prosecution of his former mob boss and close friend John Gotti. As a result, he received a five-year sentence for a racketeering charge that included 19 murders.

Forget about kiss-and-tell, says Martines, this is shoot-and-tell. It is, he and others argue, a government-approved plan to get away with murder.

He is quietly philosophical and surprisingly upbeat for a man serving four life sentences without parole. Tan and bearded, with his hair neatly combed, Martines, 42, shows up for an interview in the visitors room of the maximum-security prison wearing the standard prison-issue khaki pants and shirt, white socks and sandals.

He has been at the penitentiary in Florence—known as the Alcatraz of the Rockies—for 14 months. He is in the high-security unit, one of four facilities that make up the modern, high-tech prison complex nestled in the rolling foothills of the Rocky Mountains about 40 miles southwest of Colorado Springs. The facility, which opened in 1994, houses about 1,000 inmates. More than 250 are in the high-security wing. About 30 percent are serving from 20 years to life, according to statistics provided by prison officials.

"It's clean, the food is decent and the weather is good," says Martines, who always enjoyed the outdoors and who has a picture-postcard view of a glorious mountain range from the heavily fenced-in and barbed-wired prison facility.

Then he tells a story about a time, several years ago, before Stanfa and the shootings and the investigations, when he and his wife took a vacation in Colorado. Martines said he fell in love with the country, wanted to buy some land and relocate. He smiles at the thought of it.

"When I got sent out here to this prison, I had to laugh," he says. "I called my wife and told her, 'I finally made it to Colorado.' Of course, this isn't what I had in mind."

What Martines had in mind during the rise and fall of the John Stanfa crime family is one of the fundamental issues in his case. Federal authorities charged, and a jury later found, that he served as the acting underboss of the Stanfa organization, that he organized hit teams during an underworld power struggle with reputed Stanfa rival Joseph "Skinny Joey" Merlino, that he planned extortion attempts and, perhaps most damaging of all, that he personally attempted to murder Veasey after Veasey began cooperating with the FBI.

Because of a pending appeal, Martines said there were several issues he could not or would not talk about. But he scoffed at the notion that he was any kind of powerful mob figure, pointing out that the government's own evidence in the case indicated he was not privy to high-level mob meetings where Stanfa and others discussed key issues in the conspiracy.

"I'm innocent of a lot of the charges, most of the charges," he says. "Did I ever tell anybody to kill anybody? No. Did I ever tell anybody to beat anybody up? No. . . . So what did I do? Extortion? All right. That's 84 months [maximum sentence]. I got four life sentences."

Martines, a onetime amateur boxer and a skilled carpenter, says he copes with that fact by focusing on his appeal and by never wavering from the belief that some day he will walk out of prison. It is a tiny pinhole light at the end of a long, dark tunnel, but Martines says it is there. He has studied the case, reviewed most of the testimony, gone over all of the evidence. He brings a file folder full of documents, transcripts and newspaper articles with him to the interview room.

"I do a lot of reading," he says. "Novels. Clancy [Tom Clancy, the author of several popular thrillers]. The Constitution."

It is all part of a regimen Martines has adopted to get through each day. Accept the present for what it is, he says, and plan for a better tomorrow. He starts most days with an exercise routine, alternately running, lifting weights or doing pull-ups and sit-ups. He works in the prison commissary from noon through dinner. Then he's back in his cell reading, studying, looking for anything that will give him or his lawyer an edge in a legal battle for his life. The trial, he says, was a nightmare of misinformation and disorganization.

"It was like standing in a tidal wave with an umbrella and trying not to get wet," he said of the testimony and tapes that washed over the federal courtroom and the lack of any clear-cut defense strategy. He blasts the government witnesses as self-serving and rolls his eyes over how the jury "fell in love with the rats" despite their lengthy criminal records, checkered pasts and motives to lie. Colletti had a prior murder conviction. Veasey, despite being just 30 years old, had spent years in jail for a series of violent crimes and a history of drug abuse.

Among other things, Martines contends that the jury was prejudiced during the trial by the gangland murder of Veasey's brother, Billy, who was gunned down on a South Philadelphia street corner the day John Veasey was to take the stand. He also says that Veasey lied repeatedly from the witness stand, particularly in his description of the night he was shot. Martines said Veasey was the aggressor that night.

"I was just defending myself," he said.

Jurors, however, noting that Veasey had two bullet wounds in the back of his head, accepted Veasey's version of the events and found both Martines and Vincent Pagano guilty of the assault and attempted murder, one of more than 30 predicate criminal acts for which Martines was found culpable.

46

Martines' file is also full of newspaper articles and government reports assessing and criticizing the witness-protection program and the mandatory sentencing guidelines that now apply to all federal cases. He spreads out a series of articles, each one marked with yellow highlighting pen. He argues, pointing to the stories and reports to support himself, that prosecutors have taken over the federal sentencing system, that mandatory sentences have tied the hands of most judges, that the only way to win a sentence reduction is to bargain with the prosecution, to cut a deal, to cooperate.

"Prosecutors have all the power," he says. "They're supposed to be interested in justice, but they're really interested in winning their cases. How is that right? How is it right that I have no prior convictions and the judge has to sentence me to life without parole? Where's the rehabilitation for a guy like me? But if I kill somebody and I agree to be a rat, then the prosecutor can get me a sentence reduction?

"What kind of system is that?"

Minutes later, the interview ended. Frank Martines packed up his papers and was escorted back to his cell in one of the country's toughest maximum-security prisons.

Gotti on Trial

MARCH 8, 1992

He shot his way to the top of the mob and then used fear and intimidation to solidify his hold on power. He carried himself like a movie star, a celebrity gangster who loved the attention and the spotlight. He wore expensive clothes. Rode in a big, flashy car. And surrounded himself with a cadre of Mafia sycophants, hit men who were also yes men.

Several years ago that was the profile of Nicodemo "Little Nicky" Scarfo, the organized crime kingpin of Philadelphia. Last week, based on testimony and evidence in federal court in Brooklyn, it was the picture of John Gotti.

Gotti has been called many things: the Dapper Don because of his liking for fine clothes, the Teflon Don because criminal charges never stuck. But a month into his racketeering trial, Gotti also can be called the Nicky Scarfo of New York. He is a Mafia brother-in-blood with Philadelphia's imprisoned mob chief. And like Scarfo, who will likely spend the rest of his life in jail, Gotti is being done in by one of his own.

"Both were violent," said Frederick Martens, executive director of the Pennsylvania Crime Commission. "Both were greedy. And both created paranoia within their families . . . that led to defections."

All last week a federal courtroom in Brooklyn was center stage for Salvatore "Sammy the Bull" Gravano, once Gotti's closest friend in the mob and now the government's prime witness in a trial that could end Gotti's reign as boss of the largest and most powerful Mafia family in America. Gravano has admitted to 19 Mafia killings over the last 22 years. Ten, he said, were carried out with or on the orders of Gotti.

"He gave me permission to take him out," Gravano said of one killing.

"John told me to go along and get it done," he said of another.

"I asked permission to kill him," he said of a third.

Gravano's chilling testimony hung like a death knell in the high-ceilinged courtroom where Gotti and fellow mobster Frank LoCascio are on trial. In short, clipped phrases and with simple, direct statements, Gravano painted a picture of an organized crime family bathed in blood and motivated by greed.

Five years ago in a series of Philadelphia trials, mobsters Thomas DelGiorno and Nicholas Caramandi offered the same type of testimony. Together the two mob turncoats buried Nicky Scarfo and the Philadelphia mob, the man and the organization they had once sworn to kill for. Authorities hope Gravano will do the same to Gotti and the Gambino organization.

The parallels between the federal racketeering trial that brought down Scarfo and the Brooklyn trial that could finish Gotti are striking. In both cases, the overall charge is racketeering, and the crimes involved include murders, attempted murders and extortions. In both cases, the principal defendant is charged with being the head of an organized crime family. And in both cases, the evidence and testimony offer a window into a secret society in which killing is a tool of the trade.

Both Gravano and the Philadelphia mobsters used the same phrase to describe killing. It was "a piece of work." Only after someone had "done some work" could he be considered for membership in the organization. Gravano, in cavalier fashion, explained the rationale behind that bloody rite of passage. It was a test of loyalty, he said. And also a barometer of a person's character.

"You want to see a guy's reaction," he said, "whether he's scared to death, whether he's cool and confident and relaxed."

Gravano obviously passed the test. The first time he killed, he said, was as a mob associate in 1970. Between 1977, when he became a full-fledged member of the mob, and 1982 there were seven other killings. And in the last 10 years, there have been 11 more. One of his victims, he said nonchalantly, was his brother-in-law. Another was a close friend. In each case, he said, it was not personal, it was business.

Gravano showed little remorse over any of the killings. And when defense attorneys opened their cross-examination on Thursday, they hammered away at his obvious character flaws, depicting him as a coldblooded killer and implying, as defense attorneys had about a witness in Scarfo's trial, that he had cut a deal to save his own neck.

"It's in my best interest to tell the truth," said Gravano, who faces a maximum 20-year prison sentence after pleading guilty to a broad federal racketeering charge. Gotti, on the other hand, faces the prospect of spending the rest of his life in jail.

Nicodemo Scarfo was sentenced to 55 years after being convicted on federal racketeering charges. Coupled with two other sentences of 14 years and life, it is very likely that Scarfo, who turns 63 today, will spend the rest of his days behind bars.

A lengthy sentence for Gotti, 51, could also mean life in jail, a possibility that the New York mob boss has already considered. That became clear from a secretly recorded conversation played early in the trial. Apart from Gravano's testimony, the most devastating evidence put before the jury thus far has been a series of those conversations picked up by FBI electronic listening devices planted in Gotti's mob clubhouse in Lower Manhattan. In them Gotti talked about "whacking" a business associate who had crossed him, about severing the head of another mobster who was horning in on the family's gambling territory and about ensuring the continuation of his "Cosa Nostra." But one conversation proved especially ironic last week after Gravano took the stand.

"Don't I know they ain't gonna rest until they put me in jail?" Gotti asked an associate during a discussion about various investigators who were hounding him. "So I fight it tooth and nail to the end."

But if he did end up "in the can," Gotti said, he had designated a successor to look out for the interests of his crime family.

"I love him," Gotti said of the mobster he wanted to replace him. "I'm gonna go to jail and leave him in charge."

That man was Salvatore "Sammy the Bull" Gravano.

Mafia Prince

Salvatore Testa was a ruggedly handsome, six-foot-one, 210-pound Mafia prince. Street-smart and charismatic, he had learned the ways of La Cosa Nostra from his father, the late Philip "Chicken Man" Testa, a dour and ruthless Mafioso who amassed a small fortune through loan-sharking, gambling and drug-dealing.

By 1982, one year after Phil Testa was literally blown away in a bomb blast that rocked the South Philadelphia night, the young Testa, then only 26, had become the youngest mob capo in America. And in the turbulent two years that followed, he came into his own as the point man and field general in the bloody underworld battle that established the reign of Nicodemo "Little Nicky" Scarfo.

Scarfo was locked away in a federal correctional center in La Tuna, Texas, from August 1982 until January 1984. During that period, Salvie Testa spearheaded the Scarfo organization's battle with a rival mob faction headed by Harry Riccobene. For months at a time, hit men from the two groups would stalk each other on the streets of South Philadelphia, looking for any opportunity to fulfill the open contracts that their bosses had placed on a dozen different individuals.

Testa nearly lost an arm when a shotgun blast fired by a Riccobene loyalist blew him off a stool in front of a pizzeria in the Italian Market. But the fearless young mob captain would not be cowed. Soon after recovering from the shooting, he was back on the streets leading the charge in the mob war that ended with Scarfo atop the organization.

"Salvie was all for 'This Thing.' Knew it inside out," said Nicholas "Nicky Crow" Caramandi, who fought alongside Testa during the Riccobene war and who later became a government informant and brought down the Scarfo organization. "Knew it better than guys who were 60 years old and who'd been in it for 40 years. Because of his father. He'd been a good teacher. Salvie had nerve and he didn't care who he killed. Sometimes we used to go [on a contract] and we'd come back and tell him, 'Well, the kids were in the car, the family's in the car.'

"'I don't care who's in the car,' he'd say. 'Everybody goes.' That's the kind of guy he was.

"One Thanksgiving Day, he wanted us to go in Sonny Riccobene's house, where Robert Riccobene was havin' dinner with his family. 'Shoot everybody in the house.' But me and Charlie [Iannece] and Faffy [Frank Iannarella Jr.] made up some story that he didn't show up. Just to appease Salvie. 'Cause we didn't go for killing kids. It was something we drew a line with, but he was just so full of venom that he didn't care.

51

"He was a guy made for 'This Thing.' He loved it. He lived it. And he was very bitter about what happened to his father, about the way his father got killed, blown up with nails in him."

Testa personally killed the two men responsible for his father's death, Frank "Chickie" Narducci and Rocco Marinucci. Both were dispatched with bullets to the head and their bodies left on the streets of South Philadelphia. Testa made no attempt to hide his satisfaction in those bloody acts of vengeance. "Salvie used to say to me, I wish that mother was alive so I could kill him again, meaning Chickie Narducci," said Caramandi. "This is how much he hated this man. He had no mercy on anybody. Business was business, and killing to him was business. He was a very hard-core kid for his age."

Salvatore Testa moved up the organizational ladder quickly after the Narducci killing. He "inherited" most of his father's business, including a loan-sharking operation in South Philadelphia. He also developed a very lucrative financial arrangement with several local drug dealers, including a black organization that supplied parts of North and West Philadelphia.

The Philadelphia branch of La Cosa Nostra, like most of the New York families, paid lip service to the ban on members dealing in drugs. Along with kidnapping and counterfeiting, drug dealing was supposed to be off-limits to the Mafia's men of honor. Testa, like many of his cohorts, found a way around the prohibition. Caramandi explained the somewhat distorted logic: "You couldn't deal drugs, but you could shake down drug dealers or you could loan them money. You could do anything you wanted with them. Steal from them, rob them, make them pay a street tax. They tried to say he was dealing drugs, which he wasn't. But he was financing some drug dealers, and he was making a lot of money with them."

Testa had a house at the shore near Atlantic City. He kept a boat in a nearby marina. He made more than $1 million selling a piece of Atlantic City real estate to casino developer Donald Trump. His legitimate and illegitimate businesses had made him a millionaire. In April 1984, a front-page article in the *Wall Street Journal* described him as the most feared Mafia figure in Philadelphia and cited a law enforcement report that called him the "fastest rising star" in the Scarfo organization.

Testa loved the attention and the prestige, the stalkings and the killings. But after risking his life to solidify Scarfo's hold on the underworld, he badly miscalculated his status within the organization. He thought he had proved himself. He figured that his loyalty was beyond question. That certainly would have been the case in the days of Angelo Bruno, the courtly and low-keyed former Mafia boss, whose March 1980 murder triggered years of internecine bloodshed. But Scarfo played by a different set of rules. The very attributes that made Salvie Testa such an asset during the Riccobene war—his leadership and his fearlessness—turned him into a threat after the war was over.

In January 1984, when Scarfo came out of prison, he and Testa were, respectively, the king and the prince of the Philadelphia underworld. But in less than a month, Scarfo would turn on his young capo. And in less than a year, Salvatore Testa would be dead.

Just before Scarfo's release from prison, Salvie Testa broke off his engagement with Maria Merlino, the pretty young daughter of underboss Chuckie Merlino. Caramandi was not surprised. He and his wife had been out socially with the young couple, and only a few months earlier, in a posh South Street restaurant, they had witnessed a bitter argument between the young mobster and his fiancée.

"Salvie really didn't love Chuckie's daughter. But being the underboss' son for 25 years, he was used to being close to the top. So one day he goes to Chuckie Merlino, who now was the underboss, and says, 'I would like to go out with your daughter, take your daughter out.' Before long, they were engaged, but they wanted to wait for Scarfo to come out of jail before they married.

"By that time Salvie was in love with another girl, and he didn't want to marry Maria. And he thought when Nicky came out of jail, Nicky would take the brunt of his not marrying Chuckie's daughter because of what a good job Salvie had done during the Riccobene war. But he didn't know Chuckie the way I knew Chuckie.

"Me and Charlie White [Iannece] knew Chuckie all our lives. He's a very bitter guy and he took the broken engagement as a personal insult. I'll never forget the night when Salvie and Joe Pung [Pungitore] came into this club that we used to hang in across from the clubhouse on Camac and Moore Street. I'm sitting at the bar and Joe Pung tells me, 'Salvie just told Chuckie that he isn't going to marry his daughter.' From that moment on I knew he was a dead man.

"In the next few months, they built up things against him, saying he was going to start his own gang, he was fooling around with drugs. Chuckie got allies to convince Nicky that this fella had treason in his mind, that he was starting his own gang. But all these things weren't true. He was dedicated to Scarfo. He worked 24 hours a day.

"That's the way it is. See, we believe the organization comes before your family, before your kids, before life itself. The badge is first, this thing of ours, La Cosa Nostra, comes first, before anything. And when it comes to problems like the Riccobene war, where somebody wants to hurt our mob, it's all out. And that's the way it was for Salvie."

But as schooled and savvy as he was about the ways of La Cosa Nostra, Testa blew it when he figured Scarfo would back him in a dispute with Chuckie Merlino over the canceled wedding plans. Whether Scarfo sided with Merlino because he truly shared his sense of injured honor remains an open question in the Philadelphia underworld. There are those who believe that Scarfo, like some tribal chief, feared a Testa-Merlino alliance and was only too happy to hear that the marriage plans were off. And, seeing the young Testa as his eventual rival, Scarfo had no problem being convinced by Merlino of the need to avenge his daughter's embarrassment.

"Nicky didn't take the brunt. What happened was that Chuckie started recruitin' Faffy and Tommy [DelGiorno] to help him tell Nicky about Testa's wrongdoings. He's doing this. He's doing that. They were creating stories. This is the viciousness within. Now, there's something in it for Faffy and Tommy. Get rid of Testa, and they would become capos. So they start telling Nicky stories. 'Salvie's dealing with black people. Salvie's dealing drugs. Salvie's trying to get a gang together.' They had to come up with something to show Nicky that Testa should be dead.

"I had many conversations with Chuckie. He used to come over my house to drink wine. He'd say, 'You know I'm not mad because he didn't marry my daughter. If he would just take himself down and start all over again, he would be forgiven. You know, This Thing comes first. If he didn't wanna marry my daughter . . . he coulda did it a different way.'

"You see, the wedding was all planned. Salvie canceled out two months before it was supposed to go. They had bought gowns and they had the church. They even bought special tablecloths. There were going to be over 700 guests."

So, despite Chuckie Merlino's protestations, despite his argument that all Salvie Testa would have to do was "take himself down"—relinquish his title as capo and become a mob soldier again—Caramandi knew Philadelphia's mob prince was about to be permanently and fatally dethroned. "We knew it was only a matter of time for Salvie," he said.

The first sign came during a benefit dinner for a local charity at Palumbo's restaurant in South Philadelphia in the spring of 1984, around the same time the *Journal* was heralding Testa's rise. Nicky Scarfo took a table for himself and his top associates at the affair. Salvatore Testa was told to sit somewhere else. Then, about a month later, Scarfo and his entourage took a trip to Puerto Rico. Salvie wasn't invited. By then, Caramandi said, Testa had realized something was amiss. "He sorta got vibes," said The Crow. The order for the hit came down about that time. Caramandi and Charlie White got the ticket.

"I'm in a corner at the club that we hang at, Camac and Moore," Caramandi recalled. "Tommy comes around and says, 'You don't know what happened last night. We had dinner with Nicky. Chuckie, Philip [Leonetti], Lawrence [Merlino, Chuckie's brother], me and Faffy. Faffy buried Salvie Testa. He's gotta be killed.'

"Me and Charlie looked at one another and we knew. It was no surprise to us."

Later that day or the next, Chuckie Merlino came around to see The Crow and Charlie White. Merlino was standing in the middle of the 1800 block of Camac Street. Caramandi, Iannece, DelGiorno and Iannarella walked up and gathered around him. There they were, the mob underboss of Philadelphia and four of his top soldiers, standing in a huddle in the middle of the street in the middle of the afternoon. They met like that because, in the wake of the Riccobene violence, they feared police surveillance and hidden listening devices. They knew that even their own clubhouses could be bugged, so when important business had to be discussed, they took a walk down the block or around the corner. They figured that, while they still could be seen, they wouldn't be overheard.

"Chuckie's standing by himself and we get in a circle. He says, 'Salvie's gotta be killed,' and puts his fingers toward the ground with the sign"—his right hand with his forefinger and thumb in the shape of a gun. "'Salvie's gotta go. Nicky wants him dead. Too much treason. He's gettin' too big for his britches. He's fooling with drugs.' Then he turned to me and Charlie and says, 'You guys got any ideas?'"

At that meeting it was decided that Testa's code name would be "Brownie," that Caramandi and Charlie White would be responsible for carrying out the hit and that DelGiorno and Iannarella would supervise. "Chuckie told us, 'Try to come up with a good plan. Be careful and let's get this guy as soon as we can.'"

The meeting took place in early spring 1984, but summer would be nearly over before Salvatore Testa was dead. Part of the problem was Testa. He was a difficult target, always on the alert. And those stalking him knew that he'd be willing to shoot back. Another cause for the delay was Scarfo. The bloodthirsty little mob boss preferred to see his contracts carried out in public. "Nicky liked cowboy style. See, he didn't like walk-ins, where you take a guy in your house. He liked broad daylight, restaurants or busy street corners, anything cowboy style. He liked a lotta noise to scare people. He figured that way there would never be any witnesses because nobody would ever come forward and testify against us. And after, he liked to see a lot of publicity of the murder. Headlines and television.

"Salvie knew this. He always said Nicky liked Wild West. The more noise the better. So Salvie was very cautious. . . . He just felt bad vibes. Every time you shook his hand, he'd bring ya in close with his right hand and just pat ya down with his left hand from behind just to see if you were carrying a gun. Now, with the warm weather coming, it was pretty hard to carry a gun. We'd just have to stash it somewhere and bushwhack him, sneak it on him.

"And it's a little tough for us because we couldn't station ourselves in front of Salvie's house and wait for him to come out—he's gonna know we're the guys that's gonna do the shooting. It was going to have to be a spot he wouldn't expect, because he was very, very alert by this time. He's doing his regular business, but he knows there's something wrong. He suspects he's gonna be killed. He just can't figure out who's going to do it to him.

"And, as he looks the field over, the guys around him, he sees Joe Pungitore, his best friend, and Gino Milano. But these fellas weren't told about it. The only people that knew were Nicky, Chuckie, Philip, Lawrence, Charlie White, Faffy, Tommy and me."

At that point, Caramandi said, the only way Salvatore Testa could have saved his own life was to disappear. But that, apparently, wasn't in the kid's makeup. "He coulda just taken . . . off," Caramandi said. "Me and Charlie used to talk about that. We don't know why this . . . guy don't take off. We woulda loved to have told him, but we couldn't tell him. You know what I mean?

"He was the type of guy who, if he knew for sure, woulda went after Chuckie or Nicky and tried to kill them. This kid woulda went down in a blaze of glory. But he wasn't sure. He was aware. He was alert. But he wasn't sure."

For the next five months, Caramandi, Charlie White and eventually several other members of the Scarfo organization stalked Salvatore Testa, looking for the right time and the right place to ambush the mob prince.

Caramandi considered the Pier 30 Tennis Club on the Delaware River waterfront, where Testa played on a regular basis. But he rejected that spot as too risky. Heavy traffic in the area would make a getaway difficult. And because of the way the tennis courts were laid out, Testa would be able to spot someone before they could get off a good shot.

He looked at Testa's girlfriend's apartment and the neighborhood around it, at a vacant store at 9th and Christian in South Philadelphia where Testa was building a new clubhouse, and at a hair salon owned by Testa and frequented by many mobsters.

"Nicky, Philip and Lawrence used to come up from Atlantic City every 10 days or so to get their hair cut and get a manicure," Caramandi said. "Tommy thought about luring Salvie there. Me and Charlie had guns and a car ready. We were supposed to walk in and blast him. But they couldn't get him there."

The first serious opportunity presented itself that summer when Faffy Iannarella's wife, who was pregnant, was going to be feted at a baby shower. "Faffy's wife was going to have a baby, and so they were going to give her a big shower, in the Italian custom. People come and bring gifts. It's, like, a party. So Faffy runs into Salvie on the street, and Salvie says, 'Are you gonna be home tonight? I wanna bring ya a gift.' Faffy says, 'Yeah.'

"So now we see a golden opportunity. Me, Tommy, Faffy and Charlie get together. But now Chuckie intercedes and he says he wants Tory [Salvatore Scafidi] to do the shooting, to be at this house. Because if me or Charlie were there when Salvie pulls up, he might not want to come in. But being that Tory Scafidi hangs with Faffy, it would look normal because Faffy had bought a house and he was remodeling it.

"Anyway, Tommy says, 'Look, I got two .22 pistols with silencers. You got a place where we could practice?' I says, 'Yeah, my house, in the cellar.'

So he says, 'OK, I'll be there at six o'clock with Tory. We'll practice because sometimes the guns jam. You gotta watch the way you pull the triggers.'

"At six p.m. Tommy and Tory come to my house and we practiced. We were using homemade silencers, but they worked pretty good. After we shot a while, we decided the guns were OK. So right then and there we told Tory what to do. We knew Faffy was waiting. We said to go over to the house and stash the guns.

"Put one upstairs and one downstairs, but make sure they're accessible. We told Tory and Faffy to hang outside the house and pretend like they're working. Once Salvie gets out of his car and onto the porch, Faffy would say, 'Let me show you the house.' Then when they get him inside, Faffy would distract him and Tory would get the gun.

"So that night, Tory goes to Faffy's house and they're waiting outside. Me and Tommy go pick up Charlie because we got to take the body away if he does get him in the house. . . . We were waiting in the neighborhood, about two blocks from Faffy's house. We waited until it got dark. Salvie never showed up. We decided we'd do it the next night. We waited again, but Salvie never showed up. The following day, Salvie bumps into Faffy on the street and gives him the baby gift on the street. So that was the end of that plan."

After the opportunity offered by the baby shower didn't pan out, the shooters shifted their attention in the opposite direction. Joey Pungitore's aunt had died, and everyone, including Salvie Testa, was expected at the wake, which was scheduled for the Cato Funeral Home on Broad Street in the heart of South Philadelphia.

"Joe Pungitore was Salvie Testa's best friend out of all the fellas. He's also a made guy and was one of Salvie's top guys. So there's no way Salvie's not going to come to the funeral parlor. But Salvie knows about funeral parlors because we were gonna shoot Sonny Riccobene in one.

"Anyway, two days before the wake, we made our plans. Me, Tommy, Charlie and Tory and Faffy. Chuckie wanted Tory to do the shooting and for me and Charlie to be blockers inside the funeral parlor just in case anybody tried to interfere with Tory's escape. We'd push into them and help him get away clean. He would just drop the gun in the funeral parlor and walk out.

"So the day of the wake comes. Eleven o'clock that morning we receive a phone call to go to Chuckie's house, me and Charlie. Tommy and Faffy are there, too. Chuckie says, 'Tory got arrested this morning. He won't get out of jail until late tonight.' He says, 'Nicky's gonna be mad. I don't know what we're gonna do.'

"So we're just listening. And he's waiting for Nicky to come up from Atlantic City. Finally, Scarfo comes in with Phil Leonetti and Lawrence Merlino. We sit at the table. Chuckie starts to tell Nicky the story of how Tory got locked up after being drunk 5:30 in the morning and that he's still in jail and that they'll hold him till maybe late tonight.

"So Nicky said, 'Look, these . . . kids are irresponsible. The plan goes on as we said it would.' He looks at me and Charlie and says, 'You two guys ready?'

"We said yes. He said, 'OK, that's it.'

"That night Faffy picks me up. I got a .380 magnum. Charlie's got a .38. Tommy picks up Charlie at his house. Faffy picks me up at my house. About 25 after seven, Salvie's outside of the funeral parlor with a couple other members milling around while waiting for Nicky to come. Me and Charlie got our guns. We had jackets on. We're trying to stay away from Salvie because we know about the frisks and we want to be careful. So we're talking to other members and trying to stay away from him.

"About eight o'clock, Nicky pulls up with Lawrence Merlino, Chuckie Merlino and Phil Leonetti. We're standing on the top of the steps. He greets some people when he gets out of the car, shakes hands with people. He walks up to the top of the steps. He looks at me and Charlie and he says, 'Youse ready?' We said yes.

"We go inside the funeral parlor. We pay our respects to the dead. Now we're looking for a spot, and we're looking for some kind of signal. Charlie's on one side of the room. I'm on the other side of the room. We notice Salvie looking all around, constantly looking. And we're waitin' for some kind of signal from Tommy or Faffy to tell us, 'Go ahead.'

"A short time later, I was told to go upstairs. When I got upstairs, there's a lounge area in the front of the room and a bar. It's got 12, 13 stools. Salvie's sitting at the end of the bar, talking to somebody. I walk right next to him and I get in position right behind him. And Nicky and Chuckie and Philip are 10 feet away from me. I'm looking directly at them. They're against the wall. Chuckie's standing there and I motion to Chuckie with my head, up and down, like, let's do it right now. But he waves me off.

"So when he does that, I go to the lounge and sit down. We were all tense and I couldn't understand what happened. I was right behind him, ready to shoot him—he's talking to a guy at the bar. All I hadda do is go bing, right in the back of his head. Then about 10 minutes later, Tommy and Faffy come over, and they tell me there's too much law outside. Too many cops.

"I mean, here's Nicky, here's the boss, who wants you to do it right in front of him. It's unheard of. But these f-ing guys were so crazy that it even goes further. When we leave the funeral parlor, we all go downstairs outside and we're saying goodbye to everybody, members and nonmembers. I'm standing with Nicky, Chuckie, Philip, Tommy, Faffy and Charlie. Now, when Salvie says goodbye, he shakes hands with all of us. Chuckie Merlino shakes his hand, grabs his head and kisses him on the lips . . . for like 10 seconds. Tommy, Charlie, Faffy and me, we looked at one another. We said, 'What the f-. This guy's nuts. [Salvie's] gotta know now.' It was the kiss of death.

"We looked at the expression on Salvie. He was sorta stunned. He just couldn't figure out what . . . was going on. But this is how crazy they were. I mean, they wanted him to know."

If Testa suspected he had problems before the Pungitore wake, Merlino confirmed it with his kiss. Now it would be even more difficult for Caramandi, Iannece, DelGiorno and Iannarella to set up and carry out the hit. So, with Scarfo's approval, they decided to recruit Joey Pungitore, one of Salvie Testa's oldest and best friends.

"Joe Pung is completely unaware of the situation, which has been going on for months by this time. Now Tommy, Joe Pung and Salvie are in the numbers business and the sports business together. The plan is they're going to get Joe Pung to take him to Tommy's house, where I would be hiding behind the cellar door and would come out and ambush and shoot Salvie at the kitchen table. When we told Joe Pung about the plan, he said, 'I don't know if I could get him here, but I'll try. He's been acting funny.'

"You see, Joe Pung was all upset because this was his best friend and this was all new to him. But he had no choice—if he had said no, he would've been dead. This was an order, you know what I mean? Who's he gonna go beef to? And if he even said one f-ing word to Salvie, one iota, he woulda been dead. He knows that. He knows this game. So what was he gonna do?"

A few years later, in a debriefing session with New Jersey State Police, Tommy DelGiorno told how he recruited Pungitore on Scarfo's orders and how Pungitore had only one request. "He said he would set him up, but he didn't want to pull the trigger, do the shooting," DelGiorno told New Jersey investigators. "I told this to Scarfo and he laughed.

"'What the f-'s the difference?' he said."

The plan to lure Testa to DelGiorno's house failed, as did several other attempts that summer to set him up. Maybe it was dumb luck. Or maybe it was his guile, cunning and innate sixth sense about the ways of La Cosa Nostra. Whatever the reason, Testa outmaneuvered those plotting his death. He didn't show up for meetings. He skipped dinner appointments. He varied his routine. At one point, Caramandi had a pharmacist friend from Florida ship him knockout drops. There had been stories in the papers about hookers in Atlantic City robbing their johns after knocking them out. The hookers would conceal a drug in their mouths, then slip it into the mouth of their customers. The papers were calling them the kissing bandits. Caramandi and DelGiorno figured they'd drug Testa. The new plan was to lure him to DelGiorno's boardwalk condominium in Ocean City, New Jersey.

"Me, Charlie and Tory go down the shore to Tommy's. We put some of the liquid in a glass and some in a cup. Joe Pung is supposed to get Salvie there. When he gets Salvie there, Tommy's gonna offer him some coffee or soda. He had the glass ready and the cup ready.

"So we were waiting on the boardwalk at a pizzeria. Once this was done, we were supposed to take Salvie out, shoot him and leave him on a highway somewhere. See, the way Tommy's building was set up we coulda got him right out the door, pulled the car right up alongside the door. Practically nobody woulda seen us.

"We waited most of the day. Joe Pung showed up and said, 'I couldn't get him here.'"

The plotting and scheming had begun to take its toll. Pungitore, who was now at the center of the action, lost 30 pounds as one after another plan was set up and abandoned. Caramandi, Iannece, DelGiorno and Iannarella, who were supposedly in charge of the hit, were getting constant complaints from Merlino, Scarfo and Leonetti. "One time I'm down the shore and Leonetti tells me . . . 'I'm getting sick and tired of looking at him.'

"It was constant tension. . . . There were a lot of f-ing attempts on this guy," Caramandi said, as he ticked off several other plots, including one night when he and Charlie White waited at the bar in an Atlantic City casino where DelGiorno was supposed to bring Testa.

"We were in the casino, either the Playboy or the Sands. Me and Charlie were sitting there with our f-ing guns, looking to shoot him right there. Right in the f-ing casino. That's how desperate they were near the end. Tommy was supposed to bring him in. But he didn't show. This guy, he didn't trust no place."

And nobody. Except his best friend, Joey Pungitore.

On September 14, 1984, the crew that had been stalking Salvie Testa for months finally got it right.

"This was the plan. Joe Pung was gonna pick up Salvie at his house at 2117 Porter. And when he went there, he was gonna act very, very disturbed because he's gonna say that Wayne Grande messed up $10,000 of his money and he's very upset about it. And he wants to get it straightened out now and let's go see him now. And Grande would be at this sweet shop on Passyunk Avenue.

"So at 12 o'clock that day, Joe Pung goes by Salvie's and tells him what happened. Wayne Grande messed up his money and he wants it straightened out right away. Salvie falls for the whole story. 'Let's go get him,' he says. 'Let's go talk to him.'"

Testa and Pungitore arrived at the sweet shop shortly before one p.m. The store, which was about two blocks from the clubhouse at Camac and Moore, was being renovated. The owner, a friend of several of the young mob figures, planned to open in a few months. Wayne Grande and his brother Joe were there when Testa walked in. Salvie shook hands with each of them, patting them down in the way that had become his custom. Then he began walking toward a back room where he, Pungitore and Wayne Grande would meet to discuss the money problem. At that moment, Wayne Grande slipped behind Testa, reached under a pillow on the sofa in the front room, pulled out a pistol and pointed it toward Testa's head.

Outside on Passyunk Avenue, a crew from the streets department was breaking up a section of the sidewalk with jackhammers. No one heard the shot that ripped into the back of Salvie Testa's head. He dropped like a rock to the floor. Wayne Grande stood over the fallen mob prince and pumped another bullet into his brain. Testa's head jerked on impact, but the life had already left his body.

Wayne Grande and the others dragged the body behind the sofa, covered it with a sheet and took off, locking the door of the sweet shop behind them. Joe Grande headed back toward the clubhouse, where he met Caramandi. "It's done," he said. "It's over. He's dead."

"So now, me and Charlie call Chuckie Merlino. We say, 'Chuckie, we gotta see ya.' Boom, five minutes later Chuckie comes around, and we says, 'Salvie's dead.'

"He says, 'All right, you guys know what you gotta do. Get in touch with Tommy.' We call Tommy and tell him we're gonna go to Jersey and find a spot to dump the body that night."

"We drive to Jersey. We get off at Sicklerville Road in South Jersey. We find what's like a sand trap about four or five miles up the road. We said this spot was as good as any. This is where we'll bring him tonight."

On the way back, Caramandi and Charlie Iannece stopped at a Penneys department store, where Caramandi bought a king-size blanket to wrap the body. Iannece had already arranged to borrow a van from a friend. Tory Scafidi would be going with them when they dumped Testa's corpse.

"We drive the van right in front of the sweet shop and park," Caramandi recalled. "That night, I pick up Tory and Charlie and take them to the store. I ride around to make sure everything was OK and then wait for Charlie to give me the signal. [About] 20 minutes later, Charlie comes out. He waves to me. I pull up behind the truck and they come out and throw the body in the truck. We drive over the Ben Franklin Bridge and head to Sicklerville Road.

"I was to be used as the crash car in case they got stopped while driving there. In case a cop car stopped them, I was to smash into the cop car so that they could get away."

After dumping the body in New Jersey, Caramandi followed the van back to South Philadelphia, where it was parked in a prearranged spot. Iannece had arranged to have some associates clean out the inside of the vehicle the next day; a separate crew would clean up the sweet shop.

"Later, Charlie said to me, 'Nick, we never coulda lifted him up. It's a good thing Tory was with us. The body was stiff. We couldn't straighten the legs out. We tried to pull 'em. First of all, we couldn't find him. He was behind the couch and he was covered with blood. We couldn't get the blanket around him. We just had a big, big problem in there.'"

"The body was sitting from, like, 12 to nine. Rigor mortis musta set in . . . . And you know he's a big guy, he was like six-one, six-two, and he weighed 225 pounds. So he musta been just dead weight.

"After we made the drop, I drove everybody home. We were supposed to get changed and meet around the corner in half an hour. Then we drove down to La Cucina [a South Street restaurant that was a favorite of Scarfo's].

"Nicky's there with about 10 or 15 members: Joe Pung, Wayne Grande, Chuckie, Nicky, Philip, Lawrence, Gino Milano, Joe Grande. . . . We're all getting congratulated, congratulating one another. Nicky had ordered a buffet dinner for us, and he had some of his friends from Mexico there with him, and his girlfriend. It was like some great big party."

During the celebration at La Cucina, Scarfo walked up to Caramandi and offered his personal congratulations.

"I heard there was a lot of blood," he said.

"Yeah, it was pretty messy," said Caramandi.

Caramandi remembers one other thing about that night at the restaurant. Charlie White apparently didn't do a great job cleaning himself up after disposing of Salvie Testa's body. Tommy DelGiorno was the first to notice. "Tommy says to Charlie, 'You got blood on your neck.' So Charlie goes to the bathroom to wash it off."

Then they all headed back to the buffet table.

Who's the Pretty Boy?

DECEMBER 17, 1990

The first time New York mob boss John Gotti met Philip Leonetti, he asked, "Who's the pretty boy?" The next time they meet, Gotti may be sorry he found out.

Leonetti, the former underboss of the Philadelphia mob, is the highest-ranking Mafia figure in America to join the swelling ranks of gangsters who have turned into cooperating federal witnesses. As such, the handsome and meticulously dressed hit man is a potent weapon in the federal government's battle against organized crime.

Last week, the feds, who indicted Gotti on racketeering charges, pointed that weapon at New York's celebrity mobster, setting the stage for a courtroom encounter that could prove to be a classic. It will be Gotti, the flamboyant, outspoken "plumbing supply salesman" who federal authorities say gunned his way to the top of the Gambino organized crime family, versus Philip "Crazy Phil" Leonetti, the cold-blooded and ruthless Mafia killer who is just as deadly as a government witness.

"He's like ice up there," said one federal agent of Leonetti's appearances as a witness. "Nothing rattles him."

Leonetti, 37, began cooperating more than a year ago. But from the moment word leaked in June 1989 that he had flipped, speculation was that his value as a witness would ultimately be tested not in Philadelphia or Atlantic City, but in New York. The Scarfo crime family was already in shambles. Other mobster-witnesses, Thomas DelGiorno and Nicholas Caramandi, had helped federal agents bring down mob boss Nicodemo "Little Nicky" Scarfo and his entire organization.

Leonetti, who is Scarfo's nephew, had been caught in that web. Between 1987 and 1989, federal and local prosecutors won a series of stunning convictions in nearly a dozen organized-crime-related cases. More than 50 mob members and associates, including killers, drug dealers and corrupt union officials, ended up behind bars. Scarfo, considered by federal authorities the most ruthless Mafia boss in America, was convicted three times and, at 61, will probably spend the rest of his life behind bars.

So it was clear when Leonetti struck his deal with the FBI and the U.S. Attorney's Office that the information he would bring to the table would have to be broader in scope than what the feds had heard before. Only the delivery of that kind of information could win him a reduction in the 45-year federal prison sentence he is serving for his 1988 federal racketeering conviction.

Leonetti has already testified at three trials, all of which have ended in convictions. But those were merely tuneups. He is set to testify, sources say, in a civil racketeering case that the FBI and the U.S. Attorney's Office in New Jersey are preparing against Atlantic City Bartenders Union Local 54. While union officials adamantly deny they are involved with the mob, federal authorities have long held that the local is mob-dominated, and they say they will use Leonetti to prove it.

It will be an important case, with national implications. But even that pales in comparison to what Leonetti's value seems to be for prosecutors. The Gotti indictment may show just what they have.

Three times in the last five years, state and federal prosecutors have brought John Gotti to trial. Each time he has been acquitted. Each time he has walked out of the courtroom, smiling the smile of a New York celebrity as crowds cheered and cameras rolled and strobe lights flashed.

"HE'S A MURDERER"

Gotti's swagger and bravado—and his ability to beat the government in the courtroom—have become almost legendary in Manhattan. That, obviously, rankles investigators.

"He's a murderer. . . . He's not a folk hero," U.S. Attorney Andrew Maloney said last week after his office announced the details of the latest case. Maloney, along with the rest of the U.S. Justice Department, is counting on the "pretty boy" from Philly to help prove just that.

Leonetti is much more than just another mobster turned informant. He literally grew up in the Mafia.

"He sat at the right hand of the family boss. . . . And in addition to being the underboss, he was a family member. He was a confidant," said Special Agent Klaus Rohr, head of the FBI's Philadelphia Organized Crime Squad. Those familiar with Leonetti's testimony and debriefing sessions say that background will enable him to bring limited but important information about Gotti to the witness stand.

They say Scarfo introduced Leonetti to Gotti sometime in 1986, shortly after Scarfo promoted his nephew to underboss. It was at this meeting, says a former Scarfo associate, that Gotti made the pretty boy quip. At another meeting, insiders say, Gotti bragged to both Scarfo and Leonetti about ordering the December 1985 murder of Paul Castellano, then the boss of the Gambino organized-crime family. Scarfo mob members now cooperating with the government have said that it was common knowledge within their organization that Gotti took credit for the Castellano killing and that it was a blatant grab for power. It was, they say, the kind of move that Scarfo, who climbed to the top over 25 bodies of mobsters murdered between 1980 and 1985, admired.

VIEWED AS INVALUABLE

The Castellano murder is just one of dozens of "racketeering acts" cited in the 11-count indictment against Gotti and three codefendants. Gotti is also charged with heading the Gambino organized-crime family. That is where Leonetti will prove invaluable. He will be used to establish the existence of La Cosa Nostra, to describe its organizational structure and, in this case, to place Gotti at the head of the Gambino organization.

Leonetti's roots in the organization are deep. His mother, Nancy, was Scarfo's sister. He was raised in the same Atlantic City apartment house where Scarfo lived with his wife and three sons. In his late teens, Leonetti became an enforcer for his uncle. By his mid-20s, he was a Mafia murderer and had earned the nickname Crazy Phil. He has recounted all this and more to three juries. His delivery is cool, clear and to the point. His answers come in simple, declarative sentences. And he seldom embellishes.

During a trial earlier this year in federal court, Leonetti, after admitting his involvement in several murders, was asked by a defense attorney if he considered himself ruthless. His answer riveted the courtroom.

"I know what it is to be ruthless," he said softly. He paused, then added: "But I don't remember ever doing anything, as a matter of fact, I know for sure, I never did nothing ruthless besides, well, I would kill people, but that's our life. That's what we do."

Leonetti's testimony has included stories about his involvement in murders, beatings, extortions and union shakedowns. He has told juries about how he used brass knuckles and baseball bats to deliver "messages" to two different mob associates who had crossed the organization; about how he pulled the trigger in two murders and helped plan eight others. And he has told how, at a secret meeting in South Philadelphia in 1980, he was formally initiated into the mob.

A SWIFT ASCENT

By 1982, Leonetti has said, he was a mob capo, or captain. Four years later he was underboss. All the while, his legitimate front was his cement contracting company in Atlantic City, which gave him contacts and access to the casino industry and its labor unions. His real business was that of La Cosa Nostra.

That is what Leonetti brings to the table. He knows the how, the why and the where of the mob. He accompanied his uncle to meetings in Atlantic City, New York and other parts of the country with ranking members of other mob families. He has testified at length about meetings with Castellano and Salvatore "Sammy the Bull" Gravano, then a capo in the Gambino organization. He has told authorities about secret sessions to settle internal mob disputes, to arrange murder contracts and to discuss business opportunities in Atlantic City and elsewhere.

"He was privy to everything that [Scarfo] was considering," said Charles Rogovin, a Temple University Law School professor and former member of the President's Commission on Organized Crime. "He had access at the highest levels to decisions and discussions. He attended the meetings where things were discussed . . . at the highest possible policy level."

In the 11-count racketeering indictment handed up in Brooklyn last week, federal authorities charge that Gotti orchestrated the Castellano murder and three other mob killings; that he was the boss of the Gambino organization, and that, in addition to the murders, he was involved in loan sharking, gambling, obstruction of justice and income tax evasion. Three others—Frank Locascio, identified as the underboss of the Gambino family; Thomas Gambino, listed as a capo, and Gravano, identified as the family consigliere or counselor—were also charged.

"Once again," said a news release from Attorney General Dick Thornburgh's office, "federal law enforcement efforts have struck at the top leadership of the traditional organized crime families, those who seek profit from dealings in violence and misery." That depiction of the mob was an echo of something Leonetti said in federal court earlier this year when he was asked to describe La Cosa Nostra.

"Well," he said, "it's a secret criminal organization."

"What's the purpose of the organization?" asked the attorney.

"To make money," Leonetti replied.

"Make money how?"

"Any way we can."

Little Nicky's Big Mistake

Earlier this year, Bill Rouse shocked Philadelphia by announcing that he was abandoning his multimillion-dollar plan to develop Penn's Landing. Unfortunately, in the media swirl that followed, no one was able to ask mob boss Nicodemo "Little Nicky" Scarfo how he felt about it. And that's too bad. For if Rouse does nothing else in this city—which hardly seems likely given the number of official and corporate hats he wears—he and his now-abandoned Penn's Landing proposal will be forever linked with the Philadelphia mob.

Penn's Landing was Nicky Scarfo's Waterloo.

Back in 1986, Scarfo, blinded by greed and drunk with power, tried to shake down Rouse for $1 million. It was one of the boldest and most ill-conceived Mafia gambits in the history of Philadelphia. The leverage was a city ordinance Rouse needed passed in order to qualify for $10 million in federal funds for the Penn's Landing project. City Councilman Leland Beloff and his legislative aide Bobby Rego were the facilitators (to borrow a phrase from the government bureaucrats) of Scarfo's plan. Nick Caramandi, a mobster who would later become a major government informant, provided the muscle.

But then a very un-Philadelphia-like thing happened. Rouse was neither cowed nor cooperative. Instead, he went to the FBI. The extortion plot blew up in Scarfo's face. Indictments quickly followed. And that was the beginning of the end for the mob boss and most of his crime family.

Today, Scarfo and more than a dozen top associates sit in jail convicted of assorted murder, racketeering, conspiracy and extortion charges—while the Philadelphia branch of La Cosa Nostra collapses around them. Ten years ago, no one would have believed it possible. But that was back in the days when Angelo Bruno ran things and the local mob was viewed as virtually invincible.

Bruno, the former mob boss of Philadelphia, departed this world on March 21, 1980, when a man wearing a raincoat and carrying a shotgun blew a hole in the back of his head. Posthumously, he has become known as "The Gentle Don," a misnomer in almost all respects except one. The title fits when you compare him with Scarfo, arguably one of the most violent Mafia bosses in America.

Bruno ruled the Philadelphia mob for 21 years. He used an iron fist that he covered with a velvet glove. Scarfo saw no need for the glove. And that has made all the difference.

In many ways, Scarfo was a mob boss for the '80s, the underworld's reflection of the corporate raiders and hostile takeover artists who during this same period dominated Wall Street. Scarfo spoke the same language as these pinstriped outlaws: Greed is good, corruption is acceptable, arrogance is a virtue, get it all, get it now, take no prisoners—a philosophy that explains why the organization is now in ruins.

Angelo Bruno would never have concocted or condoned a plan to shake down Bill Rouse over the Penn's Landing deal. If he wanted a piece of the action, he would simply have called in some favors and, without anyone being the wiser, companies or people he controlled would have been in line to participate in the development. Bruno would have gotten his million dollars, but it would have been the old-fashioned way: slowly, over a period of years, through systematic graft and corruption.

So, you've got to believe that the wily old mob boss, whether he's looking up or down at the events that have transpired over the last nine years, is shaking his head in disgust over what Scarfo has done to the organization.

"The Bruno years were marked by quiet, autocratic rule," said a 1987 Pennsylvania Crime Commission report on organized crime. "Bruno, the 'docile don,' adhered to traditional principles which regarded respect and authority as character attributes. He acquired substantial loyalty during his . . . reign as boss of the family. . . . His leadership evolved into a benevolent dictatorship." In contrast, the same report labeled Scarfo "an ineffective and bumbling leader" who had "sown the seeds of his own demise" through his "exercise of naked, brutal power."

Think of Bruno and Scarfo as chief executive officers of a major corporation. The mob, after all, generates millions of dollars in revenue annually, has diversified interests, and employs, directly or indirectly, thousands of people. Look at what Bruno accomplished in 21 years as CEO. And compare that with Scarfo's eight-year tenure.

"Angelo Bruno ran a sophisticated criminal family and was able to conduct his illegal businesses with a minimum of disruption from law enforcement," said Frederick T. Martens, executive director of the Pennsylvania Crime Commission. "Scarfo has demonstrated few managerial skills other than the ability to kill people."

Bruno ran an old, established Philadelphia firm, a company that took few risks and was content to show a reasonable profit at the end of each year. He was not interested in hostile takeovers. He didn't believe in rapid expansion. You could use the fingers of one hand to tick off the documented mob murders that occurred during his years as Philadelphia's Mafia kingpin. Three, maybe four, say law enforcement officials. No bodies wrapped in trash bags and dumped on the sidewalk. No broad-daylight killings with blood running in the gutter.

Make no mistake about it, say investigators, Bruno was ruthless and vicious, when and if he had to be. But he preferred compromise and conciliation. He understood the use of power and also its limitations. He knew when to push and when to pull back. He was a Mafia diplomat. A man of honor.

"If Bruno saw you on the street, he would come up and shake your hand and say hello," says one federal investigator who has spent 20 years tracking the Philadelphia mob. "He was always very polite . . . very low-key." And so was his organization.

Bruno was a millionaire, according to most law enforcement sources, but you couldn't tell that from his lifestyle or his estate. He lived in a modest brick rowhouse on Snyder Avenue in South Philadelphia. He and his wife, Sue, were good neighbors, highly regarded and looked up to. Their children, Jeanne and Michael, grew up, married and set out on upper-middle-class lives of their own. No different, on the surface at least, from any of the other kids in the neighborhood. The sons and daughters of hard-working, first- and second-generation Italian Americans living the melting-pot dream.

Bruno worked as a salesman for a cigarette vending-machine company and reported earnings of about $50,000 a year. Sure, the company's business tripled in the Atlantic City area shortly after the casino-gambling referendum was passed in 1976. And, yes, the company did take over a $500,000 account that had been controlled for years by a competitor. So what? That was business. Bruno was a good salesman, and if he was able to drum up trade for his company, what's the big deal? That's what a salesman does.

"One of the best we've ever had, sir," Raymond Martorano, one of the owners of the vending-machine company, told the New Jersey State Commission of Investigation during a hearing in 1977. "One of the finest and [most] honest salesmen we ever had, sir."

Avuncular, taciturn, polite, diplomatic—that was Angelo Bruno. He was 69 when he was killed. He had begun talking about retiring to Florida, where his wife was said to own some property. Things were changing. There were new pressures. Atlantic City was beginning to boom, and there were those in his organization who were itching to cash in, who were tired of his cautious approach to business ventures.

One of those was Antonio "Tony Bananas" Caponigro, Bruno's consigliere, or crime family counselor. Caponigro, nearly everyone now believes, orchestrated the March 1980 assassination of the mob boss. It was a bloody grab for power that shook the foundation of the Philadelphia mob.

Scarfo was another member who was fed up with Bruno's old-fashioned ways. And while he appears to have had no role in the Bruno killing, he ultimately reaped the greatest benefit from Bruno's death and the mob fratricide that followed.

It was organized crime's version of the Peter Principle. Here was Scarfo, who had been banished to Atlantic City by Bruno in 1963, rising to the top of the heap, an incompetent junior executive who finds himself named chairman of the board. Is it any wonder that eight years later, the company is in a shambles, nearly half the membership either dead or in jail, a generation of potential leaders no longer on the scene?

Scarfo's organization has been plunged into the underworld equivalent of a Chapter 11. The mob is bankrupt. And the man who caused the collapse is a crime boss who has spent four of the last eight years behind bars, who has been convicted of extortion, racketeering and first-degree murder in three separate trials and who is awaiting trial on additional racketeering charges.

Angelo Bruno once spent two years in jail for contempt in the early 1970s when he refused to testify before the New Jersey State Commission of Investigation. It was the only significant time he ever spent in prison.

Nicky Scarfo loved the role of gangster and saw himself as a celebrity. He hung a picture of Al Capone in his office, and he molded his persona in the tough-guy image made famous by Humphrey Bogart in dozens of crime and adventure films. One of his favorites was *Casablanca*, the Bogart classic. Scarfo, while riding the crest of his power, named the Fort Lauderdale waterfront villa where he spent much of his time Casablanca South and christened a 40-foot cabin cruiser that he docked there "Casablanca Usual Suspects," a name derived from one of the most memorable lines in the film.

Married and the father of three sons, Scarfo often vacationed in Florida with a woman other than his wife. And unlike Bruno, who separated his family from his business, Scarfo wanted his sons to follow in his footsteps. His nephew, Philip Leonetti, is now the underboss of the organization and is, like Scarfo, in jail. His middle son, Nick Jr., is described by law enforcement sources as an active associate of the organization and his imprisoned father's link to the underworld.

One of Scarfo's biggest disappointments is that his oldest son, Chris, wants no part of his father's business. "He's good with these," Scarfo once told an associate, holding up his fists like a boxer. "But not with this," he added, turning his fingers into the shape of a gun, a symbolic gesture members of the Scarfo mob use to signify murder.

Until barred as an undesirable, Scarfo was a ringside regular at casino boxing matches, he and his entourage adding to the glitz and glitter that are so much a part of the Atlantic City fight scene. Typically, Scarfo would show up wearing a $300 silk suit, his thick black hair combed straight back in the style nearly everyone in the organization adopted, his nails manicured, looking for all the world like he just stepped off the pages of *Gentleman's Quarterly*.

But it is more than a question of style that separated Bruno from Scarfo. The Philadelphia mob is not in a shambles because Bruno wore gabardine and Scarfo wore silk. Bruno understood respect. Scarfo confused respect with fear. Bruno knew how to earn money. Scarfo thought he was entitled to it. Bruno was patient and intelligent. Scarfo was greedy and ruthless. The late Bill Sullivan, who headed the New Jersey State Police organized crime bureau through most of the 1980s, had a one-sentence description for Scarfo: "He's a homicidal maniac."

If you join the mob, you've got to be ready and willing to kill. That is a given. Murder is the mob's ultimate weapon. It is the final piece of leverage, the perfect negotiating tool. But you don't have to enjoy it.

For Bruno, murder was a last resort. When all else had failed, when there was no room for compromise, and no other solution, then somebody might disappear. During all his years in the mob, Bruno was never charged with ordering or carrying out a killing. Scarfo has been linked to more than a dozen.

Bruno succeeded Joseph Ida as mob boss of Philadelphia in 1959. Ida fled to Italy in the wake of the infamous mob summit meeting in Apalachin, New York, that ended abruptly when New York State Police raided the conclave. Ida left the organization in the care of his underboss, Antonio Pollina. Bruno was a capo at the time and, at least in Pollina's mind, a potential rival.

So Pollina ordered Bruno killed. But the man who got the contract warned Bruno instead. Bruno went to New York to argue his case before the Mafia Commission, a ruling council made up of the heads of the top New York families. Included in that group was Carlo Gambino, a close friend and ally.

Bruno was persuasive. The commission deposed Pollina, replacing him with Bruno. What's more, it gave Bruno the authority to do away with Pollina. Significantly, Bruno declined, ordering Pollina instead into permanent retirement. The moves solidified Bruno's hold on the organization, enhanced his standing both locally and in New York, and established the foundation for 21 years of relative stability.

Scarfo, on the other hand, headed a mob family whose coat of arms could have been a crossed set of smoking .357 magnums mounted on a blood-red shield and inscribed with the words "Kill or Be Killed." Murder was no longer the last resort, but the negotiating tool of choice. What's more, Scarfo seemed to enjoy it.

The brutal assassination of Angelo Bruno in front of his Snyder Avenue rowhouse in South Philadelphia ignited a bloody struggle for power that changed the face of organized crime in Philadelphia. In little more than a year, the local branch of the Mafia was transformed from a low-profile organization headed by a man who preferred to work in the shadows to a gang of gun-toting thugs led by a man who looked to Al Capone as an idol.

Nail bombs, bullets, knives and garrotes left a bloody trail from New York to Atlantic City as friends and family members turned on one another in a grab for power, wealth and revenge. Bruno, Caponigro, Alfred Salerno, John Simone, Frank Sindone, Philip Testa and Frank Narducci—

a generation of mob leadership and experience—were dead. And the bullets were still flying. Police have documented 16 mob murders and six attempted murders during the first two years of Scarfo's leadership.

Some were vengeance killings, others were part of an internal struggle between Scarfo and fellow mobster Harry Riccobene. Riccobene is now serving a life prison sentence for the May 1982 murder of Scarfo consigliere Frank Monte. But still others, law enforcement officials say, appear to have been nothing more than wanton and random outbursts of violence—reflections, they say, of the personality of the new mob boss.

The attempted murder of Joseph Salerno Sr. in Wildwood Crest, New Jersey, in 1982, is a prime example. Salerno's son, Joseph Jr., a plumbing contractor, had testified against Scarfo in a murder case in 1980. Scarfo, his nephew Philip Leonetti and Lawrence Merlino were accused of the 1979 murder of Margate, New Jersey cement contractor Vincent Falcone, a mob associate who had apparently failed to show enough respect to Scarfo and Leonetti.

All three were acquitted after a trial in Mays Landing, New Jersey, in which Joseph Jr. was the chief prosecution witness. The younger Salerno was then placed in the federal Witness Protection Program and was cooperating with federal and state authorities in investigations into the Scarfo organization.

Scarfo, according to law enforcement officials, wanted to silence Joseph Jr., but couldn't get to him. So he chose his father as a surrogate. "Tradition held that the mob did not harm an innocent relative or member of an enemy's family, a brother, a sister, a father," the Pennsylvania Crime Commission noted in a 1983 report that detailed the attempt on Joseph Salerno Sr. "It just wasn't done."

On the night of August 10, 1982, a man wearing a ski mask and a jogging suit knocked on the office door of a motel in Wildwood Crest owned by Joseph Sr. When Salerno opened the door, the man pulled out a gun and fired a bullet into his neck. Salerno survived the shooting, but the tradition that once protected family members in mob disputes was shattered.

The federal racketeering trial that ended in November with the convictions of Scarfo and 16 other top mob figures attributed eight murders and four attempted murders to the Scarfo organization. These included the Falcone murder, the attempt on Joseph Salerno Sr., and several other dramatic and highly publicized killings, such as the September 1984 assassination of Salvatore Testa.

Of all the killings that have occurred over the last eight years, the Testa murder was the ultimate Scarfo betrayal and, to most law enforcement sources, the most telling about the volatile mob boss.

Salvatore Testa was the son of Philip Testa, Scarfo's mentor, friend and the person most responsible for his rise from a lowly soldier to a man of importance within the organization. Philip Testa succeeded Angelo Bruno. He made Scarfo his consigliere. Together they established the reign of terror that has destroyed the mob. But Philip Testa spent just a year at the top. On March 15, 1981, as he was walking up the steps of his home on Porter Street in South Philadelphia, a nail bomb planted under the porch exploded. The blast nearly cut the mob boss in half. It also set off another round of revenge killings and paved the way for Scarfo's ascent to the top spot in the organization.

Phil Testa's son Salvie became the chief enforcer for Scarfo, planning and carrying out a series of murders that consolidated his power. But by 1984, Salvie Testa, who was featured that year as a rising mob star in a front-page article in the *Wall Street Journal*, was viewed as a rival. And so he was ordered killed.

"He got killed for no sensible reason," mob informant Tommy Del-Giorno said from the witness stand last year. "But I don't have no remorse over it because a lot of guys that I know now, the last five years got killed for no sensible reason."

Control of an organized crime family in a city like Philadelphia means power, influence and money. It means shadowy business arrangements with union leaders and politicians. It means access, directly or indirectly, to the lawyers and judges who run the judicial system. And it means millions of dollars annually.

The money comes wadded and wrapped in rubber bands. Hard, cold cash. Hundreds of thousands of dollars. Multiply this, depending on your tax bracket, by a factor of two or three, since none of it ever shows up on an income tax return. "The mob lives off people that do illegal things," said mob informant Nicholas Caramandi while testifying for the government in the extortion trial of former City Councilman Leland Beloff. And the mob apparently lives well.

Though Bruno was a millionaire when he died, according to law enforcement sources, he was a master at hiding his assets. His holdings over the years were said to comprise various legitimate and illegitimate business operations, including gambling casinos in the Dominican Republic and London, a hotel in the Netherlands Antilles, travel junket clubs in New York and Philadelphia, a New Jersey trucking firm and assorted real estate holdings in New Jersey, Pennsylvania and Florida.

Scarfo once listed his job as caretaker of an apartment building his mother, Catherine, owned on Georgia Avenue in Atlantic City. At another point, he was a salesman for a custom shirt company and, at still another point, the representative of an entertainment booking agency. Apparently, he did very well in these businesses. At the time of his arrest in the Rouse extortion case, he was returning from a stay in Fort Lauderdale, where he lived in a waterfront home valued at $850,000 and skippered a cabin cruiser worth $120,000.

Thomas DelGiorno, the former Scarfo capo who is a cooperating government witness, has told the FBI that he personally earned $1 million from his bookmaking operations between 1973 and 1986. Just before turning informant in November 1986, he "was making about $150,000 a year from the numbers and gambling businesses alone," an FBI report on DelGiorno notes. "The 'shakes' generated about $25,000 a year or more in income. They [top members of the Scarfo family] also made scores in drug deals. . . ." The "shakes" were shakedowns or extortions, a racket the Scarfo mob perfected.

Bruno had a live-and-let-live attitude about the rackets in Philadelphia and Atlantic City. He made his money; he didn't much care if you made yours, as long as everyone understood territories and boundaries. Take bookmaking and illegal gambling, for example. During the Bruno years there were dozens of independent operators. When they had to edge off some heavy betting or when they themselves were in need of money, they would go to Bruno or his people for help.

Many bookmakers are compulsive gamblers themselves, so it was often only a matter of time before Bruno, through his loan-sharking, became a "partner" in someone else's business, the debt repaid through a share in the weekly take. There were no strong-arm tactics. It was strictly business. It was a quiet, effective way to exert power and control.

Scarfo, on the other hand, decided that anyone doing business in the underworld should pay a street tax. This was assessed across the board in several sections of the city. The same tactic was used with many drug dealers.

Many of those scores and shakedowns have been detailed by DelGiorno and Nicholas Caramandi, either from the witness stand or during debriefing sessions with the FBI. DelGiorno has described how he collected "brokerage fees" totaling $300,000 for the mob in two 1983 drug deals. And Caramandi has testified that he was setting up a $2 million drug deal at the same time he was working the Penn's Landing extortion. He has also said that weekly shakedown payments from local bookmakers generated about $200,000 a year for the organization and that one-time "tribute" payments accounted for more than $50,000. A street tax on methamphetamine dealers, he said, produced an additional $400,000 to $500,000 over a two-year period.

Caramandi has also told federal authorities that he had an interest in a bookmaking operation that generated $60,000 a week and a sports betting ring that during the National Football League season produced about $300,000 a week. And he said he shared in a loan-sharking operation that had $500,000 "on the street," earning 20 percent interest per week.

The profits from all his deals, Caramandi has testified, were split among the mobsters involved. But a portion, usually 25 to 50 percent, of every score was always sent "down the shore" to Scarfo. This was known as paying tribute to "the elbow."

During a federal drug trial last year involving a $1 million methamphetamine deal, Caramandi was asked how much money he had earned for Scarfo while a member or associate of his organization.

"I brought him millions," he replied. But it was never enough.

Caramandi was arrested in June 1986; DelGiorno in October of that year. By November, both mobsters had come to the same conclusion: They had screwed up in the eyes of their boss, and they knew how he dealt with screw-ups.

Even before his arrest, DelGiorno said, he had begun to get bad vibes from Scarfo. That, he said, was what led him to cooperate with authorities. "Listen, I seen this happen to so many guys, 90 percent they think they're going to get killed, 10 percent they think they ain't," DelGiorno said from the witness stand. "I wasn't waiting for the 10 percent. . . . Since '81, I have been setting guys up to get killed. All right? I was taught by the best."

"I know Nicky Scarfo," Caramandi said. "Once he turns on you, it's all over."

Scarfo's indiscriminate use of murder to settle any score and to avenge any slight had taken its final toll. In destroying his enemies, real or perceived, he also destroyed his organization. The defections of DelGiorno and Caramandi were a turning point in the history of organized crime in Philadelphia. Their cooperation and testimony paved the way for the series of prosecutions that have placed Scarfo and most of the other major players in the Philadelphia mob behind bars.

In the last five years, 27 of the 61 identified members of the organization have been indicted on either federal or state charges. Twenty-three have been convicted. Several trials are pending. Combined with the deaths of more than a dozen other top mob figures, the prosecutions have made the collapse of the organization almost inevitable. It is, says Fred Martens of the Pennsylvania Crime Commission, comparable to removing the chief executive officer, the board of directors and most of the senior managers of AT&T. Do that, Martens says, and "I don't think you'd have the phone service you expected."

Scarfo is serving 14 years for the Rouse extortion. He and seven associates were sentenced to life in prison after their convictions in April for the 1985 murder of Frank "Frankie Flowers" D'Alfonso, a South Philadelphia bookmaker. Scarfo is awaiting sentencing on a federal racketeering conviction for which he could receive up to 55 years.

Pending also is a racketeering trial in New Jersey in which Scarfo and 12 associates, including most of those convicted in the federal racketeering case, are defendants.

Nicodemo Scarfo will probably spend the rest of his life behind bars. Most of his top associates are looking at stretches of 20 to 40 years.

No one, of course, predicts that the arrests, indictments and convictions mean the end of organized crime in Philadelphia. But the multipronged offensive that has brought about the collapse of the Scarfo organization has taken a substantial toll. It could take years to rebuild.

In development terms, it is a project of mammoth proportions, comparable in scope and magnitude to—well, to cite a handy example, the stalled multimillion-dollar development of Penn's Landing.

Mobster Ron Previte and mob boss Ralph Natale

LIFE ON THE STREETS

I once had an editor explain to me what it meant to write an "Inquirer" story. This was early in my career at the paper when we were in a head-to-head battle with the old Philadelphia *Bulletin.*

The *Bulletin* was a classic evening newspaper, the paper of record. It tried to cover everything, to be all things to all people. It failed for many reasons, not the least of which was the ever-changing reading habits of the American public. Those ongoing changes are now threatening the newspaper business in general, or so the experts claim.

We overcame the *Bulletin* in part because we were the morning paper and fit more easily into the public's reading patterns at the time. We also prevailed, I believe, because the agenda set by Gene Roberts was to find good stories and write the hell out of them.

"We zig when everybody else zags," a desk editor said to me in explaining the approach.

The idea was to try to find a different way, a more entertaining way, a more readable way to tell the same story that everyone else was covering. It was about quality and sophistication. It included assuming that our readers had the wit and intelligence to get it, to appreciate it and, eventually, to come to expect it. When you deliver on a regular basis, you build readership. That's a lesson that's getting lost today in the panic over new cyber media and the "Oh my God, kids don't read newspapers anymore and all our readers are dying" doomsday advocates who say journalism has to reinvent itself to survive.

The delivery systems may be changing, but the bottom line is still the story. Find it and report it and write it better than anyone else and the readers will come. Zig when everybody else zags.

Organized crime is a great topic for that approach. The stories are rich in detail. The characters are full-bodied. I came away again and again shaking my head and mumbling about my good fortune. You can't make this stuff up any better than it is.

The Brothers Chang

MAY 6, 2001

Each time the grainy video has flashed across the television screens in the crowded ninth-floor courtroom, John Ciancaglini, 45, has set his jaw and stared away. It is not something he wants to see. The tape is the rarest of all FBI surveillance videos—a mob hit in progress.

The victim of the March 1993 shooting was Ciancaglini's brother Joseph Jr., now 43. The attempted murder was ordered, the prosecution contends, by his other brother Michael, 30, who in turn was killed gangland-style a few months later. The tape has been played four times at the racketeering trial of Ciancaglini and his codefendants, reputed mob boss Joseph "Skinny Joey" Merlino and five others.

Now in its sixth week, the trial has included testimony about a series of plots and subplots wrapped around allegations of murder, attempted murder, extortion, and drug trafficking. None has been more compelling than the brutal and tragic saga of the Ciancaglini brothers. One dead. One crippled. And one fighting racketeering-murder charges that could send him to prison for life.

"He's crushed by this," Kathy Ciancaglini said of her jailed husband's reaction to the testimony and allegations that have swirled around the federal courtroom.

"He hates it that Michael and Joey have been portrayed as if they hated each other. That's so not true." Neither, she said, are the allegations that her husband resorted to murder to avenge Michael's death two years later.

Speaking out for the first time, Kathy Ciancaglini, 38, who has attended the trial almost every day, says her husband has been through an emotional wringer listening to and watching testimony and evidence connected to the shootings of his two brothers.

The prosecution's version is a violent tale of brother against brother, a family feud played out within a bloody South Philadelphia mob war. But that, Kathy Ciancaglini says, is a distortion of reality. Brothers fight, she said. Brothers argue. But brothers, particularly her husband's brothers, do not try to kill each other. The stories about John Ciancaglini's brothers, she said, have been especially difficult, the video excruciating.

One key prosecution witness, mob soldier Gaetano "Tommy Horse-head" Scafidi, 36, has provided detailed information to support the government's version of the shooting of Joseph Ciancaglini.

"Michael hated Joey," Scafidi said, claiming that Michael Ciancaglini ordered the hit because he believed his brother was behind a botched attempt on his life one year earlier.

In March 1992, two men wielding shotguns chased Michael Ciancaglini down a South Philadelphia street. He fled into his home. The gunmen then opened fire on his front door and front window. Scafidi testified that he was one of the gunmen who burst in on Joseph Ciancaglini a year later, shortly after he had opened his Grays Ferry luncheonette, the Warfield Breakfast & Luncheon Express.

The shooting happened at 5:58 a.m. Authorities have the precise time because of the FBI surveillance camera mounted on a pole opposite the restaurant. The bureau had also planted a bug inside.

The hit took 30 seconds. A group of shadowy figures rush into the deli. A waitress screams. Several shots ring out. The shadowy figures flee.

"I couldn't believe he would want to kill his own brother," Scafidi said.

Prosecutors contend that the brothers' blood ties had been shredded by conflicting underworld loyalties. In 1993, they say, Joseph Ciancaglini Jr. was the underboss of the John Stanfa crime family. Merlino and Michael Ciancaglini headed a group of young upstarts trying to take control of the organization. The shooting of Joseph Ciancaglini was the start of an underworld war that raged for nearly a year and claimed several other victims. Joseph Ciancaglini survived the hit but has never been the same.

An emergency medical technician testified about Ciancaglini's condition that morning, describing how one bullet had ripped through his cheek and another had blown off most of his ear, how one of his eyes had been nearly shot out. Bleeding and appearing disoriented, Joseph Ciancaglini fought with medics who tried to help him. He had to be handcuffed before they could put him on a stretcher.

John Ciancaglini, listening to the account, seemed to be fighting back tears. Kathy Ciancaglini, sitting in the crowded courtroom, sobbed quietly.

The graphic description, after two weeks of testimony from mob boss Ralph Natale, appeared to shock the jury and the courtroom. Natale's second-hand accounts of other mob hits invariably ended with one of the defendants reporting back to him that "everything went fine." Natale's was a sanitized version of a messy business. The image of Joseph Ciancaglini—mumbling, confused and bleeding from his mouth, nose and ears—was a more realistic picture.

Six months after the attack on Joseph Ciancaglini, Michael Ciancaglini was killed in a drive-by shooting. Two Stanfa gunmen, who later became cooperating witnesses, testified that they were the killers. One was John Veasey.

John Ciancaglini, the eldest of the Ciancaglini brothers, was in prison completing a nine-year sentence for extortion when his brothers were shot. (Their father, Joseph "Chickie" Ciancaglini Sr., is serving 45 years on a 1988 mob racketeering conviction. Their mother died in 1986.) There are many who believe that if John Ciancaglini had been around in 1993, he might have been able to heal whatever rift had developed between his younger brothers.

"Johnny is a diplomat," Kathy Ciancaglini said. "I truly believe had he been here in 1993, none of this would have happened. He would have kept the family together." Instead, when he came home in 1995, John Ciancaglini walked into an underworld in turmoil.

Stanfa and most of his top associates were awaiting a racketeering trial. Merlino and Natale were trying to solidify their hold on that underworld. And, according to the prosecution's version of the case, there were scores to be settled.

On October 5, John Veasey was set to take the stand as a government witness in the racketeering trial of Stanfa and seven codefendants. That morning, his brother Billy was gunned down as he left his home on Bouvier Street near Oregon Avenue, shot in the head and chest. Police said three gunmen ran up and opened fire. John Ciancaglini is charged with being one of the shooters.

"It was a brother for a brother," Natale told the FBI shortly after he became a cooperating witness. The prosecution has little, however, to corroborate Natale's account of the hit on Billy Veasey.

"My client had nothing to do with that," said F. Emmett Fitzpatrick, who is representing John Ciancaglini and who, on cross-examination, has tried to show other possible motives for Billy Veasey's killing.

Fitzpatrick has notified prosecutors that he intends to call witnesses who will provide John Ciancaglini with an alibi, but he would not comment on speculation that his client might take the witness stand in his own defense.

Though John Ciancaglini also faces three counts of extortion in the current case, it is the murder charge—the allegation that he sided with the mob faction that crippled his brother Joseph in order to avenge the death of his brother Michael—that could send him to prison for the rest of his life.

Butchie

MARCH 13, 2001

His name was Butchie. He was a low-level wiseguy who back in 1975 was suspected of skimming money from an organized crime book-making operation in North Jersey. So his friends lured him to a social club on Hudson Street in Newark, offered him a drink at the bar, and shot him twice in the back of the head. Then they dumped his body in a grave already dug in the basement of the club. They poured acid over the body, covered it with dirt, and patched the hole in the floor with cement.

As mob hits go, it was no big deal. A missing person. An unsolved murder. Now it's part of the growing saga of Peter "Pete the Crumb" Caprio, a 71-year-old North Jersey mobster who will testify for the government in the racketeering trial of reputed Philadelphia mob boss Joseph "Skinny Joey" Merlino and seven others. Pretrial hearings in the case begin today before U.S. District Court Judge Herbert Hutton in Philadelphia. Jury selection is set to begin next week.

Caprio, who has admitted his involvement in four murders—he dug the grave and owned the club where Butchie met his demise—is one of five former mob figures expected to take the stand. Another is Philip "Philly Faye" Casale, a confessed hit man with a preference for point-blank assassinations and potato chips.

Operating for years in the Newark area, Caprio and Casale trolled the bottom of the underworld, engaging in gambling, bookmaking and a series of wanton murders that had not been solved until the two men began cooperating. Casale, 56, cut a deal in the fall of 1999. Caprio flipped after he was arrested last March.

"Both have pleaded guilty and are awaiting sentencing," said Assistant U.S. Attorney Laura Kaplan, who handled both cases.

Only one of their murders, the 1996 hit on mobster Joe Sodano, figures in the Merlino case. They are also expected to testify about the overall mob racketeering enterprise that is at the heart of the case. But their stories, detailed in federal documents that have been turned over by the prosecution to defense attorneys, provide much more.

The first-person accounts, contained in more than 40 FBI documents, offer a graphically brutal picture of the life of an organized crime member. Both Caprio and Casale emerge in these self-portraits as callous and uncaring masters of that classic underworld move, the double-cross that ends in murder.

So there is Casale describing how he was casually eating potato chips while waiting to blow out the brains of an associate. And here is Caprio telling investigators how he diligently dug a grave in anticipation of Butchie's hit.

"Over a period of a couple days, [Caprio] dug a four-foot-deep hole in the basement floor," reads one report. It also notes that just before the body was placed in the hole, another mobster "shot Butchie one more time to ensure that [he] was dead."

Defense attorneys hope to use stories like those to undermine the government's case. They will allege that prosecutors have made "deals with the devil," that the witnesses have agreed to say whatever the government wants to hear in exchange for leniency when they are sentenced for the crimes to which they have confessed. Informant testimony "comes from a corrupt and polluted source," said Norris E. Gelman, a prominent Philadelphia defense lawyer who is not involved in the Merlino case.

Gelman, who successfully defended mob boss Nicodemo "Little Nicky" Scarfo in the retrial of a murder case four years ago, said defense attorneys had to convince the jury that the government's witnesses were less than credible. They have to show, he said, that the government is "taking a totally corrupt career criminal, making him an offer he can't refuse. . . . and saying this is credible testimony."

Neither prosecutors nor defense lawyers in the Merlino case are permitted to comment on specific witnesses. It is standard procedure in racketeering cases, however, for prosecutors to tell the jury that the witnesses were chosen not by the government, but by the defendants. "Swans don't swim in sewers" is one common refrain used to explain the prosecution's position that the only witnesses to a criminal conspiracy are criminals themselves.

That description fits both Caprio and Casale, who have joined a growing list of kill-and-tell hit men who have used their cooperation to avoid lengthy sentences. That list includes Salvatore "Sammy the Bull" Gravano, who admitted 19 murders; Philip Leonetti, the Atlantic City wiseguy who confessed to 10; and South Philadelphia wiseguys Thomas "Tommy Del" DelGiorno (five murders) and Nicholas "Nicky Crow" Caramandi (four).

Caprio, among other things, has admitted that he was plotting to take over the Philadelphia crime family after Merlino's arrest in 1999. The plot included a plan to kill three prominent mob figures—alleged acting boss Joseph Ligambi and mobsters George Borgesi and Steven Mazzone—by luring them to a meeting in North Jersey. Borgesi and Mazzone are among the defendants in the Merlino case.

Casale, whose criminal résumé includes a conviction for the brutal assault and sexual molestation of a 10-year-old girl in 1977, has confessed to five murders while working for Caprio and the North Jersey branch of the Philadelphia mob. Each involved a close-range shot to the head. This usually occurred while Casale was sitting in a car next to his victim.

The reasons for the hits varied. Joe Sodano, for example, allegedly was killed because he failed to show the proper respect to Merlino and then-mob boss Ralph Natale. The hit was ordered by Natale and Merlino and carried out by Caprio and Casale, according to a federal document. Casale said he had shot Sodano once in the right side of the head after luring him to a meeting in the parking lot of an apartment complex in Newark. Casale said he was sitting in the passenger seat of Sodano's sports utility vehicle.

As Sodano slumped over the steering wheel, the vehicle started to roll backward. Casale, the FBI memo reads, "exited the passenger side . . . walked around the front of the vehicle . . . opened the driver's side door . . . and shot Sodano once in the left side of the head." He then took $12,000 in cash and a piece of jewelry from Sodano. He split the money with Caprio.

Casale also admitted killing four other mob associates with shots to the head, according to the FBI. In three cases, he was sitting in a car with his victim. In the fourth, he was in a warehouse. While lying in wait for one victim in 1991, Casale said, he sat in his own car eating potato chips. After consuming his fourth bag and beginning to wonder if the target would show, Casale said, he called Caprio to ask what he should do.

"Eat more chips," Caprio replied.

The hit went down later that night. The victim was a local bookmaker who Casale said had stiffed him on a payoff. Two years later, Casale and Caprio plotted to kill a North Jersey mob associate named Billy Shear. The reason for the hit was that several mobsters believed Shear had begun to cooperate with law enforcement authorities. Casale said that Caprio had referred to Shear as "a cancer," and that Caprio said something had to be done "to stop it before it spreads," according to another FBI memo. Then he told Casale, "You gotta do what you gotta do. I think it's potato chip time."

A short time later, Casale said, he set up a meeting with Shear, saying he wanted to discuss a drug deal. Casale said he had advised Caprio that the hit was going to go down by telling him, "Tonight's potato chip night." That night, while sitting in Shear's car, Casale pulled out a gun and shot Shear in the head, he said.

"Shear began to moan, and [Casale] . . . shot Shear again," says the FBI memo, adding that after "Shear stopped moaning and slumped over," Casale took $800 from the dead man. Casale said he had given $200 to Caprio.

While extremely efficient murderers, Casale and Caprio admitted that things did not always work out as planned. Casale, for example, described his 1997 murder of Bobby Matonis, a mob associate who owned a clothing warehouse in Essex County where, rumor had it, he kept $50,000 to $100,000 in cash hidden. After killing Matonis, the only money that Casale found was $1,500 in the victim's wallet, Casale said.

The burial of Butchie also caused Caprio problems years later when the City of Newark bought the building that had contained Caprio's clubhouse. Fearing that the body would be discovered, Caprio and another associate dug a new grave at a garbage dump in Hackettstown, Warren County. Then they sneaked into the building at 140 Hudson Street and tried to dig up Butchie's remains. The body—bones and deteriorating portions of human flesh—was "stuck in the mud," an FBI memo says. Caprio and an associate "removed several leg bones, but the remainder of the body was left. More acid was poured on the body, dirt was put back, and the hole was cemented over again."

The leg bones, the FBI notes, were taken to the garbage dump and buried.

The Cop and the Wiseguy

FEBRUARY 20, 2001

It is a story more suited for *The Sopranos* than federal court; a saga of petty corruption and personal betrayal that may be as accurate a depiction of the beleaguered New Jersey mob—plagued by informants, hounded by the FBI, and decimated by a series of successful federal prosecutions—as anything the popular HBO series can offer.

Call it the tale of the cop and the wiseguy. It opens Monday in U.S. District Court in Camden.

The cop is James "Jimmy" DeLaurentis, 38, who is facing extortion charges that could end his career. DeLaurentis, suspended without pay since his 1999 indictment, is a 13-year veteran of the Hammonton Police Department who rose to the rank of supervisor of detectives. His father, Michael, was the chief of police; his brother, Joseph, a patrolman. The wiseguy is Ronald "Ronnie" Previte, 57, who for a time was known as "the Godfather of Hammonton."

Today, people who claim to know say that's a bit of hyperbole. They say what passes for the underworld in this tightly knit Atlantic County community of 12,500 residents is too unruly and too disorganized for anybody to really be in control. Previte, they say, was a major player in the local rackets. But he was a kingpin in a world populated by "low-life, low-rent fringe guys playing at being in the Mafia," according to one local resident and businessman who has followed Previte's career.

"They were just a bunch of bums and bullies," said a longtime businessman who has had several clashes with Previte in the past. Both businessmen asked not to be identified.

More to the point, Previte, despite his reputation as a knee-busting wiseguy, was a longtime secret government snitch, first for the New Jersey State Police and later for the FBI. For more than two years, beginning in February 1997, the burly, six-foot, 280-pound gangster taped hundreds of conversations in a federal investigation that led to more than a dozen arrests.

DeLaurentis ended up on some of those tapes. The conversations, federal prosecutors allege, include discussions in which DeLaurentis asked Previte to shake down a local bar owner for thousands of dollars in cash. Previte and DeLaurentis split the money, investigators say. The bribes, authorities charge, were paid to insure that the bar—the scene of frequent fights and suspected drug dealing and prostitution—did not have its liquor license revoked.

"He's gonna pay heavy," DeLaurentis told Previte in a conversation recorded over breakfast at a diner in nearby Folsom shortly after the wiseguy began wearing a wire. ". . . He's gotta go for at least 10."

DeLaurentis is charged with using Previte to collect $14,000 from the bar owner during a two-year period. His trial will be the first for any defendant arrested as a result of Previte's undercover work. Twelve others, accused of either drug trafficking or racketeering, have pleaded guilty. Nine more, including reputed mob boss Joseph "Skinny Joey" Merlino, are to be tried next month in Philadelphia.

Neither DeLaurentis nor his father, who live across the street from one another in an upscale neighborhood of modern, ranch-style homes just off the White Horse Pike, would comment on the pending case. But DeLaurentis' lawyer, Louis Barbone, hinted at a defense that would portray Previte as the originator of the extortion plot and DeLaurentis as an entrapped victim of an FBI sting gone awry. Barbone described Previte as a conniving predator who bullied his way to a lucrative lifetime of crime, all the while depending on his law enforcement handlers to protect him from prosecution.

"Ron Previte was and still is an omnipresent figure who exerts fear over everybody in town," Barbone said recently. "He ruled the police department and the community. He was a master of fear and intimidation . . . . He was and continues to be a criminal. The only difference is that now he is protected by the FBI."

Previte would hold court most nights at the same table—the second on the left as you entered the door—in the Silver Coin Diner, a popular restaurant on the White Horse Pike a few blocks from the center of town. From that perch, he ran his bookmaking and loan-sharking operations, meeting with a small group of local associates and anyone looking to do business.

"If you wanted to see Ronnie, that's where you went," said Joe Bartuccio, a friend for 40 years and a self-described member of Previte's inner circle. "And if you didn't want to see him," Bartuccio added, "you didn't go there."

Previte was well known in town, having graduated from Hammonton High School in the early 1960s. After spending 12 years as a Philadelphia police officer, he returned to the area, working for several years in the security department of an Atlantic City casino. By the late 1980s he was largely "self-employed."

Divorced, he lived alone in a sprawling ranch-style home outside of town, always drove a Cadillac, and usually dressed in casual sports clothes which he accessorized with thick gold necklaces and a large, diamond pinky ring. "Fortune favors the bold" was one of his favorite expressions.

"He's generous and above average when it comes to intelligence," Bartuccio said. "But he can be cunning and diabolical . . . Even in high school, he was always trying to stay one step ahead of everybody else."

Having grown up in town, Previte knew many of the members of the police department, including Mike DeLaurentis, who was the chief, and James DeLaurentis, who was moving up the ladder in the department.

"Jimmy was a good cop," says a police officer who worked with him. "Real good. And people liked him. But then he started hanging around Ronnie and you could see how he was being influenced. We used to wonder, what does he want to be, a cop or a wiseguy?"

The question hung over the 28-member police force, causing it to split into two factions and undermining its credibility in law enforcement circles.

"I think other agencies didn't trust us," said Frank Ingemi, a police captain at the time. Ingemi became chief after Michael DeLaurentis retired in the summer of 1998.

By the mid-1990s, with his role as an informant known only to a select few in law enforcement, Previte began showing up on FBI files as a soldier and later a capo, or captain, in the Philadelphia-South Jersey mob. The notoriety had no discernible effect on his relationship with Jimmy DeLaurentis, said Ingemi and other police sources. In fact, although there was no blood relationship, DeLaurentis sometimes described Previte as his "cousin," they said. Several also recalled how Previte and DeLaurentis would greet one another. Instead of shaking hands, they would kiss each other on both cheeks, an Old World sign of loyalty and affection that is also a common greeting in underworld circles.

"It was like Jimmy idolized him," said one fellow officer. "Ronnie drove a Cadillac. Jimmy went out and got a Cadillac. Ronnie shaved his head. Jimmy shaved his head. Ronnie started going around in loafers without socks. Jimmy would show up in the office in loafers without socks."

A low point, Ingemi said, was the annual Our Lady of Mount Carmel festival in 1996. The century-old, week-long ethnic and religious celebration attracts thousands of visitors to Hammonton each July. Built around the July 16 feast day of Our Lady of Mount Carmel, the event includes a lavish carnival highlighted by a feast-day parade.

"We march in the parade every year," Ingemi said. "We're all in uniform. Afterwards, we stop at the Sons of Italy hall for a sandwich. Usually they sit us in the back room, away from the bar. Because we're in uniform and it wouldn't look right."

That summer, Ingemi said he was with a group of officers, including Jimmy DeLaurentis. "They brought us to the back room," he said. "But when we get there, Previte's already there with a group of people. I recognized [mob boss] Ralph Natale and some other members of Cosa Nostra."

"They said, 'Hi, how ya doin'. Sit down.'"

Ingemi said he and most of the other officers left. DeLaurentis, he said, stayed.

In one taped conversation recorded in 1997, DeLaurentis happily described to Previte a chance encounter he had with Natale and several other known Philadelphia mobsters at Catelli's, a restaurant in Voorhees Township. DeLaurentis said he tried to send a round of drinks over to Natale's table.

"I says, you know, 'Send them, the whole table there, a drink for me,'" DeLaurentis said in a conversation Previte recorded on May 20, 1997. "The waiter came back and says, 'They won't take a drink. Matter of fact, they picked up your bill.'"

On another tape, DeLaurentis promised Previte that he would try to help a Natale associate who had been arrested in Bridgeton in a domestic dispute. Prosecutors hope to use those tapes at trial, but thus far a judge has ruled that they are inadmissible because they are not relevant to the charges. Several other tapes that will be played, however, include discussions in which, authorities allege, DeLaurentis and Previte plan the shakedown of the owner of the problem-plagued Choris Bar, a now-shuttered business located at 122 Railroad Avenue.

The trial is expected to last from two to three weeks, according to Assistant U.S. Attorney Mary Futcher, who declined to comment about the case. FBI agents, members of the Hammonton Police Department, including Ingemi, and the bar owner who allegedly paid the bribes are scheduled to testify. The key to the case, however, is Previte, who has pleaded guilty to an extortion charge and who will be making his debut as a government witness.

In an interview with a television reporter last year, Jimmy DeLaurentis said he was entrapped and intimidated by the hulking wiseguy who, with the FBI's blessing, ran roughshod over the town. In that interview, he called his onetime friend "a criminal with a badge."

Now federal prosecutors, who in court papers charge that DeLaurentis "used organized crime" to operate his own criminal enterprise, hope to paint that same picture of the suspended police detective.

The Wiseguy Shuffle

NOVEMBER 25, 1996

They came in fancy cars, wearing designer clothes and walking the kind of walk Philadelphia police captain John Apeldorn has seen so many times before.

Call it the South Philly two-step.

The wiseguy shuffle.

Apeldorn saw a lot of it on November 17 outside the big soirée at the Benjamin Franklin House, where reputed mob underboss Joseph "Skinny Joey" Merlino hosted a party for about 300 close friends and associates.

"These guys live for today," he said. "They don't learn from history. . . . They think they're smarter, a couple of steps ahead of the last group. Ultimately, they're going to end up in the same place."

The last group would be the John Stanfa crime family. The reference was timely.

The first anniversary of Stanfa's racketeering conviction was Thursday, just four days after the Merlino bash. The former mob boss and seven codefendants were found guilty following a dramatic 10-week trial in U.S. District Court in Philadelphia last year. Most of the charges revolved around the violent clash between the Stanfa organization and a rival faction headed by Merlino.

Stanfa now sits in a prison cell in Leavenworth, Kansas, serving life without parole while his lawyers mount an appeal. In all, 25 of 29 people targeted by federal authorities in the three-year Stanfa probe have either been convicted or pleaded guilty. Most are now doing heavy prison time. As a result, they missed the "Guys and Dolls" routine that unfolded outside the Ben Franklin as Merlino, 34, and his top associates paraded into the swank former hotel and the media and law enforcement surveillance crews recorded it all.

Inside at the private party there was a multi-course buffet dinner that started with hot hors d'oeuvres and champagne and that included, among other dishes, pasta, calimari, scampi, king crab legs, filet mignon, veal chops and porchetta. There was also a well-stocked bar, two orchestras, a string band and disc jockey Jerry Blavat, who filled the interludes with recorded music and his stylistic patter. It was a gala affair, a real—you should excuse the expression—mob scene.

What it all meant is now the topic of intense brainstorming by police and federal authorities, who were on the scene taking names, photographs and license tag numbers as the guests pulled up in Cadillacs, Lincolns and stretch limousines.

"It looked like the Academy Awards," said Apeldorn, still shaking his head in amazement three days later.

Billed as a reception to belatedly celebrate the baptism of Merlino's four-month-old daughter, the affair also has been described by authorities as a "coming-out" party for the flamboyant mob underboss. Merlino had come off a year of restrictive parole two days earlier and is now free to travel and associate with whomever he pleases. Investigators, who are trying to put together a guest list, hint that members of several other mob families came by to pay their respects. Underworld sources, however, say there was nothing nefarious about the get-together. It was what it was, said one invitee whose name shows up on all the organized crime charts.

"Sometimes a party is just a party," he said.

One person who wasn't basking in the media spotlight that Sunday night was alleged mob boss Ralph Natale, 61, of Pennsauken. On parole and under strict guidelines about where he can go and with whom he can associate, the reputed Mafia don has avoided the limelight since being released from prison in 1994 after serving 15 years on narcotics trafficking and arson charges.

Natale and Merlino were both marked for death by Stanfa during the bloody mob war that ultimately led to Stanfa's arrest and conviction. Now the two survivors sit atop the organization, authorities say, reaping the benefits of gambling, loan sharking and racketeering gambits while rebuilding a crime family left in tatters after a decade and a half of violence and prosecutions. But they both remain targets—this time of ongoing racketeering investigations in both Philadelphia and South Jersey, according to several law enforcement sources.

"We're working on things," said one high-level police source last week. "There's a lot of cooperation [between law enforcement agencies]. But these things take time. Don't expect anything too soon."

Still, he and others said, it's not a question of if, but when. Look at the history of the organization, they say. Since the gangland slaying of Mafia boss Angelo Bruno in March 1980, the Philadelphia-South Jersey mob has been a study in disorganized organized crime. With each new boss has come a higher level of violence, instability and law enforcement scrutiny. During that period, the number of gangland murders has been eclipsed only by the number of underworld convictions.

From Bruno's relatively peaceful, Godfather-like era, through the turbulent goodfella years of mob boss Nicodemo "Little Nicky" Scarfo to the comically chaotic "Pulp Fiction" that was the Stanfa mob, the Philadelphia branch of La Cosa Nostra has been on a downward-spiraling course of self-destruction.

Based on testimony and evidence presented at his trial last year, Stanfa bungled his way through the underworld, surrounding himself with a cast of misfit sycophants who looked and acted like refugees from a Quentin

Tarantino movie. These would include the hit man who botched a murder attempt because he had the wrong size shells in his shotgun; the former nude go-go dancer involved in a harebrained plot to poison Merlino by slipping cyanide into his drink at a local nightclub; and the triggerman who set himself on fire trying to torch his own getaway car.

A year later, Natale seems to have adopted the low-key, make-money-not-headlines management approach that was so successfully employed by Bruno before he was murdered. Merlino is likewise blasé, but does not shun the spotlight. The party at the Ben Franklin is just the latest example. He and his entourage of young, well-dressed associates frequent the trendy clubs along Delaware Avenue.

"Joey is a guy who dances to his own beat," said Frank Friel, a former captain and top organized crime investigator for the Philadelphia Police Department and now public safety director in Bensalem Township. "He epitomizes the new La Cosa Nostra. He enjoys the trappings."

But Friel and others in law enforcement say the high-profile lifestyle and street-corner philanthropy are only a part of the package. Merlino, they say, has earned his Mafia pedigree. He has served more than three years in prison for an armored car heist in which $357,150 was stolen (the money has never been recovered), and he is a suspect in at least three unsolved gangland shootings, including the attempted murder of Nicky Scarfo Jr. in a South Philadelphia restaurant back in 1989 and the ambush of John Stanfa and his son on the Schuylkill Expressway in August 1993. He has been wounded in an underworld ambush that left a close friend dead. And he has survived, according to testimony at the Stanfa trial, a half-dozen other attempts to gun him down, blow him up or poison him.

"He's a survivor," said Friel. "He's also been extraordinarily lucky." But he is not invincible.

"Joey is going to do what Joey wants to do, until or unless someone stamps him out," said Friel.

The question, Friel added, is whether that comes internally in another round of internecine warfare or externally from another federal racketeering indictment. The history lesson of the Philadelphia mob—the lesson apparently lost on those doing the wiseguy shuffle last week—is that one way or another, it will come.

"You get involved in this kind of thing and you end up in one of two places," said the wife of a young Stanfa crime family member convicted last year and now doing hard time. "Either you end up in jail or in the cemetery."

Dysfunctional Family

SEPTEMBER 17, 1995

It is, by any measure, the most dysfunctional Mafia family in America, an organization torn apart by its indiscriminate use of violence and lack of self-discipline. Since 1980, two of its bosses have been brutally slain. Three others have spent more time in jail than they have on the streets. Thirty members and associates, including a generation of potential leaders, have been killed. Three dozen more have been convicted and sentenced to long jail terms. And, most troubling of all from an underworld perspective, nearly a dozen members and associates have testified in court, shattering omerta, the Mafia's time-honored code of silence, and the concepts of honor and loyalty that supposedly went with it. This is Cosa Nostra Philadelphia-style: a crime family without any recognizable value system.

The depth and breadth of its problems are about to be put on public display again as jury selection begins this week in U.S. District Court for the trial of reputed mob boss John Stanfa and seven associates charged in a sweeping racketeering indictment handed up in March 1994.

"Stanfa, as head of the crime family, directed the activities of [the other defendants] in the commission of murders, attempted murders, kidnapping, extortions, loansharking, gambling and arson," the U.S. Attorney's Office said at the time the indictment was made public.

The case, based on the testimony of five mob turncoats and hundreds of hours of secretly recorded conversations, paints a picture of widespread underworld incompetence and senseless violence. Similar portraits have emerged in mob trials elsewhere in the country, leading many in law enforcement—and even some sources in the underworld—to proclaim that the American Mafia is crumbling. In the last 15 years, more than 1,200 mob members and associates have been convicted, targeted in a multipronged federal attack that has shaken the once highly secretive and seemingly invincible criminal society.

Mob bosses in most major American cities, including New York, Philadelphia, Chicago, Boston, Pittsburgh, Newark, Detroit and Kansas City, have been jailed. Mob-tainted unions have been seized by the government. Mob-controlled industries have been turned inside out. Mob informants are everywhere.

These "men of honor," who once swore a blood oath to live and die by the gun, now do their swearing from the witness stand while their agents negotiate book deals and peddle movie rights. Now the only people making offers that can't be refused are the authorities who run the Witness Protection Program and the producers who run Hollywood.

Nowhere have the factors that contributed to the American Mafia's demise been as pronounced as in Philadelphia, where scores of convictions have decimated the local organization. Based on interviews with law enforcement, legal, academic and underworld sources and on a review of thousands of pages of court transcripts and case files, those factors include:

A loss of mob-style "family values." Simply put, they don't make mobsters the way they used to.

Poor leadership. Mob bosses have, by and large, confused fear with respect, have replaced loyalty with treachery and have consistently resorted to violence to solve problems. This was particularly true in the 1980s in Philadelphia under Nicodemo "Little Nicky" Scarfo and in the New York Gambino crime family headed by John Gotti. Both are serving long federal prison sentences.

Narcotics. In theory, at least, dealing drugs once was taboo for "men of honor." Law enforcement authorities say today many Mafia families don't pay even lip service to that prohibition. Drugs mean big money. But drug dealing also brings heavy jail time, another factor that helps turn mobsters into witnesses.

Sophisticated and coordinated investigations. Federal, state and local authorities have presented a united front against the mob, sharing information, resources and, on occasion, witnesses.

"The traditional values have changed," says Patrick J. Ryan, a New York-based professor of criminal justice and former director of the International Association for the Study of Organized Crime. "The value system is different. . . . Seniority used to engender respect. Today it means nothing. . . . Obedience used to be big. Now you see guys disregarding the directives of a boss. . . . None of this is mysterious. What's happening is happening in society in general. . . . Cultures change. Societies change. We don't go and kiss our father's rings anymore."

There are about two dozen "made," or formally initiated, members of La Cosa Nostra cooperating with the government. In testimony in federal courtrooms across America, they have told a spellbinding tale of greed, treachery, violence and deceit that is at the root of the demise of the American mob.

From Phil Leonetti's cavalier comment about murder—"I never did nothing ruthless besides, well, I would kill people. But that's our life. That's what we do"—to Salvatore Gravano's description of his blind allegiance to his former boss John Gotti—"When he barked, I bit"—the words of these high-level informants have mesmerized jurors, filled thousands of pages of court transcripts and led to long prison sentences for hundreds of American mob figures.

Fifteen years ago the federal government unleashed a multipronged attack against La Cosa Nostra. According to statistics compiled by the FBI, the leaders of 20 of America's 25 Cosa Nostra families, including four of the five New York families, were convicted. These included 28 crime family bosses, 16 underbosses, seven consiglieres and 78 capos, or captains.

Taking advantage of high-tech electronic surveillance and the broad and devastating powers of the Racketeering Influenced and Corrupt Organizations (RICO) Act, prosecutors and FBI agents successfully built a series of cases that ripped away the hierarchy of most major American mob families. Three things worked in the feds' favor. They were good. They were lucky. And their timing was impeccable.

As an institution, the American Mafia has been split by a generational and cultural divide not unlike the one that has affected society. Second- and third-generation gangsters, products of middle-class America, make lousy Mafiosi. They value form over substance. They have little sense of history. They cannot deal with adversity. And they assume instant gratification as a birthright.

FBI agent Joseph Pistone, who infiltrated the Colombo crime family and posed as an aspiring wiseguy for several years in the late 1980s, told a U.S. Senate subcommittee that he saw the changes as he worked side-by-side with members of a Colombo crew in New York.

"With each generation the Mafia subculture moves closer to mainstream America," Pistone said in a 1990 appearance before the committee. "The old-timers who exhibit the strongest values of the Mafia are aging and slowly dying off. They are being replaced by younger wiseguys . . . who do not possess the same strong family values . . . . I continually heard the older members complaining about this phenomenon. They were concerned that the new members cared more about themselves than they did about the family or crew—'our thing' was turning into 'my thing' within the Mafia."

Philip Leonetti and Salvatore Gravano, two of the more celebrated Mafia turncoats now testifying for the government, are prime examples. Leonetti, now 42, was a capo in the Philadelphia crime family headed by his uncle, Nicodemo Scarfo, before the age of 30. He was underboss, or number-two man in the organization, by the time he was 33. Gravano, now 50, was a capo at age 40 and Gotti's second-in-command before age 45.

They were kids by old-time Mafia standards. Young and untested, they were nevertheless given the kind of power, authority and standing that used to be reserved for experienced "men of honor," Mafiosi who had spent 20, 30 or 40 years living "the life."

But the modern mob has thumbed its nose at tradition. Reflecting the get-it-all, get-it-now philosophy of the 1980s, leaders like Scarfo and Gotti abandoned long-range planning and patience—the marks of older dons like Carlo Gambino and Angelo Bruno—in a blatant grab for power and wealth. Younger members aligned with them became part of the new-look American Mafia. They took a high profile, grabbing expensive homes, fancy cars and finely tailored clothes with both fists. And when things got tough, some of them traded what they knew to hold onto as much of that wealth as they could.

Gravano has admitted his involvement in 19 Mafia murders. Leonetti has claimed 10. Cold-blooded hit men, they now do their shooting from the witness stand for the federal government, where they have proven to be just as deadly. Since becoming a government witness in 1989, Leonetti—handsome, articulate and soft-spoken—has testified in a dozen trials. All have resulted in convictions. Gravano, who cut his deal in 1991, has made six courtroom appearances and his conviction rate rivals Leonetti's.

Twenty-five years ago, this kind of thing was unheard of in the underworld. Fifty years ago, it was unthinkable. A mob member or associate who even flirted with the idea of cooperating knew that he was signing his death certificate, that he would end up "sleeping with the fishes." Today, guarding mob informants is a sophisticated and highly organized operation. The federal Witness Protection Program and other less publicized secretive programs run directly by the FBI or by state police organizations have wrapped a blanket of security around Mafia turncoats. Leonetti, Gravano and the others can fashion a new life out of the new identity, relocation and financial stipends their cooperation brings.

Sentenced to 45 years following conviction on federal racketeering charges, Leonetti got a substantial sentence reduction after testifying. And after a dozen federal prosecutors sang his praises, a judge knocked down his jail term to six and a half years. Leonetti ended up serving five years, five months and five days before earning parole. Less than half a year, defense lawyers later noted, for each of 10 murders in which he admitted his involvement. Gravano, who pleaded guilty to a racketeering charge and was looking at a maximum 20-year sentence, got the same kind of deal. Sentenced to five years, he was released from prison earlier this year.

Fifty years ago, Mafia members didn't testify. They couldn't. They wouldn't. Founded in 1930 by outlaw groups of Sicilian immigrants, the American Mafia was a secret society bound by tradition and culture that made cooperating with law enforcement anathema. Family and blood ties meant—and to a degree still mean—everything in Sicily.

Mafia members embraced the strict discipline and iron-clad code of secrecy that allowed the organization to survive and thrive for over a hundred years. Omerta, the concept on which the Mafia built its infamous code of silence, means "to be a man." And men, in the underworld culture of the mob and the twisted tradition of their criminal societies, didn't talk to authorities, didn't testify in court and didn't look to outsiders for help when things got tough. A man kept silent. A man took care of his problems. For a man, a jail term was a badge of honor, proof that he belonged.

That's the legacy—shined, polished and presented in its best possible light—that Vito Genovese, Lucky Luciano and their contemporaries brought to the American underworld of the 1930s. It is a somewhat glamorized version, to be sure, especially as portrayed by Hollywood and Mario Puzo. But stripped to its essence, the concepts of honor and loyalty were the major reasons the American mob survived for some 50 years despite the violence, despite the treachery and despite the greed that were always part of the package.

Early on, the American Mafia drew its membership from big-city ghettos, taking advantage of a time when options and opportunities were limited. Some first-generation Italian Americans, struggling to realize the American dream, saw the Mafia as the only avenue open to them. So they embraced the organization, made it their family. They swore a blood oath of allegiance to Cosa Nostra and its version of loyalty, honor and respect.

Fifty years later, on the surface at least, the same rules and traditions applied. Membership was restricted. Both parents had to be of Italian descent. Family ties were important. The son, nephew or brother of a "made" Mafia member usually had a leg up in cracking into the organization.

To be considered for membership in the mob, everyone, even a mob boss' son, had to "do some work." This rather innocuous phrase, informants have testified, is an underworld euphemism for taking part in a murder. It's not necessary, Gravano and others have explained, to actually shoot somebody. But you've got to play a role in a hit: set the victim up, drive the getaway car, help dispose of the body.

Some, like Gravano and Leonetti, seemed to have a particular flair for this end of the business. Other mobsters who now are cooperating have described it as a distasteful but necessary rite of passage. Nicholas "Nicky Crow" Caramandi, another Philadelphia mob informant, said, "Look, these were crazy things, but they had to be done." When he began cooperating, Caramandi admitted his involvement in four gangland killings. He served a little more than a year in prison after helping convict Scarfo, Leonetti and dozens of other local mob figures. Like Leonetti, he described murder as part of "the life." It was not, he has said again and again, a question of right or wrong. It was just a part of the underworld code. Murder was a part of the business. Everyone knew that going in.

By the 1980s, law enforcement had figured out how to attack the mob. The RICO law was in place. Prosecutors were able to establish the existence of a "criminal enterprise" and make an individual's involvement in that enterprise a racketeering offense. Multiple offenses, each carrying a 20-year prison sentence, meant long and hard jail time for those convicted. And sophisticated surveillance cameras and electronic listening devices made every meeting and every conversation a potential piece of evidence.

The new "men of honor," like Gravano, Leonetti and Michael Franzese, 44, a self-described "Yuppie don" of the Colombo crime family, found themselves caught in that new law enforcement reality. They were on the other side of the underworld's generation gap. They were not products of dirt-poor ghettos, struggling for a piece of the American pie. They were second-generation, middle-class and more at home in the comfortable suburbs of Long Island, Staten Island or Cherry Hill than in Brooklyn, Queens or South Philadelphia.

Franzese made millions running a Mafia scam defrauding the government of gasoline taxes, then hightailed it to southern California to make his mark in the movie industry. Leonetti used his Atlantic City cement company and assorted other mob gambits, like loan-sharking, bookmaking and extortion, to finance a comfortable lifestyle that included frequent trips to Florida and a luxurious condo at the Jersey Shore. Gravano, who liked to portray himself as an up-from-the-streets guy, lived with his wife and children in a stately, two-story brick home in an exclusive section of Staten Island, a home that featured stained glass windows and a backyard pool. He owned a construction company and was the point man on various mob kickback and labor racketeering schemes that generated millions of tax-free dollars each year for the Gambino organization and for himself. All benefited handsomely from involvement in the mob. None, however, was ready to pay what Mafiosi long considered the ultimate price for their lifestyle.

"You know going in that you could wind up dead or in jail," says one longtime mobster. "You accept that. These guys, they wanted it both ways."

Joe Valachi started it all in 1963. Lashing out at mob boss Vito Genovese, who he thought had ordered him killed, Valachi spilled his guts to a U.S. Senate subcommittee and a fascinated public, mentioning for the first time the term "Cosa Nostra" and detailing the workings of the secret society that ran the underworld. This was at a time when FBI chief J. Edgar Hoover was insisting that the Mafia didn't exist.

Times and law enforcement opinions have changed, but for nearly 25 years after Valachi's disclosures the government had little success in cracking the mob. A few others—Vinnie Teresa, Jimmy Frattiano, Angelo Lonardo—followed Valachi into the federal fold, but none had a substantial effect on the organization.

In the last decade, more than a dozen prominent mob members have flipped. Leonetti and Gravano head the list. From the Lucchese family there are former acting boss Alphonse "Little Al" D'Arco, underboss Anthony "Gas Pipe" Casso, and capos Anthony "Tumac" Accetturo and Peter Chiodo. From the Colombo family there are Franzese, former consigliere Carmine Sessa and the late Gregory Scarpa. From Philadelphia, in addition to Leonetti and Caramandi, there are Thomas "Tommy Del" DelGiorno, Lawrence "Yogi" Merlino, Eugene "Gino" Milano, George Fresolone—who worked undercover and taped his mob initiation ceremony for the New Jersey State Police—and, most recently, John Veasey and Rosario Bellocchi.

Each has his explanation. But most law enforcement experts believe the rash of defections is a direct result of the Americanization of the Mafia. Ronald Goldstock, former director of New York's Organized Crime Task Force, pointed to this phenomenon in prophetic testimony before a U.S. Senate subcommittee in 1988.

"When the mob was first formed in this country in 1930, it was made up of first-generation Italian Americans, either people that were born here or had come at an early age," he said. "The ties that bound members . . . together were those of honor, kinship and respect. We are now in the second and third generation of the mob, and the new members have grown up differently. They have values of their contemporaries. They are the sociological equivalent of Yuppies. Their values are not those of honor and respect; they are economic. The ties that bind them to the mob are financial in nature."

Frederick Martens, former director of the Pennsylvania Crime Commission, says much the same thing: "For the older guys, the Mafia was a way of life. For these young guys, it's a way to make money." Like any businessman, when things turn sour, they look to cut their losses.

Franzese claimed to have been born again when he rejected the mob. That and a beautiful young wife who needed him, he has said in a book about his life in the Mafia, were his reasons. Gravano and Leonetti say simply that they realized their lives of crime were a mistake. Leonetti, who has a teenage son, says his life was corrupted by the influence of his uncle, Nicodemo Scarfo, and he wants to make sure his boy doesn't follow in his footsteps.

Self-serving? Perhaps. Particularly when, between them, Gravano and Leonetti have admitted involvement in 29 murders. Indeed, some older Mafia figures who have turned have pointed to younger associates as the reason. D'Arco and Accetturo, both in their 60s, have said they were fed up with the younger generation of mobster who resorted to violence at the least provocation, who flaunted wealth and power and who had no sense of honor or loyalty.

"The problem," said Accetturo, sounding a lot like a conservative uncle, "is that these kids got too much, too soon. They were spoiled."

"This is the 'me generation' of the mob," said Louis Pichini, a former Organized Crime Strike Force lawyer who was the lead prosecutor in the 1988 racketeering trial that crippled the Scarfo organization. That case was built largely around the turncoat testimony of DelGiorno and Caramandi. The two Philadelphia mobsters testified at more than a dozen trials over a five-year period beginning in 1987 and helped prosecutors like Pichini convict more than 50 mob members and associates.

The dominoes that began falling in Philadelphia in the late 1980s set off a chain reaction elsewhere. Leonetti cooperated after being convicted in the 1988 case. Gravano agreed to cooperate because he feared Leonetti would finger him in a mob murder. A host of other New Yorkers, including Casso, who has been linked to 30 mob hits, turned to the government because of the potential testimony of Gravano.

They thought John Stanfa was the guy who was going to put it all back together. Born in Sicily and schooled in the "old ways," the stocky, barrel-chested former bricklayer emerged as reputed head of the Philadelphia-South

Jersey mob in 1991. According to several law enforcement and underworld sources, he was not the mob's first choice. Anthony "Tony Buck" Piccolo, Scarfo's cousin, had been serving as "acting boss" following Scarfo's racketeering conviction in 1988. In 1991, the Gambino and Genovese crime families in New York were said to be ready to make the appointment permanent. But Piccolo, a gentleman gambler who had ducked several earlier prosecutions and who eschewed the violent, flamboyant style that was the mark of his cousin, wanted no part of the top spot. Displaying the intelligence and foresight that had kept him out of jail for most of his life, Tony Buck looked beyond the power and prestige of being capo di capi in Philadelphia.

Piccolo, who was 68 in 1991, reportedly backed Stanfa, who had returned to Philadelphia after six years in federal prison and a brief exile in New York. It looked then like a smart move. Stanfa, just 49, had an impeccable crime family pedigree. Several law enforcement agencies listed him as a "made" member of the Sicilian Mafia before coming to the United States in 1964. Two brothers and several in-laws were Mafiosi in Sicily, according to federal and Italian law enforcement authorities. They, in turn, had ties to the Gambino crime family in New York. So did Stanfa. And, unlike many American mobsters, particularly those with Philadelphia connections, Stanfa had demonstrated his mettle. Convicted of perjury for lying to the federal grand jury investigating the 1980 murder of mob boss Angelo Bruno—he was Bruno's driver the night the mob boss was killed—Stanfa served more than six years in prison, rejecting all offers to cut a deal and testify for the government.

When Stanfa took over in 1991, law enforcement officers described him as the prototype of the new American mob boss. A Pennsylvania Crime Commission report that year warned of Stanfa's "national and international organized crime connections" and suggested that the "older values and traditions" of the Sicilian Mafia that he embodied would "regenerate an ailing American La Cosa Nostra." But by March 1994, after a bloody internal mob war that saw a series of gangland killings and a number of botched mob hits, Stanfa and most of his top associates were in jail.

It was hardly the dawning of a new era. It looked like more of the same: petty bickering, wanton violence and, at the first sign of an investigation, mobsters tripping over one another to cut a deal with the government.

"John had some people around him he shouldn't have," says one underworld source. "And he listened to some people who didn't know what they were talking about. . . . He knew what to do, but he just didn't know how to do it."

Despite his crime family bloodlines, Stanfa was an outsider to many young Philadelphia mob figures, particularly a group federal investigators say was headed by Joseph "Skinny Joey" Merlino. Stanfa's attempts to forge an alliance with Merlino, the young son of jailed Scarfo mob leader Salvatore "Chuckie" Merlino, failed. In a reflection of the "street gang" mentality that law enforcement sources say has permeated and weakened the American Mafia, Stanfa was perceived as the "new guy" trying to take over the corner. And, investigators say, Merlino and the young mob wannabes around him weren't going to let that happen. Discretion, once a hallmark of mobsters like Bruno and his New York contemporary, Carlo Gambino, had fallen out of fashion. The battle pitted brother against brother and made a mockery of the supposed Mafia code that innocent family members or friends would never be placed in jeopardy.

Joseph Ciancaglini Jr., Stanfa's crime family underboss, was wounded in a March 2, 1993, ambush that investigators and Stanfa loyalists attributed to Merlino and his top associate, Michael Ciancaglini, brother of the victim. Five months later, on August 5, 1993, Michael Ciancaglini was killed and Merlino wounded on a South Philadelphia street corner in a retaliatory attack that the feds allege was ordered by Stanfa. The Ciancaglini murder and the Merlino shooting, which Stanfa and the other defendants deny having taken part in, are part of the murder and murder conspiracy charges in the racketeering case that is about to begin. Less than a month after Ciancaglini's murder, Stanfa's son, Joe, who police said is not part of the crime family, was shot in the face in a brazen morning rush-hour ambush on the Schuylkill Expressway. John Stanfa, a front-seat passenger, escaped injury.

Less than three weeks later, Frank Baldino, a South Philadelphia bartender and neighborhood bon vivant, was gunned down outside the Melrose Diner, allegedly by Stanfa hit men. Baldino was targeted, police theorized, because he was a friend of Merlino and of Merlino's father. The Baldino murder also is part of the pending racketeering case. By the fall of 1993, the fractious and fratricidal Philadelphia mob was a shambles. The war had become a vendetta, according to conversations captured on FBI tapes, with Stanfa out to defend his honor and avenge a personal insult.

"I'm a greaseball?" Stanfa asked sarcastically in one conversation with alleged mob associate Sergio Battaglia. "I'll show who's a greaseball. . . . They think because we come from over there [Sicily], we're bigger fools than them."

In that conversation, recorded in April 1993, Stanfa talked about the way "Cosa Nostra" was supposed to be, summarizing the nearly seven years he served silently in prison: "OK, I went in like a man; I came out like a man."

In another recorded conversation, Stanfa was heard complaining in heavily accented English to two associates about the lack of "qualified" people in Philadelphia for membership in Cosa Nostra: "People should start to thinking what they're s'posed to be. No like a friend. They s'posed to be like a brother."

"It used to be that guys had to wait 20 or 30 years to get made," said Robert Buccino, a veteran mob investigator who heads the organized crime intelligence unit of the New Jersey Attorney General's Office. "They had to prove themselves. . . . Today, it's different. Today a boss is trying to put together an army, he lets anybody in."

Consider four men described as John Stanfa's young recruits, Sicilian-born Biagio Adornetto and Rosario Bellocchi and South Philadelphians Philip Colletti and John Veasey. All four were part of the organization Stanfa put together after taking over as boss. All four played a role in the violence Stanfa visited on the underworld. Now all four are preparing to testify for the government.

Adornetto scurried for FBI cover after Bellocchi tried to blow him away with a shotgun. The botched hit occurred on December 30, 1992, at La Veranda, a high-priced Delaware Avenue restaurant where Adornetto, after a falling out with Stanfa, was working as a pizza maker. That Bellocchi went on the hit with the wrong size shells in his shotgun—the gun subsequently misfired, enabling Adornetto to flee—was indicative of the way things would go over the next 18 months. An attempt three months later to kidnap a waiter friend of Adornetto who might know where the pizza maker was hiding was botched and the would-be kidnappers, Bellocchi and Gary Tavella, were arrested.

Veasey and Colletti pulled off the hit on Michael Ciancaglini and Joey Merlino in August, but left a trail that led police to their doorsteps. Veasey, according to several sources, was bragging about his role in the high-profile shootings within days of the August 5 ambush. Colletti was a suspect within hours of the shooting after committing the most basic of gangland blunders. The getaway car was found by police on fire several blocks from the scene of the Ciancaglini hit. The vehicle, a white Taurus with New Jersey tags, had been leased from a company in Hammonton to Philip Colletti.

The misadventures of Veasey and Colletti continued throughout their less than a year of involvement in the mob. Veasey has testified that pangs of conscience over the Ciancaglini murder brought him into the federal fold. Others say it was fear that he was going to be killed that prompted his epiphany. Colletti, a South Philadelphia-born plumber and longtime wannabe wiseguy, said he turned witness because he wanted to start fresh, make amends and protect his wife, their child and his parents, all of whom had been placed in jeopardy. Both men, say authorities, are examples of the "new breed" of mobster whose loyalty is primarily egocentric.

"You talk to some of these old-time Mafia members and they'll tell you, there's no philosophical core to these younger guys," said Robert Carroll, who spent 19 years prosecuting organized crime cases in New Jersey. "They get into it to make money and have a high lifestyle."

Veasey and Colletti agreed to work for the FBI, secretly recording conversations with associates. Veasey's undercover assignment ended abruptly on January 14, 1994, when Frank Martines allegedly pumped three bullets into his head during a "meeting" in a numbers house above a meat market on 7th Street in South Philadelphia. Despite the bullets in his skull, Veasey fought off two assailants, allegedly Martines and Vincent "Al Pajamas" Pagano. Veasey escaped, was hospitalized briefly and then placed in protective custody. The attempt on Veasey's life is part of the pending racketeering case. Stanfa and his codefendants deny any involvement. With Veasey cooperating, Colletti caved, negotiating a deal with the FBI in February 1994 and recording several conversations before disappearing into protective custody.

One recording, with reputed mob associate Salvatore Brunetti, was made outside Colletti's house in Glassboro on the afternoon of February 26, 1994. Brunetti, who was indicted with Stanfa and is part of a second group of eight defendants whose trial has not been scheduled, opted to talk outside despite the bitter cold for fear Colletti's house might be bugged. The recording started with Brunetti asking to borrow five dollars. Colletti responded by complaining that he was broke, in debt and that his mortgage company was foreclosing on his house.

"Sal, I'm f-ing broker than you are, man. F-ing old man hasn't given me anything. I'm not making dick. . . . I hate this s-. I got to stand out here. I can't even talk in my own house. I can't even enjoy a cup of coffee. This really sucks, Sal. This really sucks. This sucks, man. It sucks."

The fact that Colletti was cooperating became public shortly after the conversation. Like Veasey, he is now in the protective custody wing of an undisclosed prison. Colletti's family has been relocated and given new identities.

A month after the recorded conversation, on March 17, 1994, Stanfa and most of his top associates were arrested on charges in a 12-count racketeering indictment that has twice been expanded. Ten defendants in the case have pleaded guilty. Bellocchi, Veasey, Colletti and Thomas Rebbie are cooperating with authorities. So is Adornetto, who was not indicted.

Bellocchi's defection is perhaps the most embarrassing to Stanfa. He had been in jail for more than a year and was engaged to marry Stanfa's daughter, Sara. Born in Sicily, Bellocchi was supposed to be from the old school, dedicated to omerta and the ways of the Mafia. In May, like so many other wiseguys from downtown, he cut a deal with the feds and agreed to testify. In June, he pleaded guilty to a racketeering conspiracy charge, admitting his involvement in one murder, one attempted murder, three murder conspiracies and a kidnapping. The attempted murder was the botched hit on Biagio Adornetto.

Bellocchi also pleaded guilty to attempting to escape, this stemming from the time he ran from two agents in a restaurant in Ocean City, Maryland, while in protective custody. The admitted mob hit man was on the loose for about six hours before being caught. The authorities say Bellocchi ran on an impulse.

And then quickly realized he had nowhere to go.

The Last Lunch

MARCH 27, 1994

In certain circles they're calling it the "Last Supper."

In fact, it was lunch. A salad of calamari and scungilli soaked in olive oil. Some rigatoni. And then coffee, espresso and conversation—lots of conversation. This would have been Wednesday afternoon, March 16, at Pasta Blitz, a trendy Italian restaurant on the corner of 2nd and Walnut Streets.

Inside, seated at a large table by a second-floor window, according to sources, were reputed mob boss John Stanfa and several of his top associates, including ex-Philadelphia cop Ronald Previte. Outside, both the FBI and Philadelphia Police Department had the Pasta Blitz meeting under surveillance. Members of the police department's Organized Crime Intelligence Unit were taking photos. Aware of the surveillance, several men at the table smiled and waved. The cops waved back. It was a Philadelphia thing.

Most investigative sources believe the "business lunch" was arranged because Stanfa, 53, along with almost everyone else in mob and law enforcement circles, knew that a major racketeering indictment was coming soon; he needed to put his underworld affairs in order. Stanfa and about 20 others were arrested early the next morning. They have been in jail ever since—and may be for a long time to come. Investigators believe that at the luncheon and at several other meetings earlier this month, Stanfa discussed who would run the organization if he ended up in prison for any length of time.

"As long as there's money to be made, somebody's going to want to be in charge," said Philadelphia Police Chief Inspector Vincent DeBlasis, who, along with Captain Michael Lorenzo of the organized crime unit, warned last week of a new, and possibly bloody, power grab in the wake of the Stanfa arrest.

"There are a lot of ambitious people out there," added Lorenzo. "The last couple of takeovers have not been friendly, they've been hostile. . . . It's not a CEO position I would want."

Most investigative sources believe that Stanfa will try to maintain some control from behind bars. He could do this, they say, through his son, Joseph, 22, and through top associates like Previte, 50. But Previte, who was not arrested in the March 17 mob sweep, eschews the high-profile position that such an arrangement might entail, say several sources.

A 10-year veteran of the Philadelphia Police Department (he resigned in 1977), Previte surfaced about two years ago around Stanfa and is now said to be one of the mob boss' top money-makers. A resident of Hammonton, New Jersey, he operates primarily in the South Jersey area and is involved in gambling, loan sharking and extortion, investigators say.

"He's too smart to take over, even in an acting capacity," said one source. "He doesn't like all the attention."

What's more, Previte is under indictment in Camden County on extortion charges and is the target of federal and state investigations that could bring yet another round of mob indictments.

Two other names that have surfaced in the last week are William D'Elia, a reputed soldier in the Scranton-Wilkes Barre crime family once headed by the late Russell Bufalino, and Ralph Natale, a longtime Philadelphia mob figure scheduled to be released from prison next month. D'Elia, 47, is said to be Stanfa's choice as interim caretaker, even though he's an out-of-towner. Natale, 59, is perceived by Stanfa as a rival.

Police have spotted D'Elia meeting with Stanfa several times in the past. Low-key and business-oriented, he is described by state investigators as a "well-connected" mob figure who has strong ties to crime family leaders in Pittsburgh and New York as well as Philadelphia. His organized crime activities and associations have been detailed at length by the Pennsylvania Crime Commission. Reliable sources say that D'Elia was supposed to attend the Pasta Blitz meeting. He did not show up, those sources say, because he believed he was being followed by the FBI that day.

"He's the guy John wants to run the show," said one source familiar with current underworld maneuverings.

Natale, on the other hand, is a guy Stanfa wants dead. A onetime leader of the mob-dominated South Jersey bartenders union, Natale has been in jail for 14 years after convictions for arson, mail fraud and drug dealing. He is part of a group of established Philadelphia mob figures who consider the Sicilian-born Stanfa an interloper, investigators say. Stanfa was apparently well aware of Natale's views and pending prison release.

"As soon as he comes out, he has to die. . . . I don't even want to give him the time to breathe the air," Stanfa said of Natale in a conversation secretly taped in July by the FBI.

The death threat was detailed by federal prosecutor Joel Friedman during a bail hearing for Stanfa last week. Stanfa, like most of his codefendants, has been ordered held without bail. Natale, investigators say, would receive support from a young, local mob faction headed by Joseph "Skinny Joey" Merlino, who is serving three years for parole violation.

A gangland dispute between Stanfa and Merlino sparked a bloody mob war that raged for most of 1993 and left four mob figures dead and four others, including Merlino and Stanfa's son, Joseph, wounded. The indictment returned last week charged Stanfa and most of his top associates with conspiring to murder members of the Merlino faction and with the murders of Michael Ciancaglini and Frank Baldino, two Merlino associates.

None of the charges took Stanfa by surprise, according to his attorney, Edward Crisonino.

Crisonino said he discussed the pending case after being asked by Stanfa to stop by Pasta Blitz for lunch on March 16, the day before the arrests. Crisonino, who said he stayed for only part of the lunch meeting, said Stanfa wanted to surrender to federal authorities the next day to avoid the circus-like roundup staged by the FBI. Crisonino said he conveyed that offer to the U.S. Attorney's Office that afternoon but received no reply. Instead, he said, federal authorities "put on a show" the next day, arresting Stanfa and a dozen others in a series of early-morning raids on their homes, then parading the defendants before television cameras stationed outside the federal courthouse in Camden.

"It didn't have to happen that way," Crisonino said. But then not much has been going right for Stanfa and his top associates in recent weeks. Even Previte, who avoided indictment and arrest, had an unpleasant brush with the law—albeit as a victim—after the Pasta Blitz lunch. Police say that when he left the restaurant around 3:30 p.m., Previte and an associate walked to the spot near 2nd and Walnut Streets where he had parked his car. It was gone. The two-door, black 1987 Monte Carlo, registered to a friend who lives in the Hammonton area, was stolen while Previte, Stanfa and the others were eating.

"Nothing's sacred anymore," quipped one Philadelphia police official.

Previte immediately reported the theft to police, DeBlasis said.

"The vehicle has not been recovered," said the chief inspector.

Bartenders and Bad Guys

DECEMBER 30, 1990

They were Atlantic City's "goodfellas." And during the early part of the 1980s they turned the largest and most powerful union in the casino industry into a cash cow for the mob.

That is what federal authorities charged earlier this month in a lengthy civil racketeering suit aimed at the leaders of Atlantic City Bartenders Union Local 54 and mob boss Nicodemo "Little Nicky" Scarfo. In the feds' version of events, Scarfo, his crime family underboss and nephew, Philip Leonetti, and former union president Frank Gerace had the lead roles in a modern mob story of greed, corruption and murder. A union attorney termed it all "preposterous nonsense." Whatever the label, the prime source of information in the 66-page complaint is Leonetti, a confessed hit man and mob leader who has been cooperating with the federal government for the last 18 months.

"He's provided a road map of the intimate details of how Scarfo controlled that union from day one," said FBI Special Agent James Darcy, whose Atlantic County office spearheaded the Local 54 investigation.

Leonetti's story was detailed in a 21-page signed statement in which he explained how his uncle controlled Local 54. The affidavit is full of talk about "sit-downs," "murder contracts" and glimpses of the venal and petty nature of a petulant mob boss. What emerges is a picture of Scarfo as a treacherous and conniving mobster who bullied his way around Atlantic City and who thought nothing of using anyone—including his elderly mother—to advance the cause of La Cosa Nostra. Former Local 54 president Gerace, the federal authorities contend, was only too happy to go along.

Union officials last week, as they have repeatedly in the past, denied that Scarfo had any influence over their organization. Roy Silbert, who succeeded Gerace as president in 1984, called the stack of legal papers filed by the U.S. Attorney's Office "50 pounds of crap" and said the charges were without foundation. Gerace, forced to step down as president by the Casino Control Commission because of his suspected ties to Scarfo, now works for the union's international office. He could not be reached for comment but has consistently denied that he and his union were in Scarfo's pocket. The feds, however, contend that Scarfo's control of Local 54 was a classic example of the mob using organized labor to benefit organized crime.

Leonetti said that "no appointments, jobs, union cards or other favors were . . . made or given" without Scarfo's approval; that Scarfo received a monthly cash payoff—usually about $20,000—as his share of a scheme to siphon money out of the union's welfare fund, and that threats of violence and murder were used to maintain mob control of the 22,000-member labor organization. He also described another, almost trivial, type of labor racketeering. Scarfo, he said, frequently used the union's muscle to intimidate local bar and restaurant owners who were required to give him free meals and drinks or cash in exchange for the promise that Local 54 would not organize their workers.

Leonetti said there was one Atlantic City restaurant where Scarfo and anyone who was with him always ate for free. Several other restaurant owners, he said, made weekly or monthly payments to the mob boss. And when Scarfo wanted to "harass" the owner of a local bar that he felt had slighted him, Leonetti said, he told Gerace to picket the place. That alleged petty extortion is listed in the current litigation along with the alleged murders, beatings and threats used by the mob to secure a chunk of the union's multimillion-dollar treasury. A free meal or a $20,000 payoff, a picket line or a bullet in the head—it was all, say the feds, part of Scarfo's operation.

"GREEDY GUY"

"He was a very greedy guy," said a former mob associate who also is cooperating with authorities. And he built a reputation as a man who would go to almost any length, and do almost anything, to obtain what he wanted. In 1977, what Scarfo wanted was Local 54.

He had set his sights on the union, Phil Leonetti noted, shortly after voters in New Jersey approved the casino gambling referendum. Scarfo realized that the union was positioned to become the largest and wealthiest in the city, Leonetti said. He decided then that he wanted a piece of that action and in 1977 sent Leonetti and another mobster, Nicholas "Nick the Blade" Virgilio, to see Frank Gerace. Scarfo referred to Gerace as "Percy," Leonetti pointed out, because Frank had once lived on Percy Street in South Philadelphia. Scarfo, who lived in the same neighborhood, knew Gerace from those days. He also capitalized on the friendship between Gerace's mother, Lillian, and his own mother, Catherine.

SET UP MEETINGS

After striking a deal to cooperate with the mob boss in 1977, Leonetti said, Gerace met with Scarfo at least once a month to discuss union business and to take Scarfo "his end" from the welfare-fund embezzlement scheme. The mobster and the union boss used to meet at Lillian Gerace's Atlantic City home on Mississippi Avenue. But Scarfo, concerned about constant law enforcement surveillance, persuaded Gerace to have his mother move into the Georgia Avenue apartment house owned by Scarfo's mother. Scarfo also lived in that building.

"Scarfo said that if Lillian Gerace lived in the same building as Catherine Scarfo, he and Frank Gerace could meet without being seen together," Leonetti said. "Scarfo and Gerace could set up meetings through their mothers, without speaking to each other on the telephone, and Scarfo could enter Lillian Gerace's apartment to meet with Frank Gerace through the rear of Catherine Scarfo's apartment."

Lillian Gerace moved to the Georgia Avenue apartment, Leonetti said, thus facilitating the monthly meetings between Scarfo and Gerace. At that same time, he said, Scarfo was engaged in a vicious struggle to fend off attempts by Philadelphia mob boss Angelo Bruno and his associates to take over Local 54.

An angry Bruno had ordered Scarfo, then a mob soldier in Bruno's crime family, to a sit-down in 1978 at which he told Scarfo to stay away from the union. Scarfo, Leonetti said, ignored the order even though he knew Bruno might have him killed as a result. A few months later, Leonetti claimed, Scarfo spotted a known Bruno hit man lurking in the neighborhood near his apartment house. Scarfo threatened to kill the hit man, and, in preparation for a possible mob war, ordered Leonetti to build a large, cement wall behind the apartment building.

Scarfo ultimately got the upper hand in the struggle for Local 54. Bruno was killed in March 1980 in a plot hatched by several Newark-area mob figures. And in December of that year, Bruno's proxy in the battle for the union, Philadelphia Roofers' Union boss John McCullough, was killed on Scarfo's orders, according to federal authorities. By that point, Leonetti said, Scarfo had already succeeded in placing Robert Lumio, a trusted associate and soon-to-be initiated mob member, as secretary-treasurer of Local 54. Lumio, who died of cancer in 1981, is one of nearly a dozen mobsters whose links to the union are outlined in the federal suit. Scarfo, authorities say, has controlled the union ever since, continuing his domination even though he has been imprisoned since 1987 on racketeering, conspiracy and murder charges.

Not surprisingly, Leonetti's account of the mob and the union was ridiculed by both the union and defense attorneys whose clients' names appeared in the civil suit. Typical was the comment of Jeffrey Miller, whose client, Philadelphia disc jockey Jerry Blavat, was identified as a Scarfo shakedown victim. Leonetti said that Blavat paid $500 a week to keep Local 54 from unionizing Memories, a Margate nightclub and restaurant he owns. Miller said it never happened.

"It's hogwash," he said and then compared Leonetti's story, not to a popular movie, but to a current Broadway play. "There are two great fairy tales today. One is Peter Pan, and the other is Phil Leonetti. The kids are buying Peter Pan," Miller said, "and the feds are buying Leonetti."

Mob wife Brenda Colletti

GUYS AND THEIR DOLLS

I have been married to the same woman for 38 years. We have two grown daughters. I love women. I appreciate women. I find women fascinating—certainly more fascinating than men.

But I don't understand women.

What follows are several stories about women who at one point or another got involved with a wiseguy.

How and why make up one part of the story. To what degree these women understood what was going on is another.

I guess the best, and perhaps only, thing that can be said is that love made them do it.

Married to the Mob

JUNE 29, 1997

T here's a classic scene in the movie *Goodfellas* where Henry Hill's wife asks her mobster husband for some shopping money.

"How much do you need?" asks Hill, the ever-hustling, wannabe wiseguy.

"This much," says the wife, holding her thumb and forefinger about three inches apart. Hill then reaches into his pocket and hands her a wad of cash.

The scene always gets a laugh. For many people it captures the essence of what it is to be a mob wife: money, lots of money. And a nice house. A brand-new car. No bills. And a closet full of clothes. It's the underworld version of the American dream.

How much do you need? Maria Martines laughs at the thought of it. She's been there. It's not like the movies.

"I wish it was," she says with a sad smile.

Maria Martines, 42, is the wife of the former underboss of the Philadelphia mob. Her husband, Frank Martines, 43, is serving a life sentence at a maximum-security prison in Florence, Colorado, after being convicted along with mob boss John Stanfa and six others on racketeering charges that included murder, murder conspiracy, extortion and obstruction of justice.

In the long, storied history of mob prosecutions here and across the country, there has never been anything quite like the Stanfa trial that took place on the 17th floor of the federal courthouse at 6th and Arch Streets back in the fall of 1995. The trial was an organized crime classic. The testimony priceless. The witness list a string of mob informants, including three admitted hit men who looked and sounded like characters from a Quentin Tarantino movie. Who could forget the would-be assassin who botched his assignment because he had the wrong size shells in his shotgun? Or the hit man who used a car leased in his own name as his getaway vehicle? Or his accomplice who set himself on fire while torching that very getaway car?

"Goodfellas?" said a lawyer as the case unfolded. "This was dumbfellas."

But there was more. Two years of tapes, for example. Secretly recorded conversations picked up by FBI bugs. Unguarded mob talk in which Stanfa and others talked about all manner of murder and mayhem in between philosophical ramblings including the signature phrase of the case: "Goodfellas don't sue goodfellas . . . goodfellas kill goodfellas."

First Maria Martines lived through it all with Frank. Then she had to sit through it as prosecutors, with witnesses and tapes, recreated four chaotic years for the jury.

"I don't know how I did it," she now says of the 10-week trial. "If it wasn't for the Valium, I probably wouldn't have made it."

Now, without the aid of any sedatives, Martines is trying to pick up the pieces of her life, trying to come to grips with the fact that her husband of more than 20 years, a man she first kissed when she was just 11, may never get out of prison. She is equally concerned about the future of their 21-year-old son, Frank Jr., who, she admits, has not coped well. And she is unsure what, if anything, she, a high school dropout, can do to make it on her own. She never had to earn her own way; she was always Frank's wife. Clean the house, cook the meals, wash the clothes. He always provided. Now he is gone.

Frank Martines' home for the last 10 months has been the new maximum-security prison they call the Alcatraz of the Rockies. Maria Martines has been able to visit him there twice. In between trips she has sold off most of the things of value to have money to live on, has cashed in her husband's life insurance policy, has run up credit card debts to the breaking point, has had her phone temporarily disconnected, has received a notice that her electricity is about to be turned off, and has fallen months behind in the mortgage payments on their house in Yardley, which she is now trying to sell.

"Sometimes I think this is all a dream and I'm gonna wake up and everything will be the way it was," Martines says.

Sometimes she cries. And sometimes she just shakes her head in disbelief and anger.

In a series of interviews, Martines agreed to talk about her life. What emerged was an often candid, occasionally guarded look at the underworld through the eyes of a young girl, a woman, a wife and a mother. At times naive, at times cold and cynical, Martines doesn't pretend to have all the answers.

Was her husband, as the feds allege, a gangster? Her response is subtle, indirect, never quite on target. The closest she comes to responding is when she lambastes John Stanfa for abandoning "his men," for refusing to provide the money to mount a decent defense against the racketeering charges, for blocking an attempt to plead out before the start of the trial in exchange for lighter sentences and for hoarding the piles of cash he generated but which, she insists, her husband rarely got a piece of.

"He was very nice to me," Martines says of the bull-necked mob boss, "until I started asking about money. Then it was, forget about it. He only cared about himself. My husband ended up giving his life for this man. And for what?"

She says it is agony to think about her husband's life-without-parole sentence. At his age, he could end up spending more time in prison than any other defendant in the case. But there is a part of her that is bitter and angry at him for what has happened, for the life he has left her and their son, for the bills that can't be paid, for the neighbors and former friends who no longer talk to her, for the food stamps she now uses at the supermarket, for the loneliness that is so much a part of every day. Finally, she offers a cynical take on a legal system that allowed admitted murderers, Stanfa hit men in fact, to cut deals, to cooperate, to testify and to eventually walk out of prison as free men.

"They let them get away with murder," she says. "Where's the justice in that?"

Forget the movies, she says. Forget the glamour and the hype.

"Think about it," says Martines. "Look at what's happened. If anybody asked me now about this, I'd say this is no way to live, this is nothing to get involved in. Because you're going to end up in one of two places, jail or the cemetery."

Or, in the case of the wife of a wiseguy, widowed or waiting. Maria Martines was nearly a widow twice. Now she waits.

It happens over time, in small increments. It's not like your husband wakes up one morning and says, "I think I'm gonna go out today and join the Mafia." Maybe he starts out taking some bets or lending some money. Maybe he knows a guy who knows a guy and before long he's selling stuff out of the trunk of his car, good stuff at real good prices. So he earns an extra $200 here and $400 more there, and before you know it there's a steady cash flow to supplement the income from his regular job. It's subtle. Almost a seduction. But if it helps pay the bills and covers a Friday night out at a restaurant, who's going to complain?

That's not to say there isn't an underworld membership process. Frank Martines eventually hit all the rungs as he climbed the ladder, reaching, according to the authorities, the rank of acting underboss, the number-two man in the organization. If you grew up in South Philadelphia in the 1950s and 1960s, as Maria and Frank Martines did, it was easy to see the positives and ignore the negatives.

"Look, I'm not saying Frank was an angel," Maria Martines says. "He did some things he shouldn't have done, things I know he regrets, things that if he had to do over—no way. But life in prison? And guys who killed people, who pulled the trigger, are gonna go free because they testified? Because they ratted?"

Maria Tenuto Martines comes from 9th and Morris. Thirteen years of living in a white-bread suburban development in Yardley hasn't changed that. Her attitude, her syntax, her style are still very much South Philadelphia. She makes no attempt to hide it. The rowhouse where she grew up was around the corner from St. Nicholas of Tolentine, her parish church. St. Maria Goretti, the all-girls Catholic high school she attended before dropping out in the 11th grade—"I was going to go to hair-dressing school"—was two blocks away.

The house had been in her family for years. It was her grandmother's home and then her mother's and then, after she and Frank got married, it was theirs. Up on the corner there was a bar where some of the goodfellas used to hang out. Across from the bar was a pool hall, the local meeting spot for most of the guys who lived in the area. Sometimes they would hang around outside, singing a cappella, their voices echoing down the block. At nights, especially in the summer, people would be sitting out on their steps until the early hours of the morning, talking, laughing, socializing. For a young girl surrounded by family—an aunt lived across the street, an uncle was just up the block—there always seemed to be something to do, even when there was nothing to do.

"I loved living there," Martines says. "It was like a big block party every night. I wish I could go back."

Even the extraordinary seemed ordinary.

Her mother and father were divorced when she was 10. But that just gave her two houses to live in instead of one. At first, her father stayed in the rowhouse on Morris Street. He drove a truck for a living, but his real passion was gambling. Soon he was running a big poker game in his dining room. Sometimes it would go from one day into the next. A woman whose husband was one of the regular gamblers would come in and cook. The kitchen stove would be covered with big pots of gravy, spaghetti, meatballs. And the dining room table would be covered with money and poker chips.

"My God, so much money," Martines says. "Two piles. One was the house cut. The other was the pot. So much money."

And never any trouble. Except for that one time when someone drove by and blasted the door of the house with a shotgun while the game was in progress.

"Me and my girlfriend were sitting outside, right over there," Martines says, pointing to a house two doors from where she used to live. "We see this car and then this big, long gun. We couldn't believe it. We ducked behind the steps."

Later her father told her it was just a warning. The brother of one of the regular players was upset about all the money he was losing. On another occasion, she remembers, cops raided the game. But her father had gotten a few minutes' warning, and he, his customers and Evelyn, the cook, were heading out the back door while the police were banging on the front door.

"The only problem was Evelyn was so heavy, she couldn't get over the fence that separated our yard from our neighbor's," Martines recalls while giving a tour of the old neighborhood one sunny afternoon. "They hadda lift her up and over and she fell and broke her leg."

Everyone from the game, including the injured cook, scrambled into the next-door neighbor's house. When the cops knocked on that door, the woman who lived there stonewalled them.

"'Yes, whadda youse want?' she says in this real polite voice," Martines recalls. "'Nobody's here.' And she wouldn't let them in her house."

That's the way Martines remembers life in her old neighborhood. People looked out for one another. If you needed to borrow money and the bank turned you down, there was somebody in the bar or the poolroom who could help you out. If you wanted to place a bet on a ballgame or play a number, you headed for the corner.

"To me, this was an everyday way of life," she says. "It didn't faze me. Being born and raised in that neighborhood with all the gangsters on the corner, you know, you don't even think twice about it. It's just a way of life. . . . One woman on the street, her husband died. She took over his number writing. She raised four daughters that way. By herself."

Frank Martines grew up around the corner on Fernon Street. When she was 11, Maria Martines said, he took her for a walk up Moore Street over by Goretti.

"That's where all the kids used to go to kiss," she said. "Frank always says when he kissed me that night he knew we were gonna be married."

But for the longest time, they were just friends. Shortly before Maria turned 19, they started dating. In December 1974, they ran away and got married by a justice of the peace. On March 8, 1975, the day after her 20th birthday, they got married again. In church. A big reception followed in a catering hall on Passyunk Avenue. All Maria Martines remembers about it is the fight.

"No kids, right," she explains. "We had so many guests that we didn't invite any kids. We walk in the hall and the first people I see are one of Frankie's aunts and all her little kids. Naturally, all night long my relatives are coming up to me asking how come those kids were there and they couldn't bring their kids. What a night. A great way to start, right?"

They moved into the house where Maria grew up. Things were good and bad.

"We were too young," she says. "We would fight. I would scream. He would holler and break things. Later, he really mellowed out. I don't even think he realized how bad a temper he had. I look at my son now, I see the same thing. Sometimes I wonder how we made it."

The irony is that there was more money back then, early in their marriage, than later, when the feds alleged that Frank Martines had taken over the number-two spot in the mob and had access to—Maria Martines spits out the words sarcastically—"unlimited resources."

At the time they were married, Frank Martines worked as a carpenter for Amtrak. It was a good job. And on the side, he worked for Mario "Sonny" Riccobene, the half-brother of prominent South Philadelphia mobster Harry "The Hump" Riccobene. Sonny Riccobene (who was later killed gangland style) used to hang around Frank and Maria's corner, 9th and Morris. That's how Frank became one of his associates. Frank had a little money on the street—loan-shark money—and he would help Riccobene run Monte Carlo games, gambling nights for "charitable" organizations in which the mob's cut was often bigger than the house's.

"Frank was a young guy, but they liked him," Maria Martines explains. "Frank always seemed to get along better with older people. All his life, he was like that. I think, 'cause he had a lot of responsibilities when he was young."

At the time, she says, she had no idea how lucrative the loan-sharking business was. A little money could quickly become a lot of money. Then one day Frank Jr., who was about four at the time, came home from visiting his grandparents around the corner on Fernon Street and said to her, "Mommy, Daddy has all this money hidden over Grandmom's house."

"He ratted him out," Maria Martines says with a laugh.

"'Oh, yeah?' I say. See, we were living in my mother's house on Morris Street. She had moved to Jersey after the divorce. My father had remarried. And we were waiting to get enough money together to buy it. Frank kept telling me once we bought it, he was gonna fix it up. But he kept saying we needed more money. Then I find out about this money.

"Right after that we bought the house and Frank fixed it all up. Him and my father-in-law. They gutted the place. He makes it into something out of *Better Homes and Gardens.* Unbelievable."

Gambling and loan-sharking, that was what the mob meant to her. Then, on Friday morning, October 14, 1983, Frank Martines got shot. And for the first time, Maria Martines saw the other side, the darker side, of the Mafia.

For years the Philadelphia mob had operated in the shadows. It was a circumspect organization that resorted to violence only as a last resort. Angelo Bruno, the city's longtime Mafia boss, was a character right out of *The Godfather,* a Mafia diplomat with a national reputation. But after Bruno was blown away in March 1980, the crime family began to spin out of control. When Frank Martines was gunned down in 1983, the mob was in the midst of its *Goodfellas* period, headed by Nicodemo "Little Nicky" Scarfo, one of the most violent Mafia bosses in America. Eleven years later, when Frank Martines was carted off to jail, the highly structured, make-money-not-headlines organization that Bruno had run so effectively for more than two decades was a crime family of misfits and miscreants. *Goodfellas* had become *Pulp Fiction.*

"Frank was just a two-bit loan shark," Maria Martines says in recalling the day in 1983 when her husband was shot and nearly killed for being a Riccobene ally when Scarfo wanted total control. "He was still working as a carpenter for Amtrak. He would leave for work early in the morning, before seven."

On that morning, seconds it seemed after her husband kissed her goodbye, Maria Martines heard what sounded like firecrackers. Still lying in bed, she dismissed the noise as a fan belatedly saluting the Phillies, who had won a playoff game the night before. Then she heard Frank Jr. scream, and she bolted upright and headed for the bedroom window that looked out onto Morris Street.

"Ma, Ma, Daddy's shot, Daddy's shot!" Frankie Jr. was screaming.

Outside, on the pavement in front of the house, was Frank Martines, leaning up against a car, covered in blood and hollering for his wife to call the police. Martines had been shot a half-dozen times; the most serious wounds were in the chest and groin. He was rushed to a hospital in critical condition. Then, while a mob war raged on the streets of South Philadelphia, he took his wife and son into hiding. For the better part of the next year they lived with friends in a condo in Center City, ducking in and out of their home on Morris Street while mobsters aligned with Scarfo battled it out with the Riccobene faction. A year later, with the mob war over and Scarfo clearly on top, Frank Martines got out of town, moving his wife and young son into a modern, two-story house in a subdivision in Yardley. He said it was a chance to start over, a chance to put the mob behind them and build a better life.

For the better part of eight years, Frank and Maria Martines tried to become suburbanites. But then a small construction company he had started foundered. Bill collectors started to hound him. And a deal to go into the food business and out of financial trouble fell apart. Maria Martines still has copies of the business proposal her husband put together. He was negotiating with a supermarket chain that was expanding in the Yardley area. He wanted to open an Italian specialty shop inside the market, stocked with high-quality items—pastas, olive oils, cheeses, lunch meats and precooked or ready-to-cook dinners.

"Frank thought, you know, there's a lot of pampered women up here," Maria Martines said. "And he thought, you have good food, already prepared, they'll buy it. Frank was really excited about this. And the guy at the supermarket strung him along for about a year. We were all gonna work there. Then the supermarket finished expanding and what do you think? They put their own specialty shop in there. They took the idea and did it themselves. Could you believe it? Frank was sick about it."

A few months later, Frank Martines was hanging at the Continental Imported Foods warehouse in Grays Ferry. The company was also in the Italian specialty foods business, supplying restaurants and stores throughout the Philadelphia area. But Martines' presence there, federal authorities would later charge, had little to do with pasta or provolone. Continental was owned and operated by Joseph and Sara Stanfa, the 20-something son and daughter of mob boss John Stanfa. The elder Stanfa, who had done nearly eight years in prison on a perjury rap linked to the 1980 Angelo Bruno murder, was running the mob from his office at the food warehouse, police said. Throughout 1992 and early 1993, law enforcement authorities watched as a steady stream of wiseguys and wannabes turned up there on a regular basis.

"At this point, I don't know anything about anything," Maria Martines said. "One day we're in the car and Frank says he wants to stop someplace to pick up, I forget, mineral water or pasta. Something. He pulls up in front of Continental. Now I'm thinking, what is this place? I had seen it on television. Geraldo Rivera had done this show."

Rivera, in standard ambush interview fashion, had stuck a microphone in Stanfa's face outside the Continental garage. With the camera rolling, the media hit man took on Philadelphia's top wiseguy. It was classic tabloid television: lots of form, very little substance. Now Maria Martines wanted to know what her husband was doing there.

"I told him, 'You think I'm putting up with this bull again, pal, you're crazy.' I said one shooting was enough. At one point, I even told him to get out of the house, go get an apartment, go live somewhere else, 'cause I'm not dealing with this. And he's saying, 'You're crazy.'"

That was the way it went, off and on, for 18 months. Maria Martines would complain. Frank Martines would explain. It was all legitimate, he would say. Stanfa was from the old school, like Bruno. This was about making money, nothing else. Be reasonable. Be happy. Most of all, be quiet.

"I would complain, I would holler," Maria Martines said. "But he just kept denying it. . . . I don't know. . . . I guess you want to believe."

Now their social life started to revolve around a new set of friends. Stanfa would host dinners and barbecues at his house in Medford, New Jersey. There would be dinners at nice restaurants, trips to the Shore. Stanfa always treated her well. So did his wife, Lena, and their children, Sara, Joe and Maria, all of whom lived at home.

"It was a strict Italian family," Maria Martines said. "You know how, with this generation, you answer your husband back, you fight, you don't care? With them, he spoke, that was it.

"After I got to know her better, Lena got me on the side one time and said, 'This guy,' meaning her husband, 'I had eight years of peace,' meaning the time he was in jail in the 1980s. I used to feel sorry for her."

Then the bullets started flying again.

It began in March 1993, when Stanfa's underboss, Joseph Ciancaglini Jr., was shot and wounded. And it continued virtually unabated until Stanfa and most of his top associates were indicted and arrested a year later. This time it was the Stanfa organization pitted against a rival faction of young wiseguys believed to be headed by Joseph "Skinny Joey" Merlino and Ciancaglini's younger brother, Michael. According to court testimony and evidence introduced at the trials that followed, it was open warfare. Hit teams from both sides cruised the streets looking to kill one another. Six murders and more than a dozen attempted murders turned the South Philadelphia underworld into a killing field. Frank Martines, witnesses later testified, helped plan and coordinate much of the action from the Stanfa side, serving as acting underboss in place of the wounded and disabled Joe Ciancaglini. At home, however, he continued to deny that he was involved.

"I started in with him again," Maria Martines says. "It was nothing but battles. So what he would do, he would try to make it real stable here at home so that this way I wouldn't think too much. He wouldn't stay out at night or nothing like that. Forget it. He would be pacifying me. He'd go food shopping with me. He'd go to the mall with me. He helped me hang the clothes outside. He mopped the floor. This big supposed gangster."

That's how it played out, through the fall and into the winter of 1993. By the end of the year, Stanfa appeared to have the upper hand in the mob war. Merlino had been hustled off to jail for a parole violation. Mike Ciancaglini, his top associate, had been killed. Several others had gone into hiding. Early in December Stanfa hosted a big combination birthday-Christmas party at a restaurant in Northeast Philadelphia. The mob boss, who was born on December 11, celebrated his 53rd birthday in fine fashion, with the top members of his crime family toasting his health and good fortune. He appeared to be on top of the world.

A month later, the party was over.

For Maria Martines the end came with a knock on her door late on Friday night, January 14, 1994. It was Sal Brunetti, Frank's cousin, acting nervous, signaling her not to say anything, indicating that the house might be bugged. He said she had to come with him. She knew right away that her husband was in trouble. They drove to Brunetti's house in South Jersey. There, in a back room, she saw Frank lying on a bed, his face wrapped in a towel. The towel was soaked in blood. When she lifted it, Maria Martines saw a long, deep knife wound running from just under her husband's left eye all the way down the side of his face, nearly to his jaw line.

There are, of course, two versions of what happened that night. John Veasey, an admitted Stanfa hit man, testified for the government that he was lured to an apartment on 7th Street in South Philadelphia by Frank Martines and Vincent "Al Pajamas" Pagano, another Stanfa crime family member. There, he said, Martines shot him twice in the back of the head and once in the chest. Veasey had begun cooperating with the FBI a few days earlier and figured he was targeted for that reason. Despite his bullet wounds, Veasey said, he fought his way out of the apartment, grabbing a knife from Pagano during a life-and-death struggle and slashing Martines in the face. Frank Martines' version, as retold by his wife, is that Veasey— paranoid and perhaps hopped up on drugs—came at him and Pagano with the knife and that the shooting was in self-defense.

"Veasey turned the whole story around," Maria Martines said.

A jury, perhaps noting the two bullet wounds in the back of Veasey's head, chose to believe the mob informant.

For two days, Maria Martines nursed her husband while they hid out in South Jersey. Rumors abounded that Veasey, making threats from his hospital bed, planned to have her and Frank Jr. killed in retaliation. All that weekend, police and FBI searched for Frank Martines and Pagano. They went to the house in Yardley and fanned out all over South Philadelphia. Every time Maria Martines called home to check her answering machine, there would be the voice of a detective or an FBI agent telling Frank to surrender. On Monday, January 17, 1994, he and Pagano did just that.

"We got a lawyer and he brought them in," Maria Martines said.

The last time she saw her husband as a free man was when he waved from the back seat of a car outside the lawyer's Center City office on his way to the Police Administration Building. It has been 18 months since her husband was convicted; nearly a year since he was formally sentenced. In that time, Maria Martines has tried to make sense of it all, to understand how and why it all happened and to plan what she is going to do next. Two of her best friends now are Marie Piccolo and Beverly Sparacio, wives of Anthony Piccolo and Salvatore Sparacio, also convicted in the Stanfa case. They understand, better than anyone else, what she is going through, she said. Many friends of hers and Frank's are no longer around.

"It's amazing. People see the movies and they think you have this stash of money somewhere, that things are taken care of. For the first couple months after Frank got arrested, I was still getting his paycheck from Stanfa, $500. After that, nothing. Nothing. He wouldn't help anyone. He was only for himself. My husband gave up his life for that guy. I don't get it. This loyalty bull. I just don't get it."

Maria Martines says that even her husband, in his more introspective moments, admits she was right. "He says he should have listened to me," she adds, laughing sadly. But that time, she knows, is long past. The way it unfolded, there were only two possibilities. She could have been a widow.

Instead, she waits.

They Seemed Like a Nice Couple

MAY 1, 1994

S he was a former go-go dancer who had worked in an adult bookstore closed for promoting prostitution. He was an unemployed plumber who became a hit man for the mob. Yet until they disappeared into protective custody earlier this year, Brenda and Philip Colletti appeared to be a typical suburban couple, struggling to make ends meet and to raise a young son, Paulie, now four.

They lived in the Chestnut Ridge section of Glassboro, New Jersey, a community of lawns and swing sets, patios and barbecue grills less than a mile from the campus of Rowan College. Fluorescent "tot finder" decals dot many of the second-floor bedroom windows in the neighborhood. Station wagons, minivans and mid-priced sedans are parked by the curbs and in the driveways.

"They were good neighbors, they really were," said Marie Wyman, a soft-spoken widow who lived next door and said Brenda Colletti often helped her with her weeding and gardening. "There's not much else I can say about them."

Information from court records, testimony and investigative documents offers a different picture of the young couple from the one they presented to their neighbors. While they lived in suburbia, Philip and Brenda Colletti were involved with a bloody underworld power struggle that left bodies strewn across South Philadelphia.

Today the Collettis are government witnesses. He is in the protective-custody wing of an undisclosed federal prison. She is living in hiding with their son under the protection of the FBI. Both have testified before a federal grand jury that on March 17 returned racketeering indictments against reputed mob boss John Stanfa and most of his top associates. Both are expected to take the witness stand when the case goes to trial later this year or early in 1995. Their story, which is emerging along with bits and pieces of the evidence in the racketeering case, is a South Jersey version of *Married to the Mob*, with a harder, more violent edge.

Philip Colletti, 34, pleaded guilty on Monday to a racketeering-conspiracy charge. He is facing a potential life prison sentence after admitting his involvement in a series of mob murder conspiracies. He has told authorities that he was the trigger man in the August 5 killing of Michael Ciancaglini, a Stanfa crime family rival gunned down near 6th and Catharine Streets in South Philadelphia. He also has acknowledged that he was a member of one of Stanfa's extortion crews and that he was involved in planning the slayings of several other reputed mobsters, including Joseph

"Skinny Joey" Merlino, who federal authorities say headed a renegade faction of the mob balking at Stanfa's leadership.

Brenda Colletti, 27, is not formally charged with any crime. Authorities say she has been implicated in the struggle between the Stanfa and Merlino factions and in a bizarre plot, which was never carried out, to slip cyanide into the drinks of Merlino and several associates at a Philadelphia nightclub they frequented.

After a hearing in U.S. District Court in Philadelphia on Monday, Colletti was permitted to talk briefly with his wife, who had been sitting in the back of the courtroom. Tall and thin with neatly cropped, thick black hair, Philip Colletti towered over his wife as they hugged, her long, reddish-blond hair resting on his chest. They kissed and then she began to cry. But her husband stroked her hair and cheek and smiled.

"Don't worry about it," he said. "It's gonna be all right."

Philip Colletti, according to investigative sources and court testimony, was brought into the mob racketeering conspiracy about two years ago by Raymond Esposito, a Stanfa crime family soldier who lived in Gibbstown, not far from Glassboro. Evidence and testimony offered at a series of bail hearings after the March 17 indictments have offered a glimpse of the underworld turbulence raging at that time and the plots and counterplots—many bungled and some seemingly outlandish—set up by the Stanfa and Merlino groups. They included ambushes that fizzled, car bombs that failed to go off, drive-by shootings that missed their targets and one point-blank shotgun assassination attempt that was botched when the weapon failed to discharge.

"Some of this is so crazy it would be funny if people weren't getting killed," said Richard Zappile, chief inspector for the Philadelphia Police Department.

One ambush that did work was the August 5 shooting of Michael Ciancaglini and Joey Merlino. Colletti and John Veasey, who also is cooperating with federal authorities, were the shooters that day. For four days they had staked out a clubhouse near 6th and Catharine Streets where Ciancaglini and Merlino hung out. Ciancaglini and Merlino were gunned down early in the afternoon after they emerged from the clubhouse and started to walk west on 6th Street. At that point, a white Ford Taurus pulled up and two men jumped out and opened fire. Ciancaglini was hit once in the chest and died on the sidewalk. Merlino, who turned to run, was wounded in the buttocks.

A short time later, police found the Taurus abandoned and on fire near 19th and Johnson Streets in South Philadelphia. The car had been leased from an auto dealership in Hammonton, New Jersey, owned by the brother of a Stanfa associate. The lease was in the name of Philip P. Colletti. The car, police said, had been reported stolen the night before from in front of his home on Franklin Road in Glassboro. From that point, investigators say, Colletti was a suspect in the Ciancaglini hit. It would be months before the case was broken, however, and in that time Colletti continued to work for the Stanfa organization. By September his wife was also part of the bloody machinations, according to authorities.

At a bail hearing in March for Salvatore Brunetti, another Stanfa associate indicted in the racketeering case, federal prosecutor Barry Gross outlined several other mob plots believed to have been launched during the Stanfa-Merlino underworld battle. These included, Gross said, a suggestion by Brunetti that Brenda Colletti get "dressed up and go down to one of the nightclubs Merlino frequents" and slip cyanide into his drink and the drinks of any of his associates who happened to be with him. Gross said Brunetti, who worked in a laboratory, delivered the cyanide to Colletti, but she did not carry out the contract.

Philip and Brenda Colletti moved to Glassboro from Clementon about two and a half years ago and set about fixing up the red-brick and blue-shingle-sided house on Franklin Road. At the time, Philip Colletti was working as a $25,000-a-year plumber and steamfitter at Camden County's Lakeland government complex. Brenda Colletti, a onetime baker at a Dunkin' Donuts in Turnersville, had recently lost her job at the Adult House, an X-rated bookstore in Woodlynne that featured peep shows, nude dancers and sexually oriented magazines and paraphernalia.

The store, closed in May 1991 after a vice raid, was owned by Frank Crump, an underworld figure now in jail on federal drug-trafficking charges. Crump is also awaiting trial in Camden County on charges of promoting prostitution after being busted, along with several of the store's employees. Brenda Colletti, who prosecutors say was a dancer at the Adult House, was not charged in the raid, but was arrested at the same time when detectives found a pistol in her purse. A weapons-offense charge against her is pending in Camden County.

Philip Colletti left a criminal trail when he disappeared into protective custody. In addition to the racketeering conspiracy, there is a gun charge pending against him in Gloucester County and a 1981 murder conviction in Philadelphia. Colletti was arrested in September, a month after the Ciancaglini slaying, after he was stopped by state police on Route 55 in Deptford. The trooper, making what authorities say was a routine traffic stop, discovered a Browning 9-mm semiautomatic pistol and hollow-nose bullets in Colletti's car. He was charged with weapons offenses, including possession of a weapon by a felon. This was a reference to his 1981 conviction in Philadelphia for murder.

Colletti, who was born and raised in South Philadelphia, was sentenced to two years in prison after being convicted of shooting a man in a dispute over a parking space. He served less than a year and later, sources say, used the conviction and relatively light prison sentence as bragging points with his underworld friends.

"He thought he was Al Capone 'cause he got away with murder one time," said a source familiar with the investigation, who asked not to be identified. "He wanted to be a wiseguy."

Philip Colletti's life in the mob began to unravel late last year when John Veasey, the other trigger man in the Ciancaglini hit, approached the FBI. By January, when Veasey's role as an informant became public, Colletti had a problem. Shortly after that, sources say, he and his wife agreed to testify before the grand jury and become government informants.

Their life in suburbia also was coming undone. They were more than a year behind on mortgage payments, and the bank holding the note on their house had won a default judgment. Colletti, who had quit his job with Camden County in January 1992, collected a $5,500 disability payment for injuries on the job, but that hardly made a dent in the bills he and his wife had accumulated. More than $10,000 in interest alone was owed on the mortgage, according to court records. By March of this year, as the indictment of Stanfa and the others was about to be announced, Philip and Brenda Colletti and their son left Glassboro for protective custody. They have been there ever since.

Today, the Franklin Road house is closed up tight and the lawn is overgrown and sprinkled with dandelions. Other than that, it remains a picture of middle-class suburbia. A large concrete patio and brick barbecue pit dominate the fenced-in back yard. Two racing bikes stand in the corner of a back porch cluttered with wicker furniture, plastic toys, a bright-blue tot-sized two-wheeler with training wheels, and a portable gas grill. An old, midnight-blue Corvette is parked on the lawn next to the gravel driveway. A wooden Easter bunny and a plastic replica of an American flag poke out of the middle of a small flower garden next to the front steps.

The disclosure in March that there were mobsters in their midst took most neighbors by surprise. Many said they knew little about the Collettis. Few would offer their names.

"There really isn't much I could tell you," said a woman who answered the front door in the house directly across the street. "They kept pretty much to themselves."

"They were quiet," said another longtime resident. "You would see them working together in the back yard. . . . There was some talk in the neighborhood, though. People were curious because he was always home. It never seemed like he had to go to work. . . . Then after that shooting [the August 5 Ciancaglini killing], there was some talk about the car. We all read about it in the paper."

Ed Driscoll, a retired shipyard worker whose back yard butted against the Colletti home, said he had gotten to know, and like, both Philip and Brenda.

"They were just a couple of young kids trying to make it," he said. "He worked like a dog in there, cleaning and fixing that house up. We used to talk across the fence here. Nice guy. So was she. Nice. Quiet. Seemed like a decent mother. She was always out in the yard with their little boy, Paulie. She was kind of shy, actually."

Driscoll was practicing his golf game in his back yard one day last month, using an iron to chip shots into a wooded area that runs along a railroad track on the other side of Girard Road. As he spoke, four members of a special FBI organized crime task force poked around some loose masonry at the base of a patio in the Collettis' yard. The agents declined to comment on what they were looking for. Driscoll said he didn't bother to ask. A source later said the investigators were hoping to find a syringe and cyanide. Driscoll said he had not seen Philip Colletti for a couple of months. He said Brenda had stopped by the house for a few days shortly after the indictments made the papers.

"We talked, but it [the indictment] is not the kind of thing you would bring up," he said.

Driscoll said he asked Brenda Colletti how she was doing and she said she was fine.

"I told her, 'Good luck, kid.' That's the last time I saw her."

The Hit Man's Wife

OCTOBER 24, 1995

She was a housewife whose hit-man husband kept a bomb in the bedroom closet and a machine gun in the basement. She was "an exotic dancer," but not a prostitute. She lied to the police and to the FBI to help cover up a mob murder, and was ready to "take the rap" in a gun possession case in order to get her husband off the hook.

Brenda Colletti, 29, admitted that and more from the witness stand yesterday in the racketeering trial of mob boss John Stanfa and seven associates. In three hours of testimony in U.S. District Court, the auburn-haired former go-go dancer came across as a Mafia moll with an attitude. Clear, concise and to the point, Colletti detailed her involvement in her husband Philip's gangster career, described how their home in Glassboro, New Jersey, once housed a mob arsenal, and told how she was brought in on murder plots and plans to cover them up.

"If you're asking did I cover for him," she said in response to a defense lawyer's question about an alibi she supplied her husband after a murder, "the answer is yes. I covered for him. I covered for John-John [Veasey]. I covered for everybody in this mob."

When she agreed to tell authorities that a gun found in her husband's car was really hers, she said John Stanfa "patted me on the cheek and told me I was a smart girl." And when she needed money to bail her husband out of jail, Stanfa's reputed underboss and codefendant, Frank Martines, came up with the $1,500 in cash that was needed. She was asked: How many lies had she told to authorities before she and her husband agreed to cooperate with the FBI in February 1994?

"I couldn't count 'em," she said.

Colletti nonchalantly told the jury how her husband kept a homemade bomb packed with four pounds of explosive in their South Jersey home while he and other members of the Stanfa mob plotted the murders of rival Joseph "Skinny Joey" Merlino and several of his associates. There also were various weapons, including handguns and a machine gun equipped with a silencer, in the house at various times, she said. And in the backyard patio, hidden inside a cinder block, was cyanide. The testimony of the thin, self-described "exotic dancer"—who showed up in court wearing a neat, double-breasted, gray waist-length jacket over a black skirt—dominated the racketeering trial as it entered the fifth week.

In other developments yesterday:

127

Judge Ronald Buckwalter denied a defense motion for a mistrial after Philip Colletti, during cross-examination, blurted out that the brother of fellow mob informant John Veasey had been murdered recently. It was the first time the jury had heard in court about the slaying of Billy Veasey, who was gunned down gangland-style on a South Philadelpia street corner two weeks ago as his brother was about to take the stand.

The trial day ended abruptly shortly before four p.m. when defendant Anthony "Tony Buck" Piccolo, 73, fainted and slumped to the floor from the wheelchair in which he was sitting. It was the second time Piccolo has collapsed during the trial. He also passed out during jury selection. Piccolo is a diabetic with heart problems and a sleep disorder, according to members of his family. With a recess already scheduled for today for unrelated reasons, the trial is set to resume tomorrow, depending on Piccolo's medical status.

Before Piccolo's collapse, Brenda Colletti had spent nearly three hours on the witness stand recounting her involvement in a series of events that federal authorities contend were part of an ongoing turf war between the Stanfa and Merlino factions of the mob. Philip Colletti, who ended three days on the witness stand early yesterday morning, has already admitted that he was one of the shooters in the August 5, 1993, ambush in which Merlino was wounded and his top associate, Michael Ciancaglini, was killed. The jury has also heard from John Veasey, who admitted his involvement in that shooting and the September 17, 1993, murder of Merlino associate Frank Baldino. Those assaults, along with a series of other alleged murder conspiracies, are at the heart of the racketeering case against Stanfa and his codefendants. The case includes charges of extortion, obstruction of justice, gambling and kidnapping.

Brenda Colletti gave a short, straightforward account of her life and her involvement in her husband's racketeering activities. A former waitress and cashier, Colletti dropped out of school after the 10th grade and had been arrested several times on gun-possession charges, she said. She noted that while prostitution took place in some of the bars and bookstores where she danced, she was not a prostitute. She also admitted that she'd had an extramarital affair shortly before she left the federal Witness Protection Program this summer, but said that she and her husband, who has been in prison for the last 18 months, have since reconciled. Defense lawyers contend that while he was in prison this summer in a protective custody wing of a federal facility, Philip Colletti tried to hire a hit man to have his wife and her boyfriend killed. He denied this on the witness stand.

While her husband is facing a potential life sentence, Brenda Colletti could be sentenced to up to five years after pleading guilty to an obstruction of justice charge related to false information she provided authorities investigating her husband's role in the 1993 shooting of Merlino and Ciancaglini. She admitted that she'd lied to police and to the FBI after the shootings, claiming that her husband's leased automobile—which had been used in the hit and then set afire by Philip Colletti and Veasey—had been stolen the night before. She said she was ready to lie again when her husband was arrested September 3, 1993, by claiming his gun was hers. Both Stanfa and codefendant Raymond Esposito encouraged her to "take the rap," Colletti testified.

Brenda also described life with "the bomb": a pipe packed with black powder explosive and rigged with blasting caps and a remote-control detonation device. It was, she said, "all over our house." She said it was stored "in the bedroom closet . . . in the kitchen . . . in the basement." Asked if she was concerned to have it in her home, Colletti said her husband had assured her that it could not go off accidentally.

Corroborating much of what her husband had already told the jury, Brenda Colletti said he and his associates were constantly "plotting ways to murder Merlino and his crew." Once, she said, Salvatore Brunetti—a reputed Stanfa associate awaiting trial next year on similar charges—"had this great idea."

"He said I could get all dressed up and go to one of the nightclubs on Delaware Avenue and I could slip some of this cyanide into their drinks. . . . Merlino or anyone in the Merlino faction."

Brenda said her husband was "ticked off" when he heard what Brunetti had proposed and would not let her go through with the poisoning plot. She testified, "He didn't want me to get involved."

Crack Queen

SEPTEMBER 28, 1997

T he pusher had been working in one of the gatehouses, the heavily fortified neighborhood "stores" where crack cocaine and marijuana were being sold. But he was using nearly as much as he was moving. This was bad for business.

And so he was punished.

"They got him up in the room in the apartment up on Columbia Avenue," Robin Byrd recalled. "That's where they always took you if you messed up. And they stripped him buck naked and tied him to this straight-backed chair. He was just sitting there. He couldn't move. And they got one of those plastic bags, you know, that the dry cleaning comes in? And they held it up over his bare chest, and they got a cigarette lighter and started to burn the plastic and let it drip down on his bare chest. . . . He just screamed and screamed, and finally he couldn't take it no more, and he lifted himself in the chair and jumped out the window."

His name was Jack Ruby and he worked for Robert "Cush" Taylor Smith, the martial-arts-trained kingpin of one of the best organized and most lucrative drug rings in Philadelphia. This was back in the fall of 1986. While the assault—Ruby survived—attracted little public attention, it was an object lesson for those who worked for or with the Smith organization.

"That's the way Robert dealt with people who stole from him," Robin Byrd says. "He was going to teach him a lesson. You're not going to use his stuff and mess up his money."

Byrd, a John Bartram High School graduate and former Temple University student, is in a position to know. For nearly four years, she was Robert Smith's mistress. More to the point, she was the business manager of his Philadelphia drug operation. She bought or rented the tiny corner grocery stores that were converted into gatehouses and the rowhouses where workers would eat and sleep after their eight- or 12-hour work shifts. She stocked the stores with milk and bread and candy and crack cocaine. At the end of the day, she collected and counted the money.

The stores generated $10,000 to $20,000 a day in drug sales—each. There were times when the Smith organization had 10 to 12 stores up and running. It was basic economics, supply and demand. One New Year's Eve, in a store across from a housing project in North Philadelphia, customers stood in line down the street and around the block.

"It was like they were giving out welfare cheese," Byrd says. "As fast as we brought the stuff in, they'd sell it. That one night, that one store made $37,000. In one night."

Federal authorities later asserted that Smith's organization was one of the first to introduce crack cocaine into the Philadelphia area on a widespread and systematic basis. They estimated that Smith was responsible for the sale of millions of tiny vials of the highly addictive drug, as well as hundreds of kilos of marijuana and cocaine during a four-year run at the top of the Philadelphia drug world. Smith's net worth, they said, exceeded $100 million. He had a lavish home on a 100-acre estate in northern California, a mansion in Florida and another home in Brooklyn. He had a stable of horses that he kept in Ridley Creek Park, a record company in Fort Lauderdale, a fleet of luxury cars, fine clothes, expensive jewelry, and guns. Lots of guns.

But that was all before Robin Byrd became a witness.

Today Smith, 41, is serving a life sentence following his 1989 conviction on federal drug-trafficking charges. Eight of his top associates are also serving long terms. Byrd, indicted along with them, cut a deal and testified for the government, staring down from the witness stand while her former lover and his henchmen looked on.

"It was the hardest thing I ever did," Byrd says of the week she spent testifying. "I felt sick every morning of that trial. . . . But I did what I said I was going to do. I told the truth."

The truth, of course, is a complicated business. And so is Robin Byrd's story.

"It is . . . not a pretty world," Assistant U.S. Attorney Thomas Eicher, who prosecuted the Smith drug organization, told a jury back in 1989. "It is a world that is violent. It is a world that at times is shocking. But it's a real world."

Even now, a decade later, Byrd, 37, struggles to put it into words.

"Unless you're in that arena, you really can't understand how it works," she says.

She knows that she helped establish one of the most profitable and chillingly violent drug operations that law enforcement authorities had ever seen, a drug network that stretched from Kingston, Jamaica, where Smith was born, to New York City, where he grew up, and finally to North and West Philadelphia, where the organization sold crack to some of the poorest and most downtrodden residents of the city. And she knows that in the final analysis, it was her decision to cooperate that brought it all to an end. Now, after several years of living in hiding in the federal Witness Security Program, she has decided to speak out.

"I just decided I wasn't going to let this control my life," says the small, dark-haired former Philadelphian. She continues to live under an assumed name in another part of the country but is no longer formally enrolled in the Witness Security Program.

"I lived my life in fear for so long, and I'm just not going to do it anymore. . . . I just got to believe that God is going to protect me. That's the only way I see myself getting through this. I want people to know, people who are in similar situations, that you can get out, that you can do something. I was there. I know what it's like."

As she says this, Robin Byrd is sitting in the front seat of a car that is weaving through West Philadelphia, past the projects where many of her old drug customers used to live, and past the boarded-up stores and rowhouses that were so crucial to the Smith drug operation. She points to a restaurant on 52nd Street where, she says, drugs are still sold. "Robert used to supply them; he put a lot of his stuff in there," she says matter-of-factly. Two blocks away, Robin stops to observe the activity in a nondescript grocery store near a park. "Looks like it's still in business," she says. "See that place? Robert used to have his workers take samples out into the park to drum up business. The cops would bust it and as fast as they closed it, we'd open it back up again. He'd use a lot of teenage workers because he knew they'd get bail."

Another worker, a 17-year-old named Mike who had come down from New York to work in one of Smith's stores, used to smoke dope on the job. Problem was, what he smoked, he couldn't sell.

"So Robert took out his sword and they held the boy's hand out, you know, with the thumb and the first finger, the fingers he used to smoke with. And Robert just cut those fingers off with that sword so he can't use those fingers to smoke his dope no more. And they let you watch this to keep you in line, to say: This is what could happen to you."

There is an ongoing debate in Philadelphia about how best to wage war on drugs. The arguments are similar to those heard in most other cities where the poor, the uneducated, and the under-educated struggle to make their way. In this debate, some of the more vociferous members of City Council have taken on the police commissioner, arguing over police staffing levels and drug corners, putting on a great public display of anguish and frustration over law enforcement's failure to solve the problem.

Politicos are good at public displays. Solutions are another matter. They all would do well to talk with Robin Byrd. If nothing else, they would come away with a better understanding of how the drug underworld works and why it continues to flourish.

The answer, of course, is money.

Robert Smith was able to put more money into running his operation than police were in attempting to stop him. He not only paid his workers, he also housed and clothed and fed them. Bought them cars. Paid their bail. Hired their lawyers. Even, on occasion, supplied them with prostitutes. It was, in purely economic terms, the complete vertical integration of a business operation.

"He was a master at that," Byrd says. "He didn't want anyone who worked for him to worry about their everyday necessities. They needed to focus on his business. If you're focusing on the things of everyday life, you can't make him no money."

Smith also spread money around the neighborhoods where he set up shop. If, for example, he didn't own a property, he would pay some local residents to allow him to stash his drug supplies at their place.

"He'd pay someone $1,000 a month," Byrd says. "Now you're living on welfare and someone wants to give you $1,000, you're going to look out for his interests. That's what Robert did. And people looked out for him. He was like a king."

And, for part of that time at least, Robin Byrd was a queen. She grew up in West Philadelphia, near 46th and Locust Streets, the youngest of three children. Her father, a custodian for the Board of Education, and her mother, a nurse, divorced when she was seven. She, her brother and her sister lived with their mother. But they remained in contact with their father, who continued to supply financial support. They were comfortably middle-class, living in a stable home in a stable neighborhood.

Barely five feet tall and weighing less than 100 pounds, Robin Byrd hardly fit the image of the underworld moll that she would become. She looked like a high school cheerleader, not some drug lord's vamp. She had bright, expressive eyes, sparkling dark hair, and an engaging smile. More coed than coconspirator. Her older sister used to refer to her as the "goody two-shoes" of the family. Byrd still laughs at the thought of it.

"I always got good grades, always did well in school," she said. "And I never got into trouble. . . . I was, like, one of the nerds."

She was an honor student at Bartram, graduating in 1978. She started at Temple University that fall, majoring in criminal justice. A quick study, she was—and still is—charmingly sassy. Confident in her own opinions. Eager to debate and discuss any issue. She had planned on going to law school after college. But by 1984, when she met Robert Smith, things had begun piling up. Her dreams were on hold.

Robin Byrd had a three-year-old son, but was no longer living with her baby's father. She was working full-time as a cashier in a store at the Naval Shipyard in South Philadelphia and trying to resume her studies, carrying a full load of night courses at Temple's Center City campus. She was living in an apartment on Front Street in Yeadon, a small two-bedroom unit. Her mother had cosigned for the lease and was helping with the rent. She was juggling work and school and motherhood. She was getting by.

Robin met Dread, as Smith was also known, through the husband of a girlfriend. At first, they spoke on the phone. He was in Florida, where he and her girlfriend's husband had a record company. They were into reggae music. He invited her to visit him there. It would be like a vacation, he said. She said she had a job and school and a baby. He said he'd pay her for the days she lost at work and the cost of a babysitter.

On a whim, Robin decided to accompany her girlfriend to Fort Lauderdale. They were supposed to stay for four days, an extended weekend. She ended up spending 10 days in the Florida sun, wined and dined by a man who seemed to care only about what she wanted and who clearly had the resources to give it to her.

"When I left [Florida], I had $2,000 in my pocket for the work I missed," she says. "I had $500 to give my mother for babysitting. I had all new clothes. It was like, I couldn't believe it. I mean, call me naive or whatever, I just thought he was in the recording business. I mean, he did have a record company there. It was a legitimate business."

It is easy, after the fact, to question how much Robin knew. Or, perhaps, how much she wanted to know. Smith was lean and dark with dreadlocks and a lilting Jamaican accent. He was in his late 20s. Well-spoken. He drove a fancy car. Had a nice home. And he was loaded. A cynical law enforcement investigator probably would have seen the trappings of wealth that surrounded Smith as red warning flags. But should Robin Byrd have looked at him the same way? Should she have bought into the stereotype?

There was, of course, a darker side that would surface later. Robert Smith was a major operator in the Jamaican drug world, part of a notorious posse that grew out of the political turbulence that was a part of the island nation. He had been married before, at least once, possibly twice. He may have fathered as many as 10 children. A high school dropout, Smith was nevertheless a voracious reader, interested in all kinds of subjects and fanatical about learning all he could on an issue once he decided it was important. He exercised and meditated for several hours each day, and loaded his diet with fruits and vegetables. No meat. No fish. And no drugs, except marijuana.

"He was a Rastafarian," Byrd says. "They don't consider marijuana a drug. But he wouldn't put anything into his body that wasn't pure or natural."

Robin saw him again the day after she left Florida. She was visiting family members in New York. Smith surprised her, calling to say that he was also in the city and that he wanted to take her out. She was amazed. And flattered.

"I had just left him in Florida not 24 hours ago, and here he was coming to see me in New York."

He picked her up in a black Thunderbird and took her to an apartment building in Harlem, 141st Street and Lenox Avenue. It was the middle of the night and the place was alive with people. Everyone seemed to know Dread. People were going out of their way to acknowledge his presence. Young men in dreadlocks would come over from time to time and talk privately. Many would hand him wads of money.

"I can't even tell you what I was thinking," Byrd says now. "That night, I had never seen anything like it. People were coming up to him, it was like they revered him. I just don't know. . . . He swept you off your feet. I got a baby and a job and a bum who's not helping me with [child] support or anything. . . . And here is this guy wanting to pay my bills, telling me, Don't worry about nothing—you don't even have to work. . . . Lord Jesus, you don't know. I'm like, I'm going for this."

Within a month Smith had moved in with her in the apartment in Yeadon. He said he wanted to explore business opportunities in Philadelphia. He said she could help.

His name was Nathan, but they called him White Dude. He was from Canada and had once dated one of Robert Smith's nieces. Nathan came down to sell drugs for Smith in Philadelphia, one of the few white workers in the drug operation. Trying to fit in, he braided his thin, blond hair in dreadlocks. Then he got hooked on the coke he was selling.

"So when he started using, Robbie said he was a disgrace to dreads," Robin Byrd recalled. "He said there's nothing lower than a drug user. So to punish him, Robbie took a razor and started to cut off his hair. And when they got to the fine part of the hair, well, you can't cut that with a regular razor, but Robbie just kept on. And Nathan's head was all cut and bleeding."

Byrd started out buying properties for Smith in North and West Philadelphia. He was interested in small grocery stores and rowhouses. She researched property records at City Hall. Then she negotiated the purchases, either through the city directly if the property had been seized for back taxes, or with the owner listed on the deed or tax bill. After that, she would arrange the phone and electrical hookups, acquire the mercantile licenses, and set about stocking the stores with groceries and sundry items—candy, cigarettes, paper products. They also put video games in most of the stores as another way of attracting customers. Nearly all the stores were within a block or two of a housing project. Most were open 24 hours a day.

Smith had a crew of carpenters who came down from New York to renovate and customize each place. They built the steel and plexiglass partitions that enclosed the counter area. It was a security measure, he explained. They also put in trapdoors that led to the rowhouse or apartment next door. Sometimes they built labyrinths, winding hallways that led to a hidden door built to look like a wall.

At first, Robin Byrd says, she didn't know about the drug dealing. Then she found a suitcase in the closet of the apartment she was sharing with Smith. And her life changed forever.

"I had never seen it before," she said. "It had a lock on it. I called my mother and my brother and they said to pry it open."

Inside there were a dozen neatly wrapped blocks of white powder and $50,000 in cash. She put the suitcase in her car and drove to her mother's home.

"We were trying to decide what to do," Robin says. "I was going to go to the police, but I was worried that they might think I was a drug dealer."

Then the phone rang. It was Smith.

"He said, 'If you ever want to see your son again, give me back my suitcase.' I said, 'My son is in school.'"

The next voice she heard on the telephone line was that of her five-year-old son, Ralph.

"Hi, Mama," he said.

An hour later, Byrd was in a park in the Cobbs Creek section of West Philadelphia with the suitcase. Her son was sitting in the passenger seat of Smith's Corvette, eating an ice cream cone. Smith was standing nearby.

"He had gone to the school and gotten my boy," she says. "He told them he was the father, and they let him take him."

Byrd handed Smith the suitcase loaded with the cocaine and the cash. He took it, looked inside, then motioned for Ralph to get out of the car. Robin ran to her son and scooped him up in her arms.

"Hi, baby," she said, trying not to show her fear. "I lived a life of hell after that," she says.

That night, Robin remembered, was one of the first times Smith beat her. Over the next three years she was hit, stomped and whupped more than a dozen times, she says. One minute, she would be showered with gifts; the next, she would be accused of sleeping with someone else and would be thrown down a flight of steps, smacked around, or beaten.

"I couldn't get away from him," she said. "Where was I going to go? I realized when he took my son that he was a nasty, evil, violent person—anyone who would take a five-year-old and say he would kill him for his drugs and his money. What could I do?"

The explanation, of course, leads to several other questions—questions that Smith's defense lawyer, Quentin Z. Brooks, made a point of placing before the jury during the 1989 racketeering trial. Brooks, a former federal prosecutor, described Byrd as a "conniving person" with "a mean . . . cruel agenda." He said she was someone who came from a drug background, hinting that other members of her family had dealt drugs long before Smith showed up in her life, and said she had cut a deal with the government only after she was facing life in prison.

"She wanted to reap the benefits of being his main woman," Brooks said in a recent interview. "She went into it with her eyes open. Not only that, she was smart enough to turn on him and get herself the best deal she could."

Brooks scoffed at the notion that Byrd was duped, coerced or physically abused. He said she was so deeply involved in Smith's underworld and so anxious to fit in that she even adopted a fake Jamaican accent.

"She was no Jill from Chestnut Hill. She knew what she was doing. . . . She was not naive. She was very astute."

Byrd continued to work for, live and sleep with Smith after he threatened to kill her son. She helped run his business, and she shared in its profits. She even traveled to Jamaica and married one of his brothers as a ruse to get the man into the United States.

"Unless you were there, you can't understand what it was like," she says by way of explanation.

Yes, there were luxurious trappings, Byrd concedes. Smith had a Mercedes, a custom-made, $100,000 pearl-colored roadster. She drove a BMW. He owned racehorses. She shopped at Lord & Taylor. There was nothing that she wanted that she couldn't buy. Nothing that she needed that she couldn't get. But after the incident with her son, there was also constant fear and intimidation, she says.

Now the drugs were out in the open. Kilos of coke were selling for $25,000 apiece, and Smith had suppliers ready to get him all he needed. He was wholesaling to other dealers in the city. And he was bringing in cookers who worked nonstop converting cocaine to crack for sale at the stores.

"He'd fly the cookers in from all over. Set them up in the kitchen [of one of the apartments]. They'd cook it up and then leave. Then it got so productive, he brought the cookers in and just kept them here. He'd bring them in from New York and Florida, from all over. He had his own people. Just like he had his own carpenters. . . . He just was a master at the business."

Most of the drugs came down from New York, supplied by Smith's connections with the Spangler Posse, a notorious and violent Jamaican drug gang.

"People were coming in on trains," Byrd says. "Women with babies. They would hide the drugs in their baby sacks. Sometimes they would come down in a taxi."

Federal authorities later alleged that between 1985 and 1989, the Smith drug organization moved between two million and five million vials of crack. These were, in most cases, single, over-the-counter sales. The vials sold for $5 to $10 apiece, depending on the quality of the drug and the market demand. Millions of dollars more were generated from the bulk sale of cocaine and marijuana to other dealers, investigators charged. It was drugs and money.

And, when necessary, violence.

"You got to understand, where they came from, Jamaica, if you had money, you could do anything," Robin Byrd said. "And they had that same attitude here. . . . If you got in the way, if you messed up his business, he would kill you.

"What was I going to do? He would kill me and he would kill my son. So I had to decide, did I want to be a player, or did I want myself and my son to die? I know people are going to say, why didn't I go to the police, why didn't I try to get away from him. . . . Unless you're in that situation, you can't understand. Let someone take your baby and threaten to kill him and see what you would do. Put yourself in that place before you ask why didn't I do something sooner.

"I watched him maim, slice and kill people. He would say, 'This is not a joke.' Do you want to test him and try it? To survive, I learned how to play the game."

A group of corner boys from North Philadelphia didn't. They had been selling drugs right in front of one of Smith's stores at 32nd and Euclid Streets. In fact, they sometimes bought crack or marijuana from the store, then resold it on the street. This was not the way to do business.

"Robert said if they were serious, they would have opened their own store," Byrd recalled. "But they said it was their neighborhood and he should be paying them to be there. Robert wasn't going to pay nobody."

Shortly after midnight on November 30, 1986, Byrd dropped Smith off near 32nd and Morse Streets, just up the block from the store. He was wearing army fatigues and a big hat. He had a gun in his waistband.

"He just said, 'Let me off here,'" Byrd remembered. "I said, 'You're crazy.' There were, like, 10 of them on the corner and it was just him. He just told me to go home."

As she drove away, she saw Smith walking toward the corner. There were six of them on the corner, drinking wine. Hanging out. They saw the man they knew only as Cush walk toward them. He said, "You don't be selling no drugs on my corner." They said they weren't. Then he said, "You think I'm playing?" And he pulled out his gun and opened fire. The first shot struck Joel Hinnant, 19, in the stomach. He slumped to the ground, dead. His friends scattered as five more shots rang out. Joe Crawford, 20, took a shot to the leg. No one else was hit. When it was over, Robert Smith walked away.

The shooting led to a major homicide investigation. But for months, all the police knew was that they were looking for someone named Cush. The victims of the shooting were able to provide a description, but little else. Cush was a Jamaican. He was into drugs. And, said one witness, "he was like an idol around there. People talk. You hear it." It took police more than a year to match the nickname with Smith. In May 1988, he was arrested in a Sharon Hill apartment where he was living with Byrd. Later he accused her of giving him up to the cops, but she says that wasn't the case.

"It was Nathan," she says.

White Dude, his head still scarred from the dry razor cuts, had been busted for drugs. He decided to cut a deal. He told police that he knew about a major drug ring operating in the city. He said the boss of the operation was a Jamaican named Robert Smith. He said the boss was also known as Cush.

The homicide arrest came at the same time that investigators with the Drug Enforcement Administration and local police attached to a drug task force known as the Violent Traffickers Project had begun to narrow in on the Smith drug ring. In December 1988, while Smith was in jail awaiting trial on charges that he murdered Hinnant, a 72-count, 119-page federal indictment was handed up. The charges included drug trafficking, conspiracy, operating a continuing criminal enterprise, and various acts of violence, including the murder of Hinnant and assaults on several workers.

"Violence was the hallmark of this organization," said Thomas Eicher, the Assistant U.S. Attorney, when the indictments were announced. The Hinnant murder, of which Smith was convicted in Common Pleas Court, was just one example, he said. There was also the systematic intimidation of those who were part of the drug ring, including the routine "beatings and torture of workers who 'got out of line.'"

More than 20 defendants were named in the indictment. Robert Smith headed the list. Second was his brother, Everton. Third was Robin Byrd, also known as Robin Smith. She was described as one of the supervisors of the drug operation, an underboss, so to speak, who reported to and did the bidding of Robert Smith.

Robin Byrd fled Philadelphia in August 1988, three months after Smith was jailed on murder charges and four months before the federal indictment came out. She says she feared for her life. Smith was convinced she had given him up to the police, and she knew he would have her killed. She hid out in southern California with her son, living with relatives, trying to find work. Periodically, the authorities would visit her mother's home in West Philadelphia to ask about her. After the indictment, the visits became more frequent. So did the pressure. If her mother knew where Byrd was and didn't tell them, investigators said, she could be charged with harboring a fugitive.

In November, an aunt introduced Byrd to Bishop Ralph Houston of the Bethel United Holy Church of Los Angeles. He took her and her son into his home. Over several weeks, in bits and pieces, she told him the whole story. He persuaded Robin to surrender and, through church and legal contacts, set the process in motion. Shortly after the New Year, she flew back to Philadelphia. On January 9, 1989, she walked into the U.S. Attorney's Office and said she was ready to cooperate.

"I started telling them everything," Byrd says. "They told me to wait, that I should have a lawyer. But I said I didn't need no lawyer. I just wanted to tell the truth."

Robert Smith, his brother and seven codefendants were found guilty in August 1989 after a two-month trial. Byrd was the key prosecution witness. In October of that year, Smith was sentenced to life in prison with no parole. At the sentencing hearing, Judge Robert S. Gawthrop 3rd, who had presided at the trial, called the muscular, dreadlocked defendant a "foul human being," a "vicious, violent person" and "a coward at heart."

"It is my express purpose," Gawthrop added with the dramatic flourish that is his courtroom trademark, "that this defendant never get out of jail while he is still alive."

Five months later, Byrd, who pleaded guilty to drug conspiracy and trafficking charges, was sentenced to 16 months in prison—substantially less than the potential life sentence—because of her cooperation. Gawthrop described her as one of the most convincing witnesses he had ever heard.

She spent part of her prison time in a hospital, where she was operated on for stomach and intestinal problems that she attributes in part to the beatings she received while living with and working for Robert Smith. She has been operated on several times since then and continues to receive treatment for what is now a chronic medical condition. For seven years after her release from prison, Robin and her son lived under different names in the Witness Security Program. She says they lived in six cities before she quit the program for good two years ago.

"I decided I wanted to see my family, and I couldn't do that if I stayed in the program. Once you're in, they don't care about you. It's all a bureaucracy. . . . I wanted my son to know who his family is, where he comes from. . . . That's what's important."

The rest, she says, is in God's hands.

Today Byrd and her son live in another part of the country and use yet another name. It is their fifth identity and she says hopefully, their last. She has worked at several jobs—selling real estate, telemarketing, clerking, data processing—and is considering enrolling in a local college. Her son graduated from high school in June and plans to attend a university near their new home next year. Robin is deeply involved with her church and makes a point to speak whenever she can to young people, telling her story and counseling against involvement with drugs.

"They think about the money, about what they can buy," she says. "I try to tell them that's not what it's about, that that life can kill you, destroy you. It can take you away from everybody and everything that you love. . . . And I try to let people who are already involved know that they can get out. I did it. They can do it. They can have a life."

Occasionally, Byrd slips back into Philadelphia to visit her mother, other relatives and a few friends. Her arrivals are never announced; her departures, quick and quiet. For years in the Witness Security Program, she lived each day looking over her shoulder. She would get into her car each morning and then pause, anxiously debating whether to turn on the ignition, convinced that there was a bomb waiting to go off, that somehow, some way, Smith had reached out from prison to find her and kill her.

"I can't live like that anymore," she says. "I've just got to trust in God. I was the best thing that ever happened to Robbie. He was able to use me to get everything he wanted in Philadelphia. But I was also the worst thing that ever happened to him. And I know he's not going to forget it. He can't."

A man once robbed one of Robert Smith's stores in West Philadelphia, shooting one of the workers and making off with a stash of drugs and money. Later the worker, who survived, identified the man as a local bar owner. That night, Smith went to a gas station where he bought a gasoline can and filled it with fuel. Then he, Byrd, and two associates drove to the house where the bar owner and his wife lived. It was two or three o'clock in the morning.

"Robbie walked all around the house, pouring the gasoline," Byrd recalled. "He kept cussing in Jamaican . . . and saying, 'He ain't going to rob me.' That's all he kept saying. Then he lit a match and dropped it on the gasoline, and he burned the man's house up.

"I said to him, 'Robert, you got kids. The man might go after your son.' And he said, 'If he tried to do something, I'd kill him and his mother and his father and his sister and his brother.'

"I said, 'But you still wouldn't have your son.' And he said, 'It don't matter, 'cause I'd have my paybacks.'"

Caught in the Middle

MAY 11, 2003

A nnette Daidone says she doesn't know much about the Mafia or her ex-husband's alleged involvement in it. But the former Mrs. Daniel Daidone does know this: If, as the government contends, her former spouse was associated with mob boss Ralph Natale in the late 1990s, the arrangement was a money-losing proposition.

"I thought people joined the mob to make money," the Cherry Hill resident said. "Danny never made a penny. It cost us money . . . and look what it got him."

Daidone, 59, and former Camden City Council President James Mathes, 62, go on trial this week in federal court in Camden on political corruption charges linked to an attempt by the mob to corrupt and control the awarding of government contracts in the city of Camden between 1996 and 1998. Daidone and Mathes, who recently retired as affirmative action officer for the Camden Board of Education, have denied the allegations. Both are free on bail. Jury selection is set to begin Monday in U.S. District Court in Camden. The trial is expected to last at least a month.

Daidone has been described by federal authorities as the mob's "middle man" in the deals in which former Mayor Milton Milan and Mathes were targeted. Milan was convicted in December 2000 in a sweeping political corruption case that included the organized crime allegations. The primary witness in that case, mob-boss-turned-government-witness Ralph Natale, is scheduled to be the star witness in this trial as well.

The government alleges that Natale met and wooed Mathes during meetings late in 1995 at the Pub restaurant in Pennsauken, New Jersey. Among other things, Natale said he had a jeweler give a diamond engagement ring, worth between $2,000 and $4,000, to Mathes' girlfriend in exchange for the then-council member's promise to steer contracts to mob-backed companies. Natale also claimed that he used Daidone to funnel between $30,000 and $50,000 in gifts to Milan after Milan succeeded Mathes as council president, during Milan's campaign for mayor, and after Milan took control of the mayor's office on July 1, 1997.

"Danny had that appearance as a businessman," Natale said while testifying at Milan's trial in November 2000. "He could speak much better than a lot of the hoodlums that I had around me."

Daidone, a former official with the Atlantic City bartenders' union, owned a furniture store in Northeast Philadelphia at the time, according to his ex-wife. The Daidones, who were married for 26 years, divorced in 1998. He has since remarried.

"It was like he fell in love with Ralph," Annette Daidone said of her ex-husband's infatuation with the mob boss. "He'd do anything he asked him."

Annette Daidone remembers attending a Christmas party at Natale's penthouse apartment on the Cooper River. Everyone, she said, was expected to defer to the host who clearly enjoyed playing the role of "Godfather."

"It was like he expected everyone to kiss his ring. I said to Danny, 'What, are you nuts?'"

On another occasion, she went with her then-husband to meet with Natale and several of his associates at Steak 38, a Cherry Hill bar and restaurant.

"Danny had to buy the whole bar a drink," she said.

Her husband's association with the mob, she said, led to the furniture store going out of business. Among other things, she claimed, her husband furnished an office Natale opened in Pennsauken for an ill-fated bill-collection agency the mob hoped to set up. In fact, testimony at the Milan trial indicated, none of the business deals Natale tried to pull off ever came to fruition and no city contracts were ever awarded to mob-backed companies.

The evidence the prosecution used in the Milan trial and will use again in the case against Daidone and Mathes includes hundreds of secretly recorded conversations from wiretaps placed on phones and in Natale's apartment. In one conversation, Daidone complained bitterly about not receiving any contracts despite all the work he did for Milan and the Milan administration. Considered a "classic" by investigators and courtroom observers, the profanity-laced lament sounded like something out of *The Sopranos*.

"I haven't been given one contract in that city, not one," Daidone said to a business associate in a phone conversation that was taped by the FBI. "I'm [expletive] livid . . . I'm handing out [expletive] money like it's going out of [expletive] style for every [expletive] thing they asked me to do in that city. Every [expletive] thing . . . .

"I didn't have to give him no campaign money. I didn't have to buy [expletive] turkeys . . . I didn't have to go out in the cold [expletive] weather like I did . . . and hand out [expletive] turkeys to [expletive] people with snot hanging out of their [expletive] noses. But I [expletive] did it . . . And then be treated in this [expletive] way?"

The tape, which Milan's lawyer used to show no contracts had been awarded, will likely be played again for the jurors considering Daidone's fate.

Wife and Mother

SEPTEMBER 19, 1993

Maryann lost her two sons on November 11, 1986. Even now, it is a date circled in black on the calendar in her mind. The night before, her former husband, mobster Thomas "Tommy Del" DelGiorno, completed a deal with the government that would forever change the face of the Philadelphia mob. In exchange for protection for himself and his family and a plea bargain to all the crimes which he had committed, DelGiorno agreed to testify against the organization. He was the first "made member" of the Philadelphia Mafia ever to strike such a bargain.

Convincing Tommy Del to "flip" was a major coup for the New Jersey State Police and, ultimately, the federal government. Over the next two years, his testimony would bring down mob boss Nicodemo "Little Nicky" Scarfo and Scarfo's entire crime family. But his decision to cooperate—and to go into hiding—would wreak havoc with the lives of several other people close to him, people who had no criminal past and no ties to organized crime. Tommy Del's wife, Roseanne, their two young sons, Danny and Michael, and his sons from his first marriage, Tommy Jr., 20, and Bobby, 19, had to join him in protective custody.

Left behind, and perhaps hardest hit of all, was DelGiorno's first wife, Maryann Fisher. Remarried and living in a small rowhouse in the 300 block of Gladstone Street, Maryann had spent a lifetime trying to keep her sons from following in their gangster father's footsteps. Now events completely out of her control—developments that just days earlier had seemed inconceivable—were wrenching her boys away.

Bobby and Tommy Jr., after discussing the matter for hours, had reluctantly agreed to go into hiding. Both boys thought they'd be gone for six months to a year. Then they hoped—and Tommy Del let them believe—they'd be able to return to South Philadelphia. All that remained, on the night when they were to leave, was one last visit to the house on Gladstone Street. Maryann was in the kitchen cooking when Bobby and Tommy Jr. walked in.

"Sit down, have some dinner," she said.

"No, Mom, we can't," Bobby said. "We gotta talk to ya. Come on in the parlor and sit down."

Maryann sat on the couch in the tiny living room with her husband, Joe. She could tell from her boys' expressions that something was wrong. Just how wrong, she couldn't have imagined. They quickly told her that their father was going to be a witness for the government and that there was a contract out on his life. Then they said there was a chance they might be killed and that they would have to go into protective custody with their father. At first, Maryann didn't understand what they were saying. "Why?" she said. "You two live with me. That's not possible."

"Mom," Tommy Jr. said softly. "We have to leave." Maryann began to shake, then gag. She could not catch her breath. Tears welled in her eyes.

"I knew it, I knew it," she screamed. "It's all blowing up in his face. I knew it would come to this. That's why I divorced him."

For Maryann, it was a nightmare. She had fought to keep her sons away from their mobster father, and now he, with the help of the government no less, was taking them away from her. Joe Fisher reached over and tried to comfort his wife, but Maryann could neither hear what he was saying nor take any solace from his presence.

"Where is he?" she screamed, her tears turning to a bitter rage. "I'm gonna kill him. I'm gonna kill him."

Bobby and Tommy Jr. tried to calm her down. Both insisted that this was just a temporary move, that after their father had finished testifying they'd be able to return home.

"When are you going? " Maryann said between sobs.

"Tonight. In a little while."

"Where are you gonna stay?"

"We can't tell you."

"How can you go and not tell where you are? What am I supposed to do? I'm your mother. . . . That son of a bitch."

For more than an hour, the boys and Joe Fisher tried to console Maryann. Then it was time to leave. She sat sobbing quietly on the couch as they walked out the door. Memories flooded back of her babies, of her struggle to bring them up with little or no help from their father, of the sad and happy times on Gladstone Street. Of the Christmas presents. Of Halloweens and graduations and birthday parties. She was always there, while Tommy Del was nowhere to be seen. God, O God, how could this be? The only things of value she had ever taken from her first marriage were the boys. They were all that mattered to her. Their big-shot father with his money and his guns had proved to be the coward that she always knew he was. All his talk about the mob and all his gangster bull meant nothing. He could shoot people in the back. But when it was time to defend himself, he turned and ran. The hell with him, Maryann thought. But God, O God, how can he take my babies?

That night, shortly before midnight, a Winnebago camper pulled out from behind a home in the 2900 block of Broad Street in South Philadelphia. There was an unmarked New Jersey State Police car in front of the camper, and another behind it. Inside, with his wife and his four sons, was the man who would bring down Scarfo.

The DelGiornos had packed hurriedly, throwing clothes and other necessities into green trash bags and a few suitcases. The state police promised that the rest of their belongings would be sent once they were permanently situated. Tommy Del clutched a blue gym bag that contained cash and jewelry. Bobby guessed that his father had close to $200,000 on hand, although later police would say DelGiorno took about $137,000 with him into hiding. Tommy Del had also slipped Tommy Jr. a handgun, telling him to hide it. They might need the gun in the future, he said, if he decided "to go back to the old ways."

As detectives looked on, teary-eyed members of the family hugged and kissed Danny, Michael and Roe, as Roseanne was called. Bobby and Tommy Jr., still reeling from their emotional goodbyes on Gladstone Street, looked on in stunned silence as their paternal grandparents and Roe's family tried to cope with the forced departure of their loved ones. Tommy Jr.'s fiancée, Chrissy, begged to go along, but the state police refused to take her with them.

No one quite knew what to expect as the caravan pulled out of South Philadelphia. Danny and Michael, then just 10 and eight years old, were excited. To them it was the start of a great and mysterious adventure. But the rest of the DelGiornos wore more somber expressions. Tommy Del had crossed over a line that meant living the rest of his life with a Mafia murder contract on his head. Roe, as any young mother would be, was concerned about her family, especially her two young boys. Bobby and Tommy Jr., sitting in the camper as it headed north, were literally and figuratively in the dark.

In the days leading up to their secret departure, they had been repeatedly told that protective custody wouldn't be that bad, that it would be like a vacation, that in six months or so they could return to South Philadelphia. They hoped that was true. But within a week, they came to believe that, in Bobby's words, "it was all bull-." Casually at first, but on a consistent basis, the troopers who were guarding the family began to make it clear to the two older boys that they would be better off breaking all ties with the past.

"There's nothing back there for you but trouble," they would say, emphasizing that to return to South Philadelphia was to return to the lair of the mob. Their father was the biggest mob informant in the history of the Philadelphia Mafia. There was already a contract out on his life. And Scarfo had made it clear that he wasn't above holding family members responsible for the sins of their fathers, sons or brothers.

Joseph Salerno Jr., an Atlantic City plumber who had testified against Scarfo in a 1980 murder trial, was a prime example. This was the case in which Scarfo, Philip Leonetti and Lawrence Merlino were acquitted. But the jury verdict wasn't enough for Scarfo. He thought he had to make an example of the plumber. The problem was that Salerno was in hiding under the federal Witness Protection Program. Salerno's father, Joe Sr., however, was living in South Philadelphia and traveling every summer to Wildwood Crest, New Jersey, where he owned and operated a small motel.

On the night of August 10, 1982, a man wearing a designer sweatsuit and ski goggles knocked on the motel office door. When Salerno answered, the man pulled out a pistol and pumped a bullet into his neck. Though he survived the attack, a long-held Mafia tradition had been shattered.

"Based on the past, Joseph Salerno Sr. had little reason to be frightened," the Pennsylvania Crime Commission noted. "[Because] tradition held that the mob did not harm an innocent relative or member of an enemy's family—a brother, a sister, a father. It just wasn't done."

Nicky Scarfo changed those rules, and thumbed his nose at the authorities while doing it. A day after the Salerno shooting, Scarfo and several of his henchmen were spotted walking around Atlantic City wearing the same type of designer sweatsuit as the gunman who shot Salerno.

Now Tommy Del was the guy Scarfo wanted looking down the barrel of a Mafia gun. But anyone in DelGiorno's family would be an acceptable substitute. This was the bind that Bobby and Tommy Jr. found themselves in. They were paying a price—a steep and unreasonable price, they would eventually decide—for their father's life of crime. Both the FBI and the state police were insisting that they would be targeted by Scarfo's hit men because of their father's decision to become a government informant. Bobby, who had gloried in his father's role as a macho mobster, wanted to help his father. But he was being asked to give up his life—his family, his home, his friends, his very identity—to do it.

On the one hand, the detectives were telling him that if he went back to South Philadelphia, he would be killed. On the other, South Philadelphia, the place and the people, meant everything to him. He couldn't imagine living anywhere else. He couldn't imagine never seeing his family and friends again. Sometimes he thought he'd be better off dead, that maybe he should just go back home and take his chances. At other times, he and his brother would rail against their father for the spot he had put them in.

"Why doesn't he stand up like a man?" Tommy Jr. would ask. "All his life he told us never to be a rat. Now what is he?"

"Yo, Tom," Bobby would say, trying to calm down his brother and at the same time avoid the undeniable truth in what he was saying. "This is Daddy we're talking about. They were gonna kill him. What could he do?"

But for the first time, somewhere deep in his subconscious, Bobby began to question his father's way of life. For the first time, he began to ask himself if the money, the cars, the clothes, the "easy living" of a mobster were really worth it. Bobby, even more than his older brother, chafed at the confinement and restrictions that the state police imposed upon him. He was used to coming and going as he pleased. Now he had to ask permission to go outside. And a trip to the store or the movies required security clearance and an escort.

Their father took thousands of dollars into hiding. He had his wife and his two young sons with him. Bobby and Tommy Jr. liked their half-brothers, but their relationship with their stepmother had deteriorated to little more than mutual tolerance. Their friends and family were back in South Philadelphia. And as each day went by, South Philly seemed farther and farther away.

Less than a week after their clandestine departure, the DelGiornos were set up in a state police "safe house" in New Jersey. The house, in a small town in the north-central part of the state, was on a large, fenced-in estate. There was a swimming pool in the back yard and beyond the fence was a wooded area. The closest neighbor was a half mile down the road. Danny and Michael adapted immediately. For a time they didn't even have to go to school. They were with their mother and father, enjoying an extended vacation. There was a large yard to run around in and, once the weather warmed, there would be a pool to swim in.

Adding to the younger boys' excitement was the constant presence of detectives with guns and walkie-talkies and cars equipped with two-way radios and shotguns. Danny and Michael were too young and too naive to realize what Bobby and Tommy grasped almost instantly. They were prisoners. There were no bars, but this was a jail. Their every move was monitored. Any time they left the house, a detective would have to go with them. They needed permission, and an escort, to go anywhere.

Tommy Jr. would grow more hostile as the weeks went by with no indication of when, or if, the confinement would end. Bobby, who clung to the belief that he was engaged in an effort to save his father's life, fought off a foreboding sense of homesickness, denying at first what Tommy said was the reality of their situation: that they'd never be able to go back to South Philadelphia. For Bobby, that was incomprehensible.

Even before they made it to the safe house, he was dreaming about home. On the very first night, after collapsing in nervous exhaustion on a bed in a motel somewhere in New Jersey, Bobby thought about home. The tension and pressure had drained him, left him numb. All he wanted to do was close his eyes and sleep and hope. Maybe, he thought, this wasn't really happening.

"There was a state trooper driving the Winnebago and there were troopers in cars in front of us and behind us. We drove for about four hours that night. We finally pulled into this motel. There were three more undercover police cars there waiting for us.

"We all got out of the camper and walked up to the second floor. I asked one of the troopers what room was mine. He says, 'Well, Bob, we got the whole second floor, so pick two if you want.' I was so tired I walked into the first room, fell on the bed and passed out.

"I still remember what I dreamed that night. I dreamed that I was home, waking up in my own bed, running down the stairs, and my mother's in the kitchen cooking breakfast. I run up to her, give her a big hug and say, 'I'm never gonna leave you, Mom. I had this terrible dream that I left.' And my mother says, 'I'll never let you leave.'"

Then Bobby woke up. And he started to cry.

In the months that followed, as he and his brother grew bored and tired and angry while living in the safe house, that dream would come back to haunt Bobby's nights. He couldn't shake it. He would go for three or four nights without it, then a piece would return. He'd see himself in his room, or in the kitchen. He'd smell the eggs cooking and see his mother at the stove. He'd hear her voice. And then he'd wake with a start and there'd be that empty feeling in his stomach.

Bobby was 19, and he was away from home for the first time in his life. Really away. This wasn't a vacation at the shore or a trip to Florida. He missed his mother, his grandmother and grandfather. He missed his friends. He missed the schoolyard where he used to hang out and the neighborhood he grew up in. He missed being able to walk out of his house on Gladstone Street and see, sitting on a stoop two doors away, his best friend, Anthony Forline, the guy who was as close to him as his brother. He missed the Saturday night beef-and-beer parties that would bring together everybody from the neighborhood. He missed being able to walk two blocks to his grandmother's house. He missed climbing out his bedroom window at night and sitting on the roof of his mother's tiny rowhome and looking up at the stars and dreaming about the future. There were nightmares—but no dreams—in Jersey.

The DelGiornos spent their first two days in hiding at that motel. Security was so tight that when the boys wanted to go out and play football in the parking lot, they had to get clearance. It took an hour to get the OK.

"This is the kind of trouble we had to go through just to play a game of football," Bobby recalled. "First we had to wait for the OK from the supervisor who was in charge of the guard detail. Then we had to wait for him to assign two of his troopers to stand outside with us. When we finally got to play outside, I felt like a little kid. There was a cop at each end of the parking lot, like they were babysitting us.

"There was nothing for us to do but play football and eat. We stayed at that motel for two days, until my father started to complain. Then they moved us to another hotel at a ski resort. It had an indoor swimming pool, weight room and a game room for my younger brothers. But we only stayed there one night because the state police said a lot of Mafia people from New York came to that resort. That's when Roe threw a fit. She started yelling, 'I'm not living this way, going from one hotel to another. Tell 'em I wanna be put in a house or else I'm going back to South Philly.' Roe was right. We were being yanked around like yo-yos, moving around like gypsies."

Five hours after Roseanne DelGiorno's outburst, the state police told Tommy Del they had found a "safe house" where they'd be able to stay on a permanent basis. They all piled back into the Winnebago. The two state police escort cars, one in front and one in back, fell in line, and they headed out.

The house had six bedrooms, five bathrooms, maid's quarters, a den, a playroom with a ping-pong table, a weight room for exercising, and a swimming pool and cabana out back. There was a two-car attached garage and also a two-car detached garage. There were security cameras set up all over the estate, along the winding driveway that led from the road to the house and along the back and side yards. The den on the first floor served as the state police office, where a bank of video monitors allowed a trooper to scan the grounds. Somebody rich owned the place, although Bobby never found out who. Nor did he learn how the state police got access to it. The DelGiornos settled in as well as they could.

Tommy Del would be away from the home for days at a time, attending debriefing sessions or court hearings where his testimony was being used to substantiate the charges that had been lodged against Scarfo and the others and to build several other cases that state and federal authorities hoped would bring down the mob. For the law enforcement agencies that had been battling the Scarfo organization—with little success for more than five years—Tommy Del was a valuable and lethal weapon. Not so, his family. For the New Jersey State Police and, later, the FBI, the DelGiornos were a source of constant aggravation. And no one was more aggravating than Bobby.

A week after moving into the safe house, Bobby took off. He had been planning the move for two or three days and was amazed at how easy it was just to walk away. The night before, he took $15,000 in cash out of the blue gym bag where his father had hidden all the family funds. The money was from Bobby's loan-sharking and bookmaking operations, all the cash he had saved up over the last three years. He had given the money to his father to hold onto the night they left Philadelphia. Tommy Del had put it in the bag with the cash and jewelry he took into hiding. The money and the clothes he was wearing were all Bobby took with him when he left.

It was a Friday around 11 a.m. After breakfast he started for the back door when his younger brother Danny ran up to him.

"Where you going, Bob?"

"Out back in the woods to look for deer," Bobby said.

"Can I come?"

The two headed out the door, past one of the detectives, who asked where they were going.

"Out to look for deer," Danny replied.

Once in the back yard, Bobby told his younger brother to climb up into the tree house and keep watch.

"If I'm not back right away, that just means I've gone deeper into the woods," Bobby told him. "You stay up in the tree."

Bobby climbed through the fence that separated the grounds of the estate from a clump of woods and then headed out, moving in the direction of what he thought was a roadway. Ten minutes later he was out of the woods and moving toward a gas station. He asked a young girl there if she could call him a cab.

"A cab out here, are you crazy?"

It was then that Bobby realized how out of touch he was with reality. He didn't even know where he was. All he knew was that this was North Jersey, not far from New York City. And now he also knew he was somewhere without taxi service, somewhere a long way away from South Philadelphia.

"Is there a bus or a train around here that I can get to Philadelphia?" he asked.

"There's a train," she said, "but it goes to New York."

Bobby had to control his emotions, to think clearly. He had been gone less than 10 minutes, probably not long enough for anyone back at the house to get suspicious. But he was running out of time. He had to get to the train station, get to New York and then connect with a train to Philadelphia. He thanked the girl and, breaking into a trot, headed off in the direction she had indicated.

The train station was nothing more than a commuter stop, an outdoor platform that filled up each morning with office workers on their way into the city. But shortly before noon, the platform was practically deserted, adding to Bobby's feeling of isolation and contributing to his growing anxiety. For 30 minutes he sat on a bench, clutching a train ticket, expecting that any moment the gravel parking lot behind him would be filled with state police cars, sirens screaming, red lights flashing. He fingered the ticket like a rosary bead and prayed to God that the train would be on time.

Five hours later, he was getting off another train at 30th Street Station in Philadelphia. There he had no trouble hailing a taxi. A broad smile lit up his face as he jumped into the back seat and told the driver, "Take me to 2nd and Ritner." Bobby had the cab driver drop him off about a block from the neighborhood schoolyard where he and his friends always hung out. It was nearly six p.m. when he stepped out of the taxi. The sun had gone down. What had been a bright fall afternoon was turning cold. But Bobby felt a warmth that was beyond description as he began to walk the sidewalk in his neighborhood. He was home.

Bobby turned a corner and looked across the street toward the schoolyard. It was as if he had never left. There, under the lights, stood John GQ, Jimmy, Mark Pop, all his friends from the neighborhood. Bobby moved toward them, but stayed in the shadows. He scanned the streets around the schoolyard, looking for a car that might seem out of place, a car with someone sitting in it, watching. Satisfied that wasn't the case, he moved in closer. If this was a typical Friday night, the guys would be drinking beer in the schoolyard and planning what to do for the rest of the evening.

"They each had a quart of beer in their hands and they were leaning against the wall of the school," Bobby said. "I hollered over to them, 'Hey, you faggots, you got a quart of beer for me?' Everyone looked up, but they couldn't see me because it was dark and they were standing under the schoolyard lights. As I walked closer, Mark Pop yells, 'It's Bobby!' Then he runs up and lifts me in the air and he's hugging me and the other guys come running over, hugging me and asking me all kinds of questions.

"'I thought we'd never see you again,' John GQ says. 'All the newspapers are saying you, your father and your whole family's been put under protective custody.'

"While this is going on, Anthony Forline comes strolling around the corner. He sees me, runs up and jumps on me. Then he says, 'Bob, I gotta talk to you. The FBI's been to my house. They think me and you planned your escape and I was going to drive somewhere and pick you up with the $50,000. They say you stole $50,000. Your mother's going crazy. She don't believe 'em, but she's real upset.'"

Forline, in his excitement, had gotten his story somewhat twisted. It was the New Jersey State Police, not the FBI, that had questioned him.

"State police, FBI, what's the . . . difference," he said when Bobby asked him to repeat the story. Also, it was $15,000, not $50,000, and the money wasn't stolen, it was Bobby's to begin with. This was, to his way of thinking, just another example of how the authorities take a piece of information and distort it to suit their purposes. Bobby had begun to see them do that with his father. Detectives would offer subtle suggestions to Tommy Del, suggestions that Bobby and his brother later suspected were designed to ensure that their father's testimony would conform with evidence and other testimony the prosecution planned to present. It was all a game. Now Bobby decided he was going to play.

He sent Jimmy around the corner to check out his street. Sure enough, Jimmy spotted two plainclothes detectives sitting in an unmarked car on the corner. Nobody, however, was watching the alley that ran behind his mother's house. Now Bobby sent Anthony Forline back to knock on his mother's door.

"All the attention will be on you," Bobby said to his best friend. "Once you get in the house, make sure you keep my mother occupied. Make sure you keep her downstairs."

Anthony headed off for Gladstone Street. Like a quarterback in a pickup football game, Bobby started handing out assignments to the others. His plan was to sneak in the back window to his bedroom. Under a floorboard in the closet was a .357 magnum, a gun he had bought two years earlier from a local drug dealer. If Bobby was going to be walking around South Philadelphia with both the state police and the Mafia after him, he wanted to be armed.

"If anybody's gonna come up behind me and try to put some bullets in my head," he told Anthony and the others, "I want to be holding something . . . in my hand."

They gave Anthony a two-minute head start so that he could distract the detectives who were watching the street. Then Bobby, Mark Pop and Knave, another one of the guys, headed out. Knave was supposed to stand at the entranceway to the alley. If anyone came around, he would whistle. That would be a warning for Bobby and Mark Pop. John GQ stood in the schoolyard with a puzzled look on his face.

"What about me?" he asked.

"You?" Bobby said. "You got the hardest job of all. Here's 20 bucks. Go to the bar and bring back two cases of beer. Make sure it's Bud."

"And make sure it's cold," said Mark Pop.

"Me and Mark Pop started down the alley. We got to my house and both of us climb over the fence. Mark gives me a boost onto the roof that was near my bedroom. I look down and tell him, 'If you hear any yelling, just go back around the schoolyard.' As I'm walking across the roof, I'm praying the window isn't locked. I pulled on it and it opened, so I climbed in. I could hear Anthony talking to my mother, but at this point I'm most interested in gettin' the gun. I open the closet door, lift up the rug and move the floorboard and there it is. I just look at it for a few seconds, feeling so powerful. I grabbed it and, at that point, I wasn't afraid of anything or anybody. No Mafia. No nobody. I just sat there holding that gun.

"Before I go back out the window, I creep over to the top of the stairs to see what my mother was saying. I could tell she was crying. I hear her tell Anthony that she hopes I'm all right. Anthony's telling her, 'Maryann, I know your son. Bobby can take care of himself.'

"At that point I'm thinking now, here I am, right dead in the middle of everybody's life except my own. I felt like running down the stairs and just hugging my mother. But I knew if I did that, she would turn me over to the police for my own safety. The last thing I wanted was to go back to that safe house where there wasn't anything but trees and grass."

Bobby was living his nightmare. This was his house. This was his bedroom. The sounds, the smells, the feel of the place were all familiar, comforting, solid. His mother was right downstairs, sitting at the kitchen table, talking to Anthony. It was a common, ordinary scene. A piece of his past. Bobby headed for the window. He knew if he stayed any longer, he'd start to cry. All he wanted was to come home. Five minutes later he was back in the schoolyard with Mark Pop, Anthony and the others. They each had a beer in their hands and were planning their next move when a girl from the neighborhood walked up.

"Bobby, what are you doing here?" she asked.

"I live here, remember?" he said.

"But I heard there's a bounty on your head."

"And I heard there's a bounty on your ass," Mark Pop yelled, chasing her away.

"What was that all about?" Bobby asked.

No one answered.

"What's she talking about, Ant?" Bobby said.

"The word on the street is $100,000," Anthony Forline said. "That's how much for whoever kills your father or you or your brother."

The reaction of the New Jersey State Police to Bobby's disappearance indicated just how valuable law enforcement considered Tommy DelGiorno. State police detectives swarmed all over Bobby's South Philadelphia neighborhood, correctly surmising that a 19-year-old who was born and bred on the concrete sidewalks around 2nd Street would head for home. Cops staked out the neighborhood. They sat in unmarked cars on a half-dozen corners. They had surveillance posted outside his grandmother's home and, of course, they were inside and outside his mother's.

In the end it was a tearful and despondent Maryann Fisher who found Bobby and talked him into returning with the state police. But that would not occur until the morning after Bobby got his gun. He and his friends, full of bravado after polishing off both of the cases of Bud that John GQ had brought back to the schoolyard, headed for a beef-and-beer party at the Irish Club on 2nd and Mifflin that night. With detectives staked out all over the neighborhood, Bobby and his buddies partied past midnight with about 200 people. Then Bobby, drunk but still alert enough to realize he was being looked for, crashed at his friend Jimmy's house.

"They'll be looking for me at Anthony's or Mark Pop's," he told Jimmy through the drunken haze that had enveloped them all.

"You could stay with me as long as you want," Jimmy said.

A state police detective was at Jimmy's door the next morning. Word had filtered back about the party, and the police were questioning every one of Bobby's friends. Jimmy tried to hold the detective off, basically playing dumb while Bobby listened from a back room.

"Listen, you punk, this isn't some street-corner fight, this is a life-and-death situation," the detective said.

"Whose life you talking about?" Jimmy shouted back. "Bobby's? Are you kidding? . . . All you care about is that if Bobby doesn't go back, his father won't testify."

Then Bobby heard the slam of another car door and moments later his mother was inside the house, pleading with Jimmy.

"Please tell me where Bobby is," she said, her voice full of fear, anger and sadness.

Bobby walked out. He and his mother embraced. Tears filled his eyes. They streamed out of hers. Bobby was in a daze. He couldn't quite focus. In the background he heard the state police detective suggest that they all go somewhere for a cup of coffee. Somewhere where they could talk. Bobby went willingly. The somewhere was the New Jersey State Police office in Bellmawr, just across the Walt Whitman Bridge from South Philadelphia.

It was the only place they could be sure they were safe, the detective ex-plained. Bobby, his mother and two detectives sat in a small office dis-cussing the situation.

"Look, Bobby, we know it's rough," one of the detectives said, "but try to go along with us on this. We'll give you whatever we can. We'll find you a job. I understand you've got family out in Oregon. We can relocate you there. We'll pay for everything. Set you up real nice."

The only Oregon Bobby was interested in was Oregon Avenue in South Philadelphia.

"You're so busy playing cops and robbers, you're missing the whole point," Bobby said. "Don't you understand? Where I want to be is home, with my mother, with my family, with my friends."

Bobby fought to hold back the tears welling up again; this time they were tears of anger and frustration.

"How would you like it if you had to leave your family and friends and was told you'd never see them again? Tell me what you would do."

Like the night before at the schoolyard when he first asked about the murder contract, no one answered. Then one of the detectives asked the other to take Bobby's mother to another room for a few minutes. When she had left, the detective sat down behind his desk and stared directly into Bobby's eyes.

"Do you know how serious this situation is? Do you know your father has already admitted to committing 14 murders? Do you know what they're going to do to him if he doesn't testify?"

The implication was clear. If Tommy Del reneged on his agreement to cooperate so that his family could return to South Philadelphia, then the state would prosecute him for the murders he had admitted. And while the detective might have been exaggerating—Tommy Del would eventually ad-mit to his own involvement in five gangland murders—that did not change the fact that Bobby's father could face life in prison or the electric chair. The irony was that if Tommy Del did testify, then he and his family would have to remain in hiding because they were already under a death sentence from the Scarfo organization. It was a no-win situation for Bobby. And for Maryann.

All she had been thinking about for the last 24 hours, from the mo-ment the state police called and told her that Bobby had fled, was her baby turning up dead in the gutter, tortured horribly and shot in the back of the head by some Mafia goon. Now she had found him, but she couldn't protect him. For his own safety, she had to send him back to his father and the state police. She had to be content with an occasional call or letter from God knew where. She had to live her life without knowing where her boys were or what they were doing. As she sat pondering the situation in the state police office, the phone rang. It was Tommy Del. He wanted to talk with Bobby.

"He'll talk to me first," Maryann said, grabbing the receiver from one of the detectives.

Bobby, from the other room, could hear his mother screaming and knew immediately that it was his father on the other end of the line.

"This is all your fault, you son of a bitch," Maryann said. "Now I have to convince him to come back. If I do, I don't want you to lay a hand on him. Do you hear me? I don't even want you to raise your voice to him. You caused all this. If I knew where you were, I would get a gun and blow your f-ing brains out. You're nothing but a coward. Why aren't you dead?"

Quickly, one of the detectives grabbed the phone out of her hand.

"Maryann," he said, "we can't let you issue death threats. I understand how you feel, but this is a state police office here. You threaten to kill somebody, you're breaking the law. Please, try to calm down."

Bobby was handed the phone in the other room and listened while his father begged him to come back.

"Bob, they're gonna kill you if you stay in South Philadelphia," Tommy Del said. "Come back and I'll make sure you can have visitors, whoever you want, whenever you want. Who knows? In a couple of years, when this is all over, you could probably go back home."

"I'll come back," Bobby told his father. "But when this is over, I'm coming home for good."

After he hung up the phone, the state police detective told Bobby he had done the right thing. Bobby just stared at him.

"Your family's gonna come out on top of this," he said.

"The only people who are going to come out on top are you guys and the FBI," Bobby shouted. "I don't know who's worse, the mob or the police."

Bobby spent 30 minutes alone with his mother. They hugged, and she squeezed him tight. He told her he would be back as soon as his father had finished testifying at all the trials. He said the state police would arrange for her to visit with him. He said to tell Grandmom and Grandpop that he would see them soon. Then he was gone, whisked away in an unmarked state police car for a trip up the New Jersey Turnpike to Newark. There another detective in an unmarked car was waiting to take him back to the safe house. The detective was about six-foot-two and weighed nearly 250 pounds. He wore jeans, a sweater and a black leather jacket. His hair hung down around his collar. He had an earring. He was unlike any of the other members of the state police Bobby had met.

"My name's Jim," he said, reaching out to shake Bobby's hand.

"Bob DelGiorno," Bobby replied with what must have been a quizzical look in his eye.

"I work undercover, narcotics. That's why I look like this."

For the next three months, however, Jim was going to work the detail guarding the DelGiornos. Bobby liked him immediately. Even more so when they were alone in the car driving from Newark.

"Listen," Jim said, "I grew up in Jersey City so I know what it's like to be away from the city. Most of the guys on this detail don't know the difference.

"So, if you wanna get laid or just go out drinking or whatever else, just name it and we'll try to figure out a way to do it. Just do me one favor."

"What?" Bobby asked.

"Don't run away on my shift," the detective said.

Bobby smiled. Finally, he thought, an honest cop.

Over the next two years, Bobby and his brother Tommy grew more and more disenchanted with both their mob-informant father and the law enforcement authorities assigned to guard them. In November 1988, the brothers severed all ties with Tommy Del and the government. Tommy Jr., in fact, testified for the defense in a major mob racketeering trial in which his father was a key prosecution witness. Both Bobby and Tommy Jr. are now married and living in South Philadelphia, within blocks of their mother's home on Gladstone Street.

Mob boss John Stanfa

WIRED FOR SOUND

I n 1989, a mobster named George Fresolone agreed to cooperate with the New Jersey State Police. Fresolone, a burly wiseguy who was part of the Newark branch of the Philadelphia crime family, had gotten jammed up in a gambling and extortion case and appeared headed back to prison. One of the detectives working the case offered him an out.

Fresolone, who had done two years in state prison in the early 1980s, took the deal. He said he wasn't afraid of doing more time. He said he just didn't think it was worth it anymore. His mentor, Pasquale "Patty Specs" Martirano, a mob capo from the old school, was dying of cancer. And the rest of the guys in the outfit were part of that new breed of gangster who looked out only for themselves. At least that was Fresolone's take. As a result, he agreed to work undercover for the state police, wearing a wire and recording conversations.

A modern-day mobster, Fresolone wore a beeper so that he could be reached at any time. It was the perfect cover. The state police hid a miniature recorder in the device. No one was the wiser. For a year Fresolone taped conversations with dozens of mobsters from six different crime families that were operating in North Jersey.

In the end, 41 wiseguys were indicted. The tapes were so good that 39 of them, including John Riggi, then the boss of New Jersey's DeCavalcante crime family, pleaded guilty.

Fresolone capped off his year as an informant by taping his own mob initiation ceremony. Then he disappeared into the state's version of the witness protection program. He was given a new name and relocated to southern California where he went legit. He had a kid in college and another starring on the local high school football team. He bought a business, a maintenance company, and was bidding on contracts to clean office buildings and homes. I remember him laughing about how he cleaned the marble floors in Cher's house and how he did the windows for another movie star. He had gone Hollywood.

"If they only knew," he said.

Fresolone, a good guy, had a heart attack and died about 10 years after moving to California.

His taping was unprecedented at the time he was wired, but was quickly overshadowed by bigger and bolder investigations. In fact, the Philadelphia crime family might have been the most recorded Cosa Nostra clan in America in the 1990s.

The Fresolone investigation was quickly followed by the federal probe of mob boss John Stanfa built around two years of audio tapes from bugs planted in the office of Stanfa's Camden defense attorney, Salvatore Avena. The feds recorded nearly 2,000 conversations during that investigation.

No sooner was Stanfa indicted than the FBI targeted his successor, Ralph Natale. Natale's apartment, his phone and a bar where he hung out at the old Garden State Racetrack were all wired for sound.

Then in 1997, Ron Previte, the six-foot, 300-pound ex-cop who became a wiseguy, strapped on a body wire and recorded hundreds more conversations. Previte wrapped up his work in June 1999, completing a decade of audio taping that began with Fresolone. What those tapes have done in addition to providing prosecutors with devastating evidence—"How do you cross-examine a tape?" a defense attorney asked in the midst of the Stanfa racketeering trial back in 1995—is to offer an unvarnished look at the way of the wiseguy.

The secretly recorded conversations, from the mundane to the murderous, paint a picture that is more accurate than any indictment and more riveting than any courtroom testimony. This is who these guys are, in their own words, when they think no one is listening.

What follows are several articles that focused on those tapes and what they told us about the mob. The longest piece, "Mob Talk," appeared on the front page of the *Inquirer* and ran for three full inside pages on October 9, 1994, a few months after Stanfa and 22 of his top associates were indicted.

There is, of course, a story that goes with the story.

One of the keys to covering the mob, as I said earlier, is access to information. And despite what you may hear or think, very seldom do law enforcement types "leak." I can think of only one instance in 25 years when a law enforcement source gave me a document that I otherwise had no shot at getting my hands on. It was a prosecutorial memo, a lengthy outline of a case the feds were building against a labor racketeer. It was the first and only time I have ever seen such a document.

Indictments, however, are another matter. Those are public records. They basically outline the charges. More important, as a case moves toward trial, the prosecution is required by law to turn over to the defense all documents and evidence—including witness statements, affidavits and transcripts of wiretaps—that have been used to support the charges. This handing over of the evidence is called "discovery."

As a reporter I learned early on that if I could tap into that discovery process, I might have a leg up on writing about the case in which I was interested. In the Stanfa indictment, which was handed up in March 1994, I was very fortunate. There were over 20 defendants, which meant there were more than 20 defense attorneys.

Defense attorneys, I have found, are more likely to "share" information than prosecutors. And in a case with multiple lawyers all getting the same information, the likelihood increases. The more people who have the information, the more difficult it is to determine who might be providing it to the media.

A multi-defendant case provides lots of cover for criminal defense attorneys who, for whatever reason, would like to see some information made public before trial. In the Stanfa case, there also were several lawyers who were hired and then replaced, which increased the pool.

In the fall of 1994, I got a call from one of those lawyers. He asked me to stop by his office. When I got there, he showed me a pile of documents about two feet high. It was the discovery material.

To understand how valuable this was to me, you have to understand the wiretapping process. The FBI and the U.S. Attorney's Office needed court authorization to plant a bug in Stanfa's lawyer's office, which was no small thing. Lawyer-client privilege is a serious legal issue. But the feds were convinced that lawyer Sal Avena was allowing Stanfa to use his office as a meeting place for himself and other wiseguys.

An FBI affidavit outlining that proposition was submitted to the judge, who approved the bugging. The affidavit was a roadmap of the investigation, what the feds believed and what they hoped to find.

But that was just the tip of the legal iceberg. As long as the bugs were in place—and they remained in place for 24 months—the feds had to submit 10-day reports to the court outlining what they had heard. These documents usually contained snippets of conversation from mobsters who were seen meeting in the lawyer's office. And every 30 days the feds had to submit an even longer and more detailed report in order for the judge to extend the wiretap.

So we have a 24-month investigation. That's 72 10-day reports and 24 30-day reports. Along the way there were several expanded affidavits as the investigation shifted focus based on what information had been gathered. It was all there. The anatomy of the investigation.

My friend the defense attorney asked if I would like to take a look. I smiled and said better still, I'd like to "borrow" the documents for a few hours. He said fine. That afternoon I was at a Staples store in Cherry Hill, New Jersey, where an unsuspecting clerk ran off several hundred pages of what had been until that point secret documentation that would bring down John Stanfa and his crime family.

Three weeks later, "Mob Talk—Inside the Mafia of the '90s" was the banner story on the front page of the *Inquirer.* The story, in turn, became the basis for a book, *The Goodfella Tapes.*

In addition to "Mob Talk," this section includes other shorter stories that were built around secretly taped conversations and an interview with George Fresolone, who talked about what it was like to be wired for sound.

Mob Talk

OCTOBER 9, 1994

They talked of cutting out the tongue of a young South Philadelphia mobster, and of burying him and two others in quick-dry cement. They mocked an old bookie who begged for his life after a package containing a dead fish and a bullet arrived at his door. They spoke of crushing a trash tycoon in his own compactor. They ridiculed an informant who had been divorced by his wife and disowned by his family. They considered recruiting hit men from Sicily or New York to rub out dissidents in the Philadelphia underworld. La Cosa Nostra, the New York gangster told his counterparts from Philadelphia and Scranton, "is a beautiful way of life if we respect it."

Mob talk. It went on day after day, from October 1991 to September 1993, in the second-floor Camden law offices of Salvatore J. Avena where the FBI had secretly planted microphones. The federal probe resulted in the indictment of Philadelphia mob boss John Stanfa, Avena and 22 others on racketeering charges in March 1994. Four defendants pleaded guilty. Twenty, including Stanfa and Avena, pleaded not guilty and are awaiting trial. Avena, one of the few defendants permitted bail, denies he was part of any criminal enterprise and, through his lawyer, says he will challenge the bugging of his office as a violation of lawyer-client privilege.

A review of more than 100 official documents and partial transcripts shows that the bugs planted in Avena's second-floor suite gave authorities an uncommon look inside organized crime in the 1990s, as described by key figures in three La Cosa Nostra families. From a listening post a block away, FBI agents got it all—in candid, profane and sometimes humorous detail—from individuals the FBI describes as major Mafia figures, including Salvatore J. Profaci, a capo of New York's Colombo family; William D'Elia, a major figure in the Scranton-Wilkes Barre Bufalino family; and Stanfa and several of his Philadelphia lieutenants.

They heard one mobster targeted for death because he'd "gotten cute" with Stanfa's 26-year-old daughter, Sara. They listened as Profaci bragged of muscling in on supermarket pasta sales and D'Elia boasted that he'd paid $50,000 to a Pennsylvania environmental official. They got a detailed account of a botched City Line kidnapping. They heard about a multimillion-dollar civil suit that threatened to expose mob involvement in trash hauling, and the scramble by representatives of three crime families to settle the issue in what they called "the court of honor" rather than "the court of law." They heard talk of rattling mob informant Philip Leonetti the next time he testified by having his elderly grandmother show up in court. They listened

163

to a cynical eulogy for another informant killed after he "foolishly" returned to the Philadelphia area. And through it all, they heard John Stanfa, by turns paranoid and powerful, arrogant and afraid, sounding like some tragic Shakespearean figure, a leader unsure of his followers, fearing for his life and unable to sort out the truth in the machinations of those around him.

The balding and barrel-chested 53-year-old crime boss was caught on tape in the midst of a bloody underworld power struggle with young mob renegades Joseph "Skinny Joey" Merlino and Michael Ciancaglini. Stanfa, the tapes make clear, wanted Merlino and Ciancaglini out of the way. He also wanted peace. He couldn't sleep, he feared his own assassination, and he questioned the loyalty and competence of those around him. The only thing Stanfa seemed to fear more than the Merlino faction was the FBI. The mob boss and his top associates knew they were targets of an ongoing investigation. They just didn't know how imperiled they were.

By October 1992, the FBI bugs had been in place for a year and would stay for nearly another. Every 10 days, as required by law, the FBI gave the U.S. Attorney's Office reports summarizing the tapes and offering excerpts. Armed with those reports, the prosecutors sought court permission each month to keep bugging and taping. Stanfa tried to take precautions, talking in code, seldom using the phone. Avena had his office "swept" for bugs on a regular basis. On October 22, 1992, an electrician assured him, "It's clean." It wasn't. What follows is some of what the FBI heard.

ONE WAY OUT

John Stanfa was out of options. For months, the mob boss had tried to resolve a festering dispute with an underworld faction led by Joey Merlino, 31, and Mike Ciancaglini, 30. He had been rebuffed, insulted and ridiculed. Now, Stanfa decided to act.

"You can deal with nobody no more," he told an associate in a June 22, 1993, conversation in Avena's law office. "You can trust nobody."

There was, Stanfa said in his fractured English, only one way out:

"What it comes down to here is they f- me or I f- them. That's where we are. . . . What I want to do, I have to take these two guys' head . . . . Then, whatever happens, happens."

Six weeks later, on August 5, 1993, Merlino and Ciancaglini were gunned down outside their South Philadelphia clubhouse. Ciancaglini died on the sidewalk. Merlino, wounded, remained atop the rival faction. The civil war that Stanfa had spoken of avoiding, a generational and cultural conflict rooted in greed and treachery, had flashed into the open.

"I'm the target, I know that," Stanfa said at one point in 1993. "I gotta leave or die." He said later: "I got a lot of pressure . . . and nobody try to cut the weight. At nighttime I can't even sleep good. I sleep little bit. I wake up thinking this way, that way. . . . I don't trust nobody either."

He feared visiting a wounded colleague because he might be trapped and assassinated in a hospital elevator. He mused about whether to strike first, because: "I can't live like that."

Of the young mobsters causing this agita, Stanfa offered only disdain. Greed and avarice drove the younger generation of gangster, Stanfa maintained in a conversation with his consigliere, Anthony "Tony Buck" Piccolo.

"They have no shame," Stanfa said. "They know nothing." For them, he added, "money is like a curse."

"They got no brains, either," said the 71-year-old Piccolo. "No shame and no brains."

Some of his own associates, Stanfa conceded, weren't much better. "They don't even know where to start, believe me," he said. The Sicilian-born Stanfa then bemoaned the decline of the Mafia, the loss of its old codes of loyalty and respect.

"I [was] born and raised that way. I'm gonna die that way, but with the right people," he said. "Over here, [it's] like kindergarten."

TRASH AND CASH

"See, Sal, the difference is, he is a street guy. You're not a street guy. . . . They're two different breeds. In other words, when this guy is making moves and you're doing it straight, you don't have a shot."

It was December 15, 1992, and reputed Scranton mob leader Billy D'Elia, 48, was holding court for Avena, Profaci, Stanfa and Piccolo in Avena's wood-paneled conference room. The mob sit-down had been called to discuss a multimillion-dollar civil suit Avena had filed against a business partner, reputed mob associate Carmine Franco. Avena, an avuncular 68-year-old noted for his measured and mannerly courtroom style, was about to get a lesson in conflict resolution, Mafia-style.

The Camden lawyer had sued Franco, his business partner in Philadelphia-based AAA Waste Disposal Corp., claiming Franco was robbing him blind. Franco had countersued, claiming it was Avena who'd brought threats and mob influence into the business. The case was headed for trial, which the mob leaders feared would risk exposing the mob's silent partnership in the lucrative trash business. (Franco, who pleaded not guilty to unrelated racketeering charges in New Jersey in August, has been identified by Pennsylvania and New Jersey law enforcement agencies as a front for the Genovese crime family in the waste disposal business. Through his lawyer, Franco consistently has denied the allegations.) In a conversation taped six months earlier, Profaci had said that Franco was a big money-maker for New York's powerful Genovese crime family, and that its leaders had begun to complain about Avena's suit.

"They're saying that we are the cause of destroying everything that they've created in Philadelphia," the solidly built, dark-haired Profaci, 58, said. "And plus, by blowing Carmine out of the water, we are destroying their number-one earner in the whole organization."

The lawsuit, Profaci told Avena, was not the way to do business.

"Goodfellas don't sue goodfellas," he said. "Goodfellas kill goodfellas."

D'Elia, who had been brought in from Scranton to mediate, echoed the point.

"The answer," said the burly, six-foot-four, 240-pound gangster, "was that when he [Franco] was standing by the [trash] trucks, somebody should have bumped him in and let them compact him." This, Profaci noted, could have drawn the ire of the Genovese family. D'Elia said there were ways around that.

"You know what they say in New York, don't you?" D'Elia asked.

"Accidents happen," Profaci said.

"'Oops, we didn't know,'" replied D'Elia.

"Oops is right," said Profaci. "Shame on us."

Now, they told Avena, the only solution was for him to accept a $2 million settlement from Franco, a deal Profaci had worked out with the Genovese organization.

"Better to win small than to lose big," counseled Stanfa, concerned about a conflict with the Genovese family. "They got all the power. They can run an army, OK?"

The more soft-spoken Piccolo also urged Avena to settle.

"It's no longer about Carmine Franco," the tall, silver-haired consigliere said. "It's about making sure no one gets hurt. . . . This could be a f-in' tragedy."

Avena didn't seem to realize it, but his business might not have been the only thing at risk. Three days after the D'Elia conference, Piccolo and Stanfa were picked up on tape in Avena's office privately discussing the lawsuit. Stanfa said Avena had better accept the deal.

"I know, John," replied Piccolo. "He [Avena] don't understand."

"They gonna say to Sal, 'Do this,'" Stanfa said, apparently referring to the New York mobsters, "or they do this."

"Or we have to do it," Piccolo added ominously.

The FBI's report noted dryly: "Stanfa and Piccolo's comments are believed to refer to killing Avena." Told last month of the FBI's account of the conversations, Franco's lawyer, Michael Critchley, labeled it "baseless gossip."

"My client . . . never was nor is he presently a member of any organized crime group," Critchley said. "He is a hard-working individual who through sheer individual effort has achieved a degree of success in the solid waste business. . . . It's an American success story, not an organized crime story."

The Avena-Franco civil dispute was settled out of court in April 1993.

STALKING BIAGIO

It was an affair of the heart with a decided underworld twist. The lesson for a pizza man named Biagio Adornetto: Don't date the boss' daughter.

The lesson for the Stanfa mob: Make sure the ammunition fits. The stalking of Adornetto was tracked by federal authorities from their Camden listening post.

On December 21, 1992, Stanfa and Piccolo sat in Avena's law library and talked about a hit. FBI agents heard that someone named "Biagio" was the target. They surmised it was Adornetto, whom they called a "shooter and confidant" of Stanfa's, according to an FBI summary. What agents didn't know was where, when or why the hit would take place.

"Something cooking?" Piccolo asked.

Stanfa replied, "This is him. This time, forget her. I don't take no f-in' chances for nobody."

"Get Biagio?" Piccolo wondered.

"He gotta go," replied Stanfa.

"Got a date?" asked Piccolo.

"Do it tonight, or not, tomorrow night," said Stanfa.

"Oh, Jesus Christ," Piccolo sighed.

Nine days later, on December 30, 1992, a masked gunman walked into the posh La Veranda restaurant on Columbus Boulevard. The masked man approached Adornetto, who was baking pizzas, pointed a shotgun at him and pulled the trigger. The gun misfired. Law enforcement officials say the hit man had put the wrong size shells into the chambers, and they fell out. The gunman ran from the restaurant, reloaded and came back. By then, Adornetto had scrammed out the back door, the first steps in a flight for his life that would lead him to the FBI.

Nine more days elapsed before the FBI heard additional details of the bungled shooting. In a conversation picked up on January 8, 1993, Stanfa gave Piccolo a concise critique of the La Veranda hit: "They f-ed it up."

Piccolo reacted in English and then in Italian: "Oh, Christ Almighty, John. Chissu disonorato [This dishonored person]."

"They put a shell and took it out," Stanfa said, explaining how the shotgun had misfired. Then he bemoaned the lack of a backup shooter: "They weren't backing the hit."

Over the next three months, the Adornetto affair bedeviled Stanfa. Whatever could go wrong, did go wrong. And all the while, the FBI tapes rolled. Stanfa had his organization frantically searching for the pizza maker, calling in help from mob sources in New York and Sicily.

"You go look for him," Stanfa beseeched Tommaso Gambino, a Sicilian acquaintance who had come to Camden from New York. "Los Angeles. Put in your mind that he's far away . . . like Los Angeles, Chicago or New York."

Meanwhile, Stanfa's associates began to gossip about why the mob boss wanted his former confidant dead: Adornetto apparently had made unwanted advances toward Stanfa's older daughter, Sara.

"I didn't know that Biagio was threatened, the thing with the shotgun," Sal Avena told Piccolo on March 4, 1993, in the law office conference room.

"He got cute with John's daughter," Piccolo whispered.

167

"Biagio?" Avena said in surprise. "Made a pass at his daughter?"

Two weeks later, on March 19, two of Stanfa's henchmen, Rosario Bellocchi, 25, and Gary Tavella, 36, were arrested for trying to kidnap a waiter at the San Marco restaurant on City Avenue. The waiter, a Sicilian named Fernando Vincenti, was a friend of Adornetto's, and Stanfa apparently hoped he could be persuaded to tell where Adornetto was hiding. Like the hit at La Veranda, the San Marco kidnapping lacked a certain professionalism.

Witnesses spotted Vincenti being forced into a van on the restaurant parking lot. A high-speed police chase ended on the Schuylkill Expressway with Bellocchi and Tavella arrested. A gun was found in the van, along with masking tape, a blanket and rope. Vincenti, police said at the time, was probably going to be killed and dumped somewhere. By the end of the month, the waiter had returned to Italy, and the charges against Bellocchi and Tavella had been reduced to gun possession. Both received minor jail terms, but the escapade had undermined Stanfa's reputation in the underworld.

"It's all we needed," bookie Salvatore "Shotsie" Sparacio was heard complaining to Piccolo in April 1993, back at Avena's office. "That's another nail in the coffin. . . . Just when we thought we had everything smooth. F-in' morons like this do this s-. It's bad for everybody."

Stanfa realized he had lost face. Adornetto couldn't be found. The bungled shooting and kidnapping had become symbols of Stanfa's ineffectiveness and had emboldened the young Merlino group.

"He took us for a bunch of cuckolds," said Tommaso Gambino in his native Sicilian.

"Even the little Americans [the Merlino faction] have started to bust my balls here because they see that nothing has been done," Stanfa replied. "And I'm banging my head against the walls. . . ."

It was worse than he thought. By this time, Adornetto had begun cooperating with the FBI and was in protective custody. The San Marco incident was resurrected in the racketeering indictment returned in March. Bellocchi and Tavella, along with Stanfa and several others, were named in a conspiracy to kidnap Vincenti. Like Stanfa, Bellocchi and Tavella are being held without bail.

For Bellocchi, stalking Adornetto may have been more than just business. At a preliminary hearing in March, defense attorneys described the short, wiry and dark-haired Sicilian as a young, hard-working immigrant who came to this country in 1990 to find employment and a better life. Among other things, they said, he had found romance. Bellocchi, according to court testimony, is engaged to marry Sara Stanfa.

PIZZA AND PASTA

In late 1992, the talk at the Camden law offices turned to the price of pasta. Sara Stanfa and her brother Joseph, then 23, are owners of record of Continental Imported Food Distributors Inc., a South Philadelphia company that sells upscale Italian food products to area stores and restaurants. John Stanfa is employed as a salesman. Salvatore Profaci had been involved behind the scenes in the food distribution business since the 1970s, according to state and federal authorities. His son was involved with a New Jersey-based food distributor that Profaci referred to as "my company."

From the tapes, the FBI heard how mobsters "sell" their products. Profaci was more than a little upset when Continental, Stanfa's company, began to sell products to local pizza parlors. That's not how business was done, Profaci explained during a September 1992 meeting.

"I'm in all the pizza shops," the Colombo crime family capo said. "And if I'm not there today, I will be there tomorrow.

Later that day, Profaci detailed his sales technique to John and Joe Stanfa. The prearranged meeting stemmed from a dispute over the sale of De Cecco pasta to Shop Rite supermarket stores. Stanfa, according to Profaci, had begun selling De Cecco products to four Shop Rite stores in the Philadelphia area at prices lower than those Profaci was able to offer. Profaci didn't like that. He claimed he couldn't match Stanfa's prices because he'd had to pay someone—he didn't say who—to get shelf space in the stores. He said he'd also paid to have a certain brand of cheese well displayed. The mob pasta sit-down was later summarized in a report filed by FBI agent Charlotte Lang, supervisor of the Philadelphia office's organized crime squad, which was coordinating the Avena office surveillance.

"Stanfa's sale to the four stores at a lower price could jeopardize the entire 274-store chain to whom Profaci sells," Lang wrote of the meeting that day. "Sal Profaci pointed out to Stanfa that the kickbacks involved in selling to the chain kept Profaci from meeting Stanfa's price . . . [and] that when he went to Shop Rite with Grande Ricotta, he had to pay $65,000 to get shelf space, but could not remember how much he had to pay for the shelf space for De Cecco macaroni."

Profaci went on to say that before selling to any other supermarket chains, Stanfa should first consult with him about the price.

"Profaci reminded Stanfa that this sort of price-fixing is illegal," Lang noted in her report, "but that among themselves they could fix the price in advance. Avena interjected that any agreement to set a price is illegal and instructed the others that they should never admit that they had discussed prices."

A month later, FBI agents picked up another conversation about pasta prices. This time, Stanfa appeared to capitulate to Profaci.

"John Stanfa said they, in the food business, should be working together, not cutting each other's throats," Lang wrote. ". . . Stanfa went on to say there were many calls from Shop Rite, but Stanfa would not sell to them. . . . Stanfa let the opportunity go because he did not want a misunderstanding with the Profacis."

Authorities say there is no indication that either food company, Italy-based De Cecco or Grande Corp. of Wisconsin, was aware of Profaci's hidden interest in firms that distributed their products. Mary Ellen Gowin, a spokeswoman for Wakefern Food Corp. of Elizabeth, New Jersey, the parent company of Shop Rite, said the company was unaware of the kickback allegations. She said Wakefern does not distribute either De Cecco or Grande food products, though individual Shop Rite stores may purchase them from other suppliers.

BRIBES AND KICKBACKS

La Cosa Nostra, said Salvatore Profaci, "is a beautiful way of life if we respect it." Billy D'Elia agreed.

"The way it's supposed to be. It's not an instrument to make money."

Yet making money, anywhere, anyhow, was a topic that dominated most of the conversations picked up in Avena's office. That gave federal investigators a rich supply of new leads.

Profaci's secret interest in legitimate food distributorships—one FBI report alluded to his attempting to extort his way into a company—is now part of an investigative file. So are other stories about bribes and kickbacks that surfaced again and again on the Avena tapes. All are being evaluated by federal authorities with an eye toward further prosecutions. On one tape, D'Elia, the Scranton mobster, boasted that he once paid $50,000 to a state Department of Environmental Resources official to protect an illegal trash-dumping operation. D'Elia also said he and a former union leader were receiving a commission on all the trash Carmine Franco was dumping at an upstate Pennsylvania landfill. Stanfa discussed an illegal trash-dumping scheme in which he said he, Profaci and D'Elia would share in a skim of "$6 per ton" in a venture that could generate "150 tons a day."

There was also talk of $200,000 or $250,000 paid by Franco to obtain the rights to a private trash-hauling contract for the Italian Market in South Philadelphia. Franco, according to Avena, said he had to make the payment to Genovese and Gambino family interests in New York. In another conversation, Avena questioned whether Franco was simply pocketing the money.

"He took with both hands," Avena said bitterly. "Hundreds and hundreds of thousands."

Based on the conversations, one FBI report read, "It is believed that Franco overcharged customers and generated cash to pay bribes to unlawfully dump trash and debris and to pay off the LCN [La Cosa Nostra] in order for him to continue to do business." (A spokeswoman for Franco's trash company said the Italian Market's private hauling contract was obtained through a standard business transaction with the previous contractor. There were no bribes and no mob involvement, she added.)

A DEAD FISH AND A BULLET

"Today, we got to create a whole new image. You got to get public apathy on your side . . . You got to softsoap everything and get out of the limelight. Not create problems that get in the limelight." Salvatore "Shotsie" Sparacio had it right.

This was in November 1992, before the war broke out and the Stanfa organization started to unravel. In conversations dating to the previous summer, the stocky, gray-haired Sparacio, 71, was the voice of reason: counseling against violence, against making headlines, arguing in favor of a quiet, smoothly run crime family whose only concern ought to be making money.

"We ain't looking for trouble," the bookie said.

He urged the organization to take better care of its bookmaking and loan-sharking, proven money-makers when run properly.

"The gambling business, I been in it all my life," he said. "I wish I could get out. . . . We got the f-in' reputation, we got the heat, and we can't make a dime."

Sparacio, who controlled a bookmaking and loan-sharking operation in South Jersey, clearly was not a Stanfa favorite. For a time, Sparacio thought he was going to be killed. In September 1992, the FBI heard Avena and Piccolo discussing Sparacio's fears. Avena said Sparacio had been warned to "watch his back." Piccolo said that Sparacio and an associate each had received a package containing a dead fish and a bullet.

At Sparacio's urging, Avena set up a meeting with Stanfa on September 8, 1992. Before Sparacio arrived, FBI tapes picked up Stanfa complaining about Sparacio's lack of backbone. During some earlier problem with the young mob dissidents, Stanfa said, Sparacio was nowhere in sight. Now, when things had settled down, he was pledging his loyalty. Shortly after three p.m., Sparacio arrived at the office and entered the law library. He told Piccolo and Stanfa about the warnings he'd received.

"I'm here to plead my case," he said.

Stanfa dismissed Sparacio's concerns. If he was going to have him killed, Stanfa told Sparacio, he would not warn him. The FBI reports reach no conclusion about who had sent the dead fish and the bullet.

BETTER THEM THAN US

At the same time he was assuaging Shotsie Sparacio, Stanfa was formally initiating Joey Merlino and Mike Ciancaglini into the crime family, according to the FBI. The "making" ceremony came in September 1992 after a peacekeeping meeting in which the differences between the young dissidents and the Stanfa organization had been worked out, at least for the moment. Past problems—the January 1992 murder of Stanfa soldier Felix Bocchino and a failed retaliatory ambush of Michael Ciancaglini in March—were supposedly forgotten and forgiven. Ciancaglini's brother Joe, 35, was named underboss

171

by Stanfa, another move aimed at bridging the gap between the two groups. Not everyone was happy with those developments.

"Tony Buck" Piccolo, the low-keyed elder statesman of the Philadelphia mob, saw too much arrogance and bravado in Merlino and compared him to former mob boss Nicodemo "Little Nicky" Scarfo, whose penchant for violence had decimated the organization in the 1980s.

"You can't afford to have these fellas around you, John," Piccolo told Stanfa on December 1. "They'll destroy everybody."

Stanfa and Piccolo talked of murdering one of the young mobsters, although it wasn't clear which one.

"See, we do that guy, we gonna start a war," Stanfa said. "The problem is, we gonna start, you know. . . . We gonna give the satisfaction. We start to kill each other."

Piccolo replied in Sicilian: "Better them than us."

Through the first three months of 1993, Stanfa tried to maintain control over his fragmenting organization. The Adornetto affair was a fiasco, but two other hits were carried out with precision. Rod Colombo, 29, a former California bodybuilder who had become a mob enforcer, was shot and killed in Audubon, New Jersey, on January 7, apparently for stealing from Stanfa. And on January 28, Mario "Sonny" Riccobene, 60, a mob informant from the Scarfo era who had left the federal Witness Protection Program and returned to the area, was gunned down in the parking lot of a Brooklawn, New Jersey, diner. Riccobene's passing was duly noted three days later at the Camden law offices.

"How about Sonny?" Avena remarked on February 1.

"Yeah, a damn fool all his life," said Sparacio.

"It's tragic," said Avena, "the way he [messed] up everything, including his family. . . . Really sad."

"It is sad," Sparacio agreed. "They create sadness in their life."

"Not to say that [the murder] was deserving, don't misunderstand me, but this violence," Avena added.

"Well, it figures to end," Sparacio predicted.

The Riccobene murder was a piece of mob business that everyone in the organization—young or old, Stanfa or Merlino loyalist—could understand. Riccobene had signed his own death warrant in 1984 when he agreed to cooperate and testified for the government in a series of mob trials. Among other things, he helped convict his own half-brother, Harry "The Hump" Riccobene. Six weeks after the Mario Riccobene hit, the Avena tapes were again buzzing about a rumored clash of brother against brother. And the war that Stanfa had hoped to avoid appeared inevitable.

Shortly before six a.m. on March 2, two masked gunmen walked into a South Philadelphia luncheonette on Warfield Street, just up the street from Stanfa's Continental warehouse, and opened fire on Joey Ciancaglini, Stanfa's reputed underboss and Mike Ciancaglini's brother. Shot five times in the head and neck, Ciancaglini somehow survived. But Stanfa's tenuous hold on the organization was broken. No one has been charged with that shooting. At first, Avena, Sparacio and Piccolo speculated that it came either from the Merlino faction or from the still-missing pizza man, Biagio Adornetto. Within a month, the consensus at Avena's office was that Joey Merlino and Mike Ciancaglini were behind the hit. Now the talk turned to war.

On April 16, Luigi "Gino" Tripodi, whom the FBI called a Stanfa capo, told Piccolo of a new plot.

"Mike [Ciancaglini] and Joe Merlino are gonna kill me and John [Stanfa]," said an agitated Tripodi. "They plan to kill me first."

"Watch yourself," said Piccolo. "Be careful. . . . Sons of bitches. I knew it was going to come to that."

In another conversation, Piccolo told Avena, "You're dealing with cowboys. These are not rational people." Both men saw the toll events were taking on Stanfa.

"He looks all disheveled, he looks tired," Avena noted on April 28.

"Got a lot of trouble," Piccolo replied. "Trouble. Guys going haywire down there."

"That thin fella, right?" asked Avena, referring to Joey Merlino.

"Him and the other guy," Piccolo returned.

"The brother?" Avena asked, referring to Mike Ciancaglini.

"They better do something fast," Piccolo said of Stanfa. "I mean, it's out in the open."

Conciliation had failed. The other side was gaining strength. Stanfa seemed to reach a decision: It was time to strike back. What followed were tapes in which Stanfa detailed plans to kill Merlino, Ciancaglini and Gaeton Lucibello. All three, Stanfa said on April 29, 1993, should be shot and then their bodies should be dropped in bags of quick-drying cement.

"This way the concrete hardens and we'll go dump them," he said. Stanfa, a former bricklayer, knew about cement. Lucibello, whom the feds described as a onetime Stanfa loyalist, was marked for a particularly brutal end in Stanfa's ramblings. Stanfa told his associate Sergio Battaglia, "I got to put one right here, with my own hands, in the mouth. The motherf-er. You know what I'm going to do? Get a knife. I'll cut his tongue and we'll send it to his wife." Battaglia suggested disposing of the corpses in different locations: "Maybe we'll take one to New York, one down to Delaware. We spread them out."

The next day, Stanfa told Piccolo and Sparacio: "From Mr. Nice Guy, I'm gonna be Mr. Bad Guy. . . . Today, maybe it's the times, you can do no more with these guys . . . I put it this way: Me, you, him, oldtimers. That's a different way. They got a different school. . . . They have no respect for you, your family, anybody. . . . No respect at all."

Stanfa then outlined a strategy: an ambush at 6th and Catharine Streets, where Merlino and Ciancaglini were opening a clubhouse.

"It's the only way to go," Piccolo agreed. "All right, Sam?"

Sparacio, who was also called Sam, reluctantly replied, "Yeah, if it's gonna work."

Piccolo said there was no alternative: "All of us, not just him [Stanfa]. . . . They could take us all out."

ALONE AT THE TOP

John Stanfa was about to go to war. But he wasn't sure who would follow him into battle. Luigi Tripodi had taken a trip to Italy. Ray Esposito, another reputed mob soldier, was complaining of heart trouble. And Sparacio was beginning to openly question Stanfa's leadership.

"Things look worse and worse every day," Stanfa told Tony Piccolo. "I don't know what I gotta do. I'm by myself."

Sparacio could not be relied on, he said. Tripodi was a "stupid guy." And Esposito "keeps saying, 'Oh, my heart. Oh, I taking medicine.'" Sparacio's doubts were no secret around the law office.

"It's a dog-eat-dog thing," the bookie had told Piccolo. "It's over. It seems like it's just over. You got wild sons-of-bitches like this that gonna destroy it all together, that wanna eat everybody. Even us."

"They want to eat everything starting with us," Piccolo replied.

Sparacio had counseled Stanfa against the planned counterattack on the Merlino faction: "You don't have the right nucleus to put the thing to guns. What do you do? You go out and challenge somebody? We all lose if we don't do it right. . . . We all lose."

And he had privately told Avena that he thought Stanfa had lost control and ought to step down.

"He don't have the strength to control it," Sparacio said. "Made too many mistakes from the beginning."

"Well, who then is it?" Avena asked. "These young guys?"

"Yeah. . . . At least if they get in there, you know where you stand," Sparacio replied. "You make a pact. You go along with the program. . . . Let's face it, comes a time, you gotta step aside. He didn't handle the situation from the beginning. All wrong. All wrong. And he can't rectify it. 'Course, I ain't gonna tell him that."

By then, Stanfa had made up his mind. Late in June 1993, he met with his friend Tommaso Gambino, the son of imprisoned Mafia heroin trafficker Rosario Gambino, a longtime Stanfa associate. Stanfa had asked the younger Gambino to enlist help in New York. But Gambino told him no one was available and suggested Stanfa travel to Sicily and recruit new members there. Stanfa said if he left, his position as boss in Philadelphia would be in jeopardy.

"I'm all alone," Stanfa said on June 22. "It's no one else. It's me. If it goes well, it's me. If it goes bad, it's me. . . . What I want to do, I have to take these two guys' head. . . . Then, whatever happens, happens." He went on to tell Gambino: "You know what's needed here? A demolition."

On August 5, 1993, as they walked along Catharine Street about 100 yards from the corner clubhouse they had recently renovated, Mike Ciancaglini and Joey Merlino were shot. Like the Adornetto shooting attempt and the Vincenti kidnapping, the ambush was not a gangland classic. Merlino survived with a wound in the buttocks. And within hours, Philip Colletti, one of the two shooters, was a prime suspect. Although the getaway car was torched several blocks away, police quickly traced it: The car had been leased in Colletti's name.

Back in Camden, the men in the law office talked of the potential aftermath. Sparacio was beside himself. He and Avena agreed that Stanfa had not heard the last of Merlino.

"That's why [when you] start out doing something, you got to finish it," Sparacio complained two weeks after the shooting. "Anymore, everything's just shoddy."

The next day, the FBI heard Avena and Piccolo wax philosophic about the generational war that had pitted Stanfa against Merlino. The conversation started out as a discussion about Salvatore "Wayne" Grande, another Scarfo-era mob soldier who had begun cooperating with authorities. As a result, Piccolo said, Grande's father had disowned him and his wife had divorced him and refused to speak with him.

"What a cross to carry for the rest of their lives," Avena said of Grande's family.

"Certainly, sure," Piccolo agreed. "The stigma, that stays. It's a shame."

Then Avena asked Piccolo why he thought so many young mob associates had sided with Merlino against Stanfa.

"Where's the inducement? " Avena wondered. "I mean, obviously people don't believe in tradition, then."

Piccolo said he believed many younger associates thought Stanfa would be too strict, too hard-line when he took over. Ironically, Piccolo noted, that wasn't the case: "He's been very liberal with them."

"Everything was fair game, Sal. Whichever way they wanted to go, that's the way they went. Beating people up. Shaking people down. . . . They really got carried away, Sal."

NOBODY WINS

John Stanfa and his son, Joe, traveled to work at their Continental Imported Foods warehouse in the Grays Ferry section of South Philadelphia the same way each morning. A driver would pick them up at their home in Medford, New Jersey, then head south and over the Walt Whitman Bridge to the Schuylkill Expressway. The Stanfas usually arrived for work around eight a.m. On the morning of August 31, 1993, they were delayed.

In the midst of rush hour, a white van pulled alongside the gray, late-model Cadillac in which Stanfa and his son were riding as it approached the Vare Avenue exit. Suddenly two 9-mm machine pistols were pointed out of makeshift portholes cut in the van's side. Stanfa's car was sprayed with gunfire. The mob boss, riding in the front seat, ducked as the window by his head shattered. His son Joe, in back, did not react as quickly and took a bullet in the chin. Joe Stanfa, who was rushed to the Hospital of the University of Pennsylvania, eventually recovered. As in the Joe Ciancaglini shooting that started it all, no one has been charged in the expressway ambush.

Law enforcement officials called the shooting a blatant breach of underworld protocol. Gunfire in rush-hour traffic was insanity, they said; what's more, Stanfa's son, not a member of the crime family, should never have been targeted. On tape, the men in the Camden law office agreed.

"These things are unprecedented," Shotsie Sparacio told Avena just hours after the shooting. "You never touch the family. . . . Crazy. Total . . . insanity. . . . Nobody wins. Everybody's in a no-win situation. This guy [Stanfa] must be beside himself."

Sparacio and Avena then spoke of the old mob protocol that said a member's family was never put at risk.

"Family was always taboo," Sparacio said. "There's no brains behind nothing. Maniacs. . . . There's nowhere you can turn to make sense out of anything. Before, people mediated things, ironed something out. I don't know where it's gonna lead."

Two more mob shootings would rock South Philadelphia before the summer ended. On September 15, Stanfa ally Leon Lanzilotti was wounded near 8th and St. Albans Streets. And on September 17, Frank Baldino, identified as a friend of Merlino's, was killed in the parking lot of the Melrose Diner. By then, the FBI had shut down its electronic surveillance of Avena's law office and federal prosecutors had begun presenting evidence to a grand jury. That, plus an intense street-level crackdown by the Philadelphia police organized crime unit brought an end to the open warfare.

Merlino, picked up on a parole violation, was packed off to prison in November. And on March 17, Stanfa, Avena, Sparacio, Piccolo, Esposito, Tripodi, Battaglia and a dozen others were arrested on racketeering charges outlined in a 12-count indictment based in large part on the Avena tapes. (Profaci and D'Elia were not named in the indictment. Both are targets of ongoing investigations, according to law enforcement officials.) By that time, both Colletti and John Veasey, the other shooter in the August 5 ambush of Merlino and Mike Ciancaglini, were cooperating with the FBI. Colletti and Veasey are expected to testify for the government when Stanfa and the others are brought to trial sometime next year. So is the pizza man, Biagio Adornetto.

A SILENCE BROKEN

John Stanfa grew up in the Sicily where omerta, the Mafia code of silence, was sacrosanct and where turncoat testimony was a vile aberration. But this was Philadelphia, where so many mobsters are now singing for the government that omerta could be the title of an aria. So when Veasey and Colletti became government witnesses—flipped, in mob parlance—no one seemed surprised.

In June 1993, in the midst of all the war talk, Piccolo and Avena were picked up discussing Phil Leonetti, Scarfo's nephew and former underboss. Leonetti, one of six former members of the Scarfo organization to turn informant, had become the government's favorite witness. Tan, well-dressed and poised, he had just testified in a Toms River, New Jersey, case in which four New Jersey Mafia figures were convicted. Leonetti had been relocated in the federal Witness Protection Program along with his mother, his wife and his son. Rumors abounded of the good life he was living, and of the cash—millions, it was said—he and his mother had been permitted to take with them into hiding.

"Son of a bitch, Leonetti, they can't shake him," Piccolo said of the ex-mobster's cool demeanor on the witness stand.

Piccolo and Avena then talked of ways to rattle Leonetti if he ever appeared in court against them. One way, Avena said, was to bring Leonetti's elderly grandmother—Nicky Scarfo's mother, Catherine Scarfo—into court when Leonetti took the stand.

"I understand if he appears here, she wants to come down," Avena said.

"How about that clown?" Piccolo went on. "He's got that Rolex watch from that jeweler friend of his. . . . How nice. He had about $5 million in cash. . . . And he testifies like that."

"Son of a bitch, ain't he, Sal?"

"Son of a bitch."

Dumbfellas

NOVEMBER 5, 1995

T he demise of John Stanfa began on the campus of La Salle University in the fall of 1990. With clock bells chiming in the background, Eddie O'Hanlon, a skinny accounting student $3,925 in debt to a bookmaker, met with Tommy Marrone, a bulky young collector for the mob. O'Hanlon, 20, was broke, scared and begging for time. He also was wired for sound. Thus the three-year investigation that brought mob boss Stanfa and his top associates to trial began with Marrone's words.

"You went in and you bet $3,900 this week with no f-in' money?" he asked O'Hanlon as they sat outside a classroom building on the leafy campus. "I mean, are you out of your f-in' mind, or what? You're not playin' with little kids here."

But O'Hanlon wasn't dealing with mental giants, either, evidence later showed. The Marrone tape was one of more than 100 played in the racketeering trial of Stanfa and seven codefendants, which is expected to end this week in U.S. District Court. The tapes, and testimony from a rogues' gallery of witnesses, gave the jury a picture of life inside the crime family, a sometimes frightening yet often comical portrait of disorganized organized crime. There has never been a mob trial quite like this. If there's a screenplay here, it won't go to Martin Scorsese or Francis Coppola. This is for Quentin Tarantino. Or Woody Allen.

"Dumbfellas," one lawyer has called it. How else to explain getaway cars that wouldn't start, bombs that wouldn't explode, a poodle's head in a refrigerator freezer or a rottweiler named Al Capone? How else to capture the wisdom of wiseguys and their associates talking—on tape—about the life?

"Goodfellas don't sue goodfellas. Goodfellas kill goodfellas."

"If you're a midget, they could put you on the highest mountain, you'd still be a midget."

"You can't put the s- back in the donkey."

And how else to portray the brooding, Sicilian-born Stanfa, who on some tapes sounded like King Lear, besieged and betrayed, and on others like Don Corleone, asking for God's help as he plotted to slaughter rivals? The jury will consider all that and more in its deliberations later this week or early next.

Stanfa, 54, and his reputed underboss and codefendant, Frank Martines, 41, face potential life sentences if convicted of all the charges against them. Anthony "Tony Buck" Piccolo, 73; Salvatore "Shotsie" Sparacio, 73; Vincent "Al Pajamas" Pagano, 66; Raymond Esposito, 51; Sergio Battaglia, 27, and Herbert "Herbie" Keller, 27, could get from 40 to 80 years. Eight other reputed Stanfa associates—including Camden lawyer Salvatore J. Avena, in whose offices the FBI secretly taped most of the conversations played for the jury—are scheduled to be tried next year on similar charges. If you want to understand why the American Mafia is in disarray, look no further than the story, as told by the prosecution, of Stanfa's rise and fall.

"SEE, IT AIN'T THE MONEY"

Eddie O'Hanlon's father did the feds a favor: He persuaded his scared son to contact the FBI. After taping the meeting at La Salle with Marrone, authorities moved on to bug a South Philadelphia bookmaking operation and then a bakery in Runnemede, New Jersey, where Shotsie Sparacio's betting ring was believed to be based. Initially, Sparacio was the target of the investigation. A gambler all his life, he had clear ideas about how those who bet and those who accepted bets should behave. O'Hanlon had violated that code. "Shame on him and anything he ever does," Sparacio said on tape. "He's a thief. That's a disgrace, a guy going to college to try to have some character or class. . . . See, it ain't the money . . . ."

Soon, wires set up by the FBI and Pennsylvania and New Jersey State Police picked up mob shakedown attempts. And the investigation of Sparacio led to Avena's law office, where FBI agents saw a parade of mobsters showing up on a regular basis. After a federal court approved a request to bug the law office, what had started as a gambling investigation expanded into a racketeering investigation.

"LA COSA NOSTRA'S VERY SACRED"

A framed poster hangs in Salvatore Avena's wood-paneled office, a reproduction of the World War II "Loose Lips Sink Ships" publicity campaign. In dark and brooding grays and blues, it shows a ship sinking in turbulent seas. A sailor bobbing in the water is holding a hand up desperately for help. The caption: "Somebody Talked." For nearly two years, sitting in comfortable leather chairs underneath that poster, the reputed leaders of three mob families did just that. These were men of honor and proud of it: Stanfa, Piccolo, Sparacio, Salvatore Profaci—a capo in the Colombo family and the son of the late mob boss Joe Profaci—and William D'Elia, a reputed leader of the Scranton-Wilkes Barre branch of La Cosa Nostra. All ended up on tape.

"You know, to me La Cosa Nostra is very sacred . . . ," Profaci said. "And it's no honor when we kill one another . . . [unless] a guy's a rat."

'Cause he deserve it," agreed Stanfa.

"Of course, that's honorable," added Piccolo.

In another meeting, Stanfa lamented the mores of the younger generation of Philadelphia mobsters, particularly the rival faction allegedly headed by Joseph "Skinny Joey" Merlino, with whom the Stanfa organization would eventually go to war.

"They can't even shine our shoes," Stanfa said in Italian. "We know where we come from . . . ," the reputed mob boss added. "First comes honor and respect. Without these requisites, you're not a man. Instead, these people are competing in the cuckold contest."

He, Piccolo and Profaci complained about a lack of competent people for La Cosa Nostra.

"We don't want quantity, we want quality," Stanfa said.

"EVERYBODY'S GOT A GOOD SIDE AND A BAD SIDE"

John Veasey was one of the people Stanfa recruited. It was not, in retrospect, a quality hire. Veasey, 29, turned out to be just the kind of young, self-centered gangster Stanfa had railed against. He was, however, a great witness.

A street-corner raconteur with a beguiling demeanor, the admitted hit man became the centerpiece in the government's case against Stanfa, mesmerizing the jury. Veasey admitted that he was a shooter in the August 5, 1993, ambush in which Merlino was wounded and Michael Ciancaglini was killed, and in the September 17, 1993, slaying of Frank Baldino. Merlino and Ciancaglini topped a "hit list" put together by Stanfa and Martines, Veasey testified. A hardheaded former South Philadelphia drug addict, Veasey went to work for Stanfa in July 1993, turned to the FBI in January 1994, and buried his older brother Billy—slain gangland-style on a South Philadelphia street corner—just five days before he took the stand.

No one has been charged in the Billy Veasey shooting, which some investigators say may have been meant to silence his brother. If it was, it didn't work. Veasey seemed to enjoy the spotlight and grew more animated the longer he was on the stand. He told the jury that he had renamed his rottweiler "Al Capone" and his pit bull "Frank Nitti" after joining the mob; that he had once used a power drill to poke holes in a man who had threatened him; that he had set fire to his injured hand to hide involvement in the torching of a car used in a mob hit, and that the tattoo on his back of a pistol and two bullets was to commemorate his two mob murders.

"Everybody's got a good side and a bad side," he said. Veasey brought both to court.

When he referred to his late mother, Veasey paused and made the sign of the cross. But when he talked of murdering Ciancaglini and wounding Merlino, he said he wasn't paid enough. Veasey said he refused to murder a Stanfa rival's young son because he had children of his own. But he admitted that he had been arrested several times for assaulting his commonlaw wife. Of codefendant Sergio Battaglia, a Stanfa favorite who talked tough but never got involved in murders, Veasey said, "He wouldn't throw a grape if he worked for Welch's."

Veasey said that on January 11, 1994, he agreed to wear a wire and co-operate with the FBI but was shocked three days later when, he alleged, Martines and Pagano lured him to a meeting and shot him.

"Yo, Frank, what the f- are you doing?" he said he screamed after Martines pumped a bullet into the back of his head. Veasey said he was shot three more times before fighting Martines and Pagano off with a knife and escaping. And when a defense lawyer asked if it were true that Veasey had once fed a live chicken to his pit bull, he replied, "No. It was a rooster."

"I PUSHED THE BUTTON"

Besides Veasey, jurors heard from James "Jamo" Lynch, who taped conversations with Martines and Pagano while working for the New Jersey State Police; Thomas "Santa Claus" Rebbie, who helped dispose of guns used in the Baldino hit; Philip Colletti, who teamed up with Veasey in the Ciancaglini and Merlino shootings; Colletti's wife, Brenda, a former nude dancer, and Rosario Bellocchi, a hit man who was once engaged to Stanfa's daughter.

It was Lynch, with a history of robbery and drug convictions, who admitted under cross-examination that he once tried to intimidate an extortion victim by cutting off her poodle's head and leaving it in her refrigerator. It was the bearded, white-haired Rebbie, a grandfatherly figure with a history of drug dealing, who said that at the time of his arrest he was carrying a knife for protection and a set of handcuffs for "sexual content." Philip Colletti talked of the botched hits during the Merlino war, including a half-dozen occasions when a homemade bomb—an eight-inch pipe stuffed with four pounds of explosive—failed to detonate after being placed near Merlino's car.

"I pushed the button, Sergio pushed the button, Herbie pushed the button," he recounted.

Colletti, a dark-haired Barry Manilow look-alike, shrugged and grimaced through three days of testimony. He told of a gun hidden in a frozen loaf of bread, of revolvers and rifles wrapped up as Christmas gifts. Like Veasey, he chided Keller and Battaglia, claiming that they once went to the trouble of having a car stolen but then couldn't get it started on the morning of a planned hit. Brenda Colletti, as clear and concise as her husband was rambling, was a Mafia moll with an attitude. The auburn-haired former stripper told the jury of her home life: the bomb stored in her bedroom closet, the machine gun in the basement, and the plan for her to dress in something slinky, go to a nightclub and slip cyanide in Merlino's drink. And Rosario Bellocchi, last of the key government witnesses, told the jury that he murdered South Philadelphia gambler Francesco DiGiacomo on Stanfa's orders but botched another hit because an associate had put wrong-size shells in his shotgun. "I pull the trigger—nothing," he said.

"I HEARD SCREAMING . . . I HEARD SEVERAL GUNSHOTS"

Early on March 2, 1993, Stanfa underboss Joseph Ciancaglini Jr. was gunned down at the Warfield Breakfast & Luncheon Express in the Grays Ferry section of South Philadelphia. The shooting left Ciancaglini permanently disabled. It was a seminal event in the war between the Stanfa and Merlino factions and ended any chance for reconciliation. And like so much else, the FBI got it on tape. A bug had been planted inside the luncheonette about a month before. A camera, mounted on a pole outside, was focused on the front door. FBI agent Paul J. Hayes Jr. was on surveillance from about a mile away shortly before six that morning.

"I heard screaming . . . and I heard several gunshots," he testified before the videotape and audiotape were played for the jury. The taped action takes no more than 15 seconds.

The camera picked up a passing car. And then three or four men—shadowy figures because of their dark clothes and the early hour—ran in the front door. There was a scream, several shots, another scream and another staccato blast of gunfire. Then the men are seen running from the luncheonette. The sound of the shots, like the chimes of the La Salle clock on O'Hanlon's tape, seemed to hang in the air of the federal courtroom. The trial resumes tomorrow.

Goodfellas Don't Sue Goodfellas

MARCH 11, 1996

S alvatore Avena: "Did I do somethin' wrong?" Salvatore Profaci: "Well, we started a lawsuit. Goodfellas don't sue goodfellas . . . . Goodfellas kill goodfellas."

Of all the quotes on all the tapes from all the conversations made during the FBI's four-year probe of the Philadelphia mob, none compares to New York mob leader Sal Profaci's succinct and chilling explanation picked up by an FBI bug on June 2, 1992, in Sal Avena's Camden law office. Law enforcement authorities say it captured the essence of wiseguy life.

"We couldn't make this stuff up," said one federal prosecutor more than a year ago of what has become the signature phrase of the investigation.

Francis Ford Coppola and Mario Puzo rode to fame and fortune on a similar line—"We'll make him an offer he can't refuse"—but that was make-believe. This was real life. Or maybe it was life imitating art. Sometimes the FBI agents monitoring the conversations in Avena's downtown Camden office suite couldn't be sure. Now it's up to a U.S. District Court jury in Philadelphia to decide. The trial of Avena and four codefendants, which opened last week, is set to resume today before Judge Ronald Buckwalter.

In some ways, the case is a rerun of last fall's federal racketeering trial that ended in the convictions of mob boss John Stanfa and seven codefendants. Once again, the tapes—more than a hundred secretly recorded conversations picked up by FBI bugs planted in Avena's office from October 1991 to September 1993—will be crucial to the prosecution. And once again they will be bolstered by the testimony of mob turncoats who murdered and extorted for Stanfa and then became informants in order to win reductions in their own pending jail terms.

Reputed mobsters Luigi "Gino" Tripodi, Salvatore Brunetti, Giuseppe Gallara and Gaeton Lucibello are also on trial. Each will mount a separate defense against the various charges that they face: racketeering acts that include murder, murder conspiracy, extortion and obstruction of justice. But if Stanfa, the bull-necked Mafia don, was the dominant defendant in last year's trial, then Avena, the avuncular 69-year-old lawyer in whose office most of the incriminating tapes were recorded, is the central figure this time. And if, as most courtroom observers believe, Stanfa's presence was a detriment to his codefendants, then part of the overall defense strategy in the current case will be to turn Avena's presence into an asset.

"The evidence will show Mr. Avena is a lawyer gone bad," Assistant U.S. Attorney Robert Courtney 3rd, one of four federal prosecutors trying the case, told the jury in opening arguments last Monday. "He crossed over the line."

"These tapes will show you that Mr. Avena was doing his job," countered Avena's lawyer, Edwin Jacobs Jr., in his opening. "He did all the things that a good criminal attorney is supposed to do."

So, as the tapes are played and the mob talk echoes through the 17th-floor courtroom, the question that hangs in the air and that could go a long way to determining the outcome of the case is this: Was Sal Avena a mobster or a barrister, consigliere or legal counsel?

A man noted for his polite and courtly manner, Salvatore J. Avena has operated his law practice for decades out of a nondescript second-floor suite of offices at 519 Market Street in downtown Camden. Along the way, he has represented a coterie of criminal defendants, including the late Philadelphia mob boss Angelo Bruno as well as Stanfa, Anthony "Tony Buck" Piccolo and several other reputed South Jersey mob figures.

Unlike some other well-known mob lawyers—Bruce Cutler in New York or Bobby Simone in Philadelphia, for example—Avena is not a flamboyant or aggressive courtroom advocate. His is a more studied, low-key approach. Competent and effective are the words often used to describe his practice. His standing with many of his more notorious clients was enhanced by his family background: His father, John Avena, had been a Philadelphia Mafia boss in the early 1930s. He was murdered, gangland-style, when Sal Avena was 10. Piccolo, who was convicted with Stanfa last year, alluded to that in one conversation recorded by the FBI.

"I mean, this fellow comes from an honorable family," Piccolo said, defending Avena's reputation in what authorities say was an underworld dispute. "And here's his father that gave his life for this family. Jesus Christ, don't we respect each other anymore? I mean, Christ almighty, he does favors. . . . He don't take advantage of anybody. He breaks his neck for everybody, and this is the way he's gonna be treated?"

But there was more to Avena than his alleged mob ties, which made his March 1994 arrest and indictment on racketeering charges along with Stanfa and the others all the more startling to those who knew him. Raised by a widowed mother in South Jersey, Avena worked picking vegetables and on a conveyor-belt assembly line at the old RCA plant while earning his bachelor's and law degrees, Jacobs told the jury last week. After serving in the Army, he started a 46-year legal career that included a stint as a deputy New Jersey attorney general, a municipal director of public safety and a lawyer for several police unions. His work with those unions resulted in lifetime membership in South Jersey police groups, Jacobs said. What's more, say many who know him, he is a genuinely nice guy, one who could talk at length about law, philosophy, good restaurants or his six grandchildren, on whom he clearly dotes. But federal prosecutors say the tapes tell another story.

"John, you act like you're getting dissatisfied with me," Avena told Stanfa in one conversation that prosecutors say showed Avena's complete fealty to the mob. "If you want me to put my brains in the toilet, I'll put my brains in the toilet."

On another tape, Avena is heard telling Piccolo, "There's gonna come a day when I'm gonna ask for the badge," a reference, authorities claim, to Avena's desire to be a formally initiated mob member. And on others, prosecutors contend, Avena counseled Stanfa about a mob war with a rival faction headed by Joseph "Skinny Joey" Merlino, urging him to take a tough stance.

"I say use the whip when it's time," Avena said in a May 6, 1993, conversation. "I don't think you're showing the kind of strength you should." In another, he told Stanfa to "go in the back door."

Those conversations and others like them, prosecutors argue, show that Avena was more than a lawyer, that he went, in Courtney's words, from "representation to participation" in the violent criminal enterprise that was the Stanfa crime family.

Jacobs, in his opening, argued that much of what Avena said was distorted and taken out of context because of whom he represented. Avena, he said, was charged not because of what he did—which Jacobs has repeatedly described as functioning as a defense attorney—but because of the people he did it for: members of organized crime. Another defense contention holds that Avena was "a victim" of organized crime, a contention that gets to the heart of the "goodfellas" tape and Sal Profaci's lengthy discussions about La Cosa Nostra.

Law enforcement officials privately concede that some of the best conversations picked up during the two years Avena's offices were bugged had only marginal importance to the substantive charges leveled against Stanfa, Avena and the others. They are, however, crucial to a description of La Cosa Nostra as a criminal enterprise, an issue that is at the heart of the overall racketeering charge in the case and that Profaci, unwittingly, provided commentary on almost every time he opened his mouth.

"La Cosa Nostra's a beautiful thing if we respect it," he said in one conversation in which he lamented the loss of values and tradition within the organization.

"There's no honor when we kill one another," he said at another point. "Unless a guy's a rat," he amended.

"Sure," said another wiseguy.

"Then it's honorable," said a third.

The powerfully built Profaci, a gravelly voiced but well-spoken Mafia diplomat, had more than a passing interest in Avena's problems. Profaci's son was married to Avena's daughter. The New York mobster, son of the late mob boss Joseph Profaci, and the Camden criminal lawyer are in-laws. That, in part, explains the sometimes highly emotional conversations between the two. Profaci, in fact, dominated most of the discussions in which he took part, whether they were with Avena or with Stanfa, Piccolo and the other mob figures who authorities say met regularly in Avena's office to discuss and plot mob strategy.

On December 5, 1991—to the delight of FBI agents monitoring the tapes—Profaci outlined the mob's interest in a dispute between Avena and Carmine Franco, partners in two Philadelphia-based trash businesses. Franco has been identified by law enforcement authorities as an associate of the powerful Genovese crime family and a point man for the mob in the highly lucrative trash-hauling and waste-disposal business. Franco, through his lawyer, has denied that allegation. To the dismay of Profaci, Stanfa and the other wiseguys picked up on tape, Avena filed a lawsuit against Franco in January 1992. A few months later, Franco filed a counterclaim. Each accused the other of defrauding the business. And each alluded to the other's alleged mob ties.

Eventually, the suit was settled out of court. Terms of the settlement have never been disclosed. But for nearly 16 months, FBI agents got a behind-the-scenes account of how Profaci and other mob figures tried to iron out the problem "in the court of honor" rather than the "court of law." Profaci said he didn't want to see Avena cheated, but he also said it was important to quietly end the litigation so the mob's hidden interest in the trash business would not be exposed. Otherwise, he implied, Avena's life could be in jeopardy.

"I'm trying to keep us alive, that's what I'm trying to do," Profaci said in one conversation picked up by the FBI as the dispute escalated.

In his opening, Jacobs said that Avena's decision to sue Franco demonstrated his independence from the mob and that despite pressure from organized crime, including possible death threats, Avena continued to seek an equitable and legal settlement.

Avena's perceived role in the dispute—as either a willing mob associate or a victimized mob target—could be crucial to how the jury interprets the tapes. The legal arguments will revolve around what was said and what was meant. For example, Jacobs was quick to point out to the jury last week that later in the infamous and oft-quoted "goodfellas" tape cited by the prosecution, Avena balked at Profaci's proposal to settle the suit quietly.

Avena: "What do you want me to be, some dunce?"

Profaci: "I don't wanna hear it. . . . I don't wanna hear it."

Avena: "You want me to be some dunce . . . sittin' on the side of the desk."

Profaci: "I am just tryin' to guide us through this thing in one piece, OK?"

Avena: "I don't know what that means."

Profaci: "Because it's. . . . If you're no longer around, or I'm no longer around, we're gonna suffer tremendous. Our family suffers tremendously. . . . Whatever your financial damages will be, we will look to see how it's got to be compensated for. . . . That's . . . evidently, that's the new rules of the game."

Avena: "Well, I'm not gonna play those rules, Sal."

Wired

JULY 11, 1999

The recording device sometimes malfunctions. The conversations don't always go the way they are supposed to. The only constants are the uncomfortable presence of the tiny machine taped to your groin and the knowledge that if it is discovered you could end up a dead man. That, says someone who ought to know, is a thumbnail sketch of the last two years in the life of Ron Previte.

Previte, 55, the latest Philadelphia-area mobster-turned-informant, taped hundreds of conversations for the FBI in a two-year undercover investigation that ended on June 28 with the arrests of reputed mob leaders Ralph Natale, Joseph "Skinny Joey" Merlino and nine others on drug conspiracy charges, according to law enforcement sources. Whisked into protective custody shortly before the arrests, the six-foot, 280-pound former police officer is now being guarded and debriefed by federal authorities. But another mobster who played the same role in a similar investigation nine years ago says he knows what Previte went through and can predict what lies ahead.

"After the first couple of times you get used to wearing it," George Fresolone said of the body mike and recording device that becomes an unwelcome part of the anatomy. "But every single day you're out there, you always have the fear in the back of your mind, God forbid, of getting caught."

Fresolone, 45, lived with that fear for a year while he secretly tape-recorded hundreds of conversations for the New Jersey State Police. That investigation ended in August 1990 with the arrests of dozens of mobsters from six crime families. The Fresolone investigation was so successful that all but one of the 41 defendants charged in the case pleaded guilty rather than go to trial. The one defendant who did, interim Philadelphia mob boss Anthony "Tony Buck" Piccolo, was convicted.

"You can't argue with tapes," Fresolone said in a telephone interview last week.

He was the Tony Soprano of his day, moving around the same areas of North Jersey that are now the backdrop of the highly successful and oft-quoted—"What, no freakin' ziti?"—HBO television series. A bulky wiseguy who grew up in the Down Neck section of Newark, Fresolone was a mob money-maker who specialized in monte and dice games, bookmaking, loan-sharking and related financial gambits. He was also an accomplished card-counter who loved the blackjack tables in Atlantic City where, he once boasted, he won tens of thousands of dollars for himself and his mob mentor, the late Pasquale "Patty Specks" Martirano. Now living in another part of the country with his wife and three children, Fresolone is one of the few Philadelphia crime-family informants who has made a successful transformation from wiseguy to working stiff.

"I got a mortgage, I got bills," Fresolone said. "I go to work every day. I got a life."

His advice to Previte is to plan for the future and make a clean break with the past. Too many other informants, he says, couldn't do that.

"You can't sit around all day looking over your shoulder, worrying somebody's going to shoot you," Fresolone stated. "I took what I learned on the streets and used it to make a new life."

Fresolone notes the fact that his family is with him made the transition easier. Previte is divorced with two married daughters and has gone into protective custody alone.

"It's extremely hard to change from that lifestyle to average Joe Citizen," Fresolone observed.

A few years after being resettled and given a new identity, Fresolone went to work for a service industry contractor. He eventually bought the business and now spends his days bidding on jobs and working the ones he is awarded. For security reasons, he asked that neither his business nor his location be disclosed.

"My wife used to complain that my hands were softer than hers," Fresolone says with a laugh. "Now my hands are like sandpaper."

His oldest son is now in college. His daughter has graduated from high school and his youngest son is a sophomore standout on the football team.

"My wife spends $400 a week food shopping," he said. "My kids can eat. We got bills just like everybody else. They come due, you gotta pay them. But I wouldn't trade it for anything."

Fresolone enjoys the typical middle-class life he has built for himself and his family. When his oldest son got a driver's license, he said, he and his wife were nervous wrecks. Even today, three years later, he sheepishly confesses that he can't go to sleep when his son is out until he hears the car pull into the driveway. An avid sports fan, Fresolone coaches a youth basketball team and religiously follows his younger son's high school football career.

"They were running raffles at the games to help raise money for the team," Fresolone recalled. "Fifty-fifty tickets. They had some kids go into the stands to sell them. They were making 40, 50 bucks. The kids didn't care. They didn't know how to do it. You gotta hustle. One day I said, 'Let me try to sell those tickets.' I went up and down the stands. I hit up everybody. I raised 300 dollars. Now every week I sell the tickets. If they only knew. . . ."

Fresolone began cooperating in 1988 shortly after he, Martirano and three others were indicted on racketeering charges in New Jersey. Martirano, who was suffering from what proved to be a fatal bout with cancer, went on the lam to duck the arrest. Fresolone, on bail, became the eyes and ears of the highly regarded North Jersey boss of the Philadelphia crime family. Aware that Martirano was dying and fed up with what he describes as the internal treachery, deceit and wanton violence that were the marks of then-mob boss Nicodemo "Little Nicky" Scarfo, Fresolone struck a deal with the New Jersey State Police.

He began wearing a wire in the summer of 1989 and for a year moved through the underworld, recording conversations that linked top mob figures to extortion, loan-sharking, gambling and labor-racketeering operations. Fresolone capped his undercover work by recording his own mob making (or initiation) ceremony. It was, he admits, a bittersweet moment. The ailing Martirano was barely able to generate enough strength to prick Fresolone's finger with a pin in order to draw the blood that is part of the mob initiation rite. Martirano died a few weeks later. Shortly after attending the funeral, Fresolone, along with his family, was moved to another part of the country as dozens of shocked mobsters were arrested and the undercover operation was made public.

"The tapes were extraordinarily powerful," said David Brody, the state prosecutor who ran the Fresolone case. "When you can put the words of the targets themselves in front of a jury, you've got a strong case. . . . Fresolone had access at the highest levels [of the mob]."

Nine years later, Fresolone can still recall most details of the investigation. He can still feel the heat and sweat generated by the listening device strapped to his groin and the irritating rash that occasionally developed. He remembers the chill he felt when an underworld rumor about an undercover operation swirled around the mob circles in which he was traveling. And he recalls with a laugh the time he and another informant, working for another agency, were taping some of the same targets and nearly taped one another. Five years ago, Fresolone wrote a book, *Blood Oath*, about his life on a wire. He has been trying for several years to pitch a movie deal. Now, with the success of *The Sopranos*, he also is touting himself as a possible consultant for the HBO crime show.

Two months ago, Fresolone was a guest speaker at a law enforcement seminar in Lake Tahoe where he told more than 200 investigators from various state and local police agencies about life in the underworld. It's not like it used to be, he said. Honor and loyalty have been replaced with greed and treachery. There will always be a mob, he assured them, but it is no longer monolithic. Fresolone said he was brought into the underworld by Martirano and the late Antonio "Tony Bananas" Caponigro, another larger-than-life North Jersey mobster who was the crime-family consigliere.

"If Bananas were alive, if he had become boss, we wouldn't be having this conversation," Fresolone said. "That's how much I believed in that man and 'This Thing.' But it's over. That's why I did what I did."

Now, Fresolone says, he looks forward, not back. That, he added, is the best advice he can give to someone like Previte who is just beginning a journey that Fresolone has been on for nearly a decade.

A Tale of the Tapes

JULY 4, 1999

I t's another tale of the tapes. And this time, there's video to go with the audio.

Five years after Philadelphia crime boss John Stanfa and most of his crew were brought down by a series of highly incriminating conversations picked up on a secret FBI listening device, the mob is again in crisis because of the recorded words of its leaders. Omerta, the Mafia's once-sacrosanct code of silence, is, in Philadelphia at least, like the Liberty Bell, cracked and inoperative. "Speak into the mike" has replaced "forgetaboutit" as the signature phrase of the organization.

Last week, Stanfa's alleged successors, Ralph Natale and Joseph "Skinny Joey" Merlino, found themselves jackpotted by an FBI undercover operation: A confidential informant wore a body wire and recorded dozens of conversations in which the mob leaders allegedly approved a series of drug deals.

"If you think the Stanfa tapes were good, wait till you hear these," one investigative source boasted after Natale, Merlino and nine other reputed mobsters were arrested on Monday.

Federal authorities declined to comment about the specifics of the investigation except to say that it continues. In fact, according to several sources, more indictments are expected. Natale, Merlino and the others were arrested on Monday in two drug conspiracy cases. Merlino, 37, was accused of authorizing three cocaine deals by a group of Boston associates who were unknowingly dealing with a cooperating witness and an FBI undercover agent. Natale was charged with approving a series of methamphetamine deals conducted by a group of associates, including the cooperating witness. Though authorities have refused to identify that witness, sources in both law enforcement and the underworld have confirmed that it is Ronald Previte, 55, a onetime Philadelphia police officer-turned-wiseguy.

Previte, formerly of Hammonton, New Jersey, was a top operative for Stanfa who aligned himself with Natale, 68, and Merlino after Stanfa was arrested in 1994. Though there was some speculation at the time that Previte was cooperating with New Jersey authorities, he nevertheless managed to move up the organizational ladder in the Natale-Merlino organization. He was listed as a capo, or captain, in a 1998 crime family chart put together by federal and state investigators. By that point, he had already been wearing a wire for the feds for more than a year.

Over two years, law enforcement sources said, Previte taped hundreds of conversations in meetings with Natale, Merlino and other top mobsters. The arrest complaints and indictments made public last week offered snippets of conversations from various meetings. But everyone knows that if and when the cases come to trial, there will be much more. In several talks, authorities say, Natale set up and approved methamphetamine deals. In others, they charge, Merlino approved a series of cocaine transactions.

The cocaine deals were carried out, according to the indictments, by four Boston-area mobsters who were working with Merlino. Previte was able to introduce them to an FBI undercover agent in Boston who was posing as a businessman who dealt in stolen property and drugs. In a series of meetings that were picked up on audio and video, the hapless Beantown wannabe wiseguys discussed cocaine deals, stolen furs, stolen jewelry and a diamonds-for-drugs deal. Money changed hands, and the cocaine was delivered while the tapes were rolling. Merlino and the others pleaded not guilty to the charges last week. Through his lawyer, Joseph Santaguida, Merlino has contended that he was unaware that the Boston deals involved narcotics.

"He was conned [by Previte]," Santaguida said last week.

The indictment, however, alleges that Merlino accepted $6,000 in cash from the cooperating witness as his take from the drug deals and that on June 8 the witness told Merlino he was traveling to Boston again and would have $10,000 to split with him when he returned.

"Joseph Merlino pointed to his nose, which the CW [cooperating witness] understood to be a reference to the cocaine deal, and stated, 'That's good, but be careful up there with Bobby, that's a bad pinch,'" according to the arrest complaint. Bobby was identified as Robert Luisi Jr., 38, the Boston-area mob figure through whom Merlino was allegedly working.

In another tape made in Boston, Luisi and the witness talked about dealing cocaine and complained that they had to go over the head of a top Merlino associate, George Borgesi, in order to set the cocaine-trafficking operation in motion. Borgesi apparently had nixed any drug-dealing, but Luisi and the witness indicate on the tape that Merlino then approved it.

"To his credit, Borgesi told them to stay away [from dealing drugs]," one law enforcement source said last week.

Borgesi, contacted at his South Philadelphia pasta warehouse, declined to comment. His lawyer, Michael Pinsky, said Borgesi, 35, is "100 percent adamantly opposed to drugs and anybody who deals in them."

On the tape, Luisi and the witness said much the same thing.

"He told me straight out no," Luisi said in a conversation in which he and Previte discussed Borgesi. The conversation was held on April 28 in Boston, according to a 29-page affidavit unsealed in U.S. District Court in Massachusetts last week.

"The other guy above him [Merlino] says go ahead," Previte replied.

"I know. No disrespect to George," Luisi commented.

"No disrespect to nobody," Previte added.

"It's what the other guy says anyway . . . It's what he wants," Luisi noted.

In that same conversation, Luisi indicated that Merlino had given him the "green light" for the cocaine deal. In two deals, the FBI undercover agent in Boston bought a total of three kilograms of cocaine from Luisi and his associates for $74,000. Another deal, for four kilograms at a cost of $96,000, was under discussion when the arrests were made. In addition to the drug deals, sources say Previte recorded a number of other conversations that will figure into gambling, loan-sharking, extortion and hijacking cases that are still to come.

A New Jersey law enforcement source said last week that Previte was a money-maker and that because of the steady flow of cash he brought to Natale and later to Merlino, both men tended to overlook the possibility that he was cooperating with law enforcement.

"As long as you grease their palms, they'll overlook things," said the source, who asked not to be identified.

Previte began cooperating after deciding that the days of the mob were over. He chose to jump before he was pushed; that is, before he was killed or indicted, the source said. Previte realizes the defense will try to challenge his character and background once he takes the witness stand, another law enforcement source said. He has a reputation for violence and has been arrested several times. He has also admitted to being involved for years in a wide range of underworld activities that include extortion, gambling, prostitution and narcotics. But for at least some of that time, Previte's activities were part of an undercover operation. And no matter what his character, the case—as it did in the Stanfa investigation—will revolve primarily around the words of the wiseguys themselves.

"They can say what they want [about Previte]," one investigator said last week. "The tapes will tell the story."

Blood and Honor: Inside the Scarfo Mob— The Mafia's Most Violent Family

"Forget about it! This is the best gangster book ever written."

—Jimmy Breslin

"The best mob book ever."

—*Penthouse* magazine

Blunt and graphic, *Blood and Honor* is a firsthand account of the rise and fall of Philadelphia's notorious Scarfo organization, told from the perspective of wiseguy-turned-witness Nick Caramandi. To this day, Caramandi is a prime target for hit men because of his incriminating testimony and continues to survive only under government protection.

Mobfather: The Story of a Wife and a Son Caught in the Web of the Mafia

"George Anastasia has crafted a gangland masterpiece. You see the murderous Philadelphia mob through the eyes of a turncoat and relive the daily horror of life in his home from the words of the wife and son whose lives he nearly destroyed."

—**Jerry Capeci, columnist, GangLandNews.com**
Former columnist, *New York Daily News*

CAMINO BOOKS, INC.
P. O. Box 59026
Philadelphia, PA 19102
www.caminobooks.com

Please send me:
_____ copy(ies) of *Blood and Honor: Inside the Scarfo Mob—the Mafia's Most Violent Family*, $17.95
_____ copy(ies) of *Mobfather: The Story of a Wife and a Son Caught in the Web of the Mafia*, $17.95
_____ copy(ies) of *Mobfiles: Mobsters, Molls and Murder*, $17.95

Name _____

Address _____

City/State/Zip _____

All orders must be prepaid. Your satisfaction is guaranteed. You may return the books for a full refund. Please add $5.95 for postage and handling for the first book and $1.00 for each additional.